IT'S GREAT TO BE HERE!

John,
Thank you for all you do for all of us. This is a special time in your life. Enjoy every day with family and friends.
Semper Fidelis
Richie Moran

By Richie Moran

With an assist from Steve Lawrence

Foreword by ESPN's Jeremy Schaap

Production/Design: Maria Bise
Cover Illustration: © 2012 Pat Lopez

Editorial Director: Steve Lawrence

It's Great To Be Here
ISBN 978-0-9961448-3-4

Printed in the United States of America

MomentumMedia Sports Publishing
20 Eastlake Road
Ithaca, NY 14850
(607) 257-6970
info@MomentumMedia.com

Table of Contents

Dedication

This book is dedicated to my wife, Pat, to whom I said "I do" on February 11, 1961. Like everything else I have accomplished, it would not have been possible without her.

It is also dedicated to our children, Kevin, Jennifer and Kathy, and their spouses, Melissa Van Buren, Lou Sposito and Bill Rogers.

My deep gratitude also goes out to our grandchildren, Kylie, Ryan, Chase, Lindsay, Adrienne, Eamon, Quinlan and Finn, all of whom fill me with pride every day of my life.

Bios

Richie Moran

- 29 seasons as Cornell's head coach, 257-121 (.680)
- Three undefeated seasons (1970,'76 and '77)
- Three National Championships (1971, '76,'77)
- 15 Ivy League championships
- 42 consecutive NCAA victories (NCAA record)
- 39 consecutive Ivy League victories (conference record)
- Only shutout victory in NCAA tournament history (14-0 over W&L, 1976)
- 3-time USILA Coach of the Year (1971, '77,'87)
- USILA Man of the Year (1975)
- 117 All-Americans – 202 All-Ivy players
- Recipient of the Spirit of Tewaarton Award (2012)
- Named Head Coach Emeritus at Cornell (2015)
- Numerous Halls of Fame
- One of two coaches to win a national championship as a player (Maryland, 1959) and as a coach
- Founder and leader of Irish Lacrosse Foundation (2001-present)
- Awesome dad
- Even more awesome grandpa

Steve Lawrence

- Sports columnist at the *Ithaca Times* since 1992
- 2,000-plus published articles
- 2-time winner of the NY Press Association's Better Newspaper Contest (Sports Features)
- Dad to three wonderful daughters

Foreword

In 1976, when I was six years old, my father, Dick Schaap, who had played lacrosse at Cornell in the 1950s, took me to see the team play at Rutgers. The Cornell team of the 1970s was one of the greatest lacrosse teams ever assembled—but I didn't know that. I didn't know anything about lacrosse, other than the stories my father had told me about playing against Jim Brown, which filled him with pride and were also a source of some form of post-traumatic stress.

After the game, which Cornell won, 14-6, my father took me into the locker room. I can't remember if he addressed the team, or just offered congratulations, or said nothing. What I do remember is Richie Moran.

Anyone who has spent time with Richie has felt that unique magnetism, that energy, that enthusiasm, how Richie wraps you in his embrace and makes you feel better about everything, especially yourself. That's what I remember about meeting Richie for the first time—and it's still the way I feel whenever I think about him.

Since that spring day in New Jersey in 1976, I have been fortunate to interact with just about every famous coach in North American sports, and many beyond. I followed my father into the business and I've been privileged to cover pretty much all the major sports and all the big events. But 40 years later, I have yet to encounter any coach or any manager who surpasses Moran. When I think of the ultimate coach, I think not of Belichick or Bowman or Phil Jackson—I think of Richie Moran. Richie happens to be one of the all-time greats based strictly on his record, but more important no coach at any level has cared more about his players or has been more invested in their success, beyond the game, and in their lives.

That point was driven home for me in September 2001, after Eamon McEneaney was killed on 9/11 at the World Trade Center. I've seen sorrow and I've been to many funerals, but I've never seen anyone as grief stricken as Richie the day he eulogized McEneaney. McEneaney might have been Richie's greatest player, but he was also a son to him—and I think he felt, and still feels, that all his players are sons to him.

In the final years of his life, my father had a home in Ithaca and nothing gave him greater pleasure than spending time with Richie. They would hang out, play golf, barbecue. Being with Richie always made my father feel especially alive. That's the Richie effect on everyone. I couldn't have identified that phenomenon when I was six, but even then I think I could sense it. Some coaches find success through their passion for perfection, or their technical acumen, or their ability to inspire fear. Richie was great, will always be considered great, because of his capacity for love, to love and be loved.

In my book, that's the best kind of greatness.

– Jeremy Schaap, ESPN

Co-Author's Intro

I admit it… there have been times when my phone rings, I see who is calling, and I (with varying degrees of guilt) say to myself, "Not now."

My phone rang recently, and the Caller I.D. conveyed, as it often does, that Richie Moran was calling. I eagerly took the call, expecting another request to meet up for lunch, or coffee, or perhaps to celebrate the birthday or retirement of one of our many mutual friends. Richie stays on top of things like that, he knows how much it means to people when their special days are remembered, and he follows through.

This call, however, fell into the category of "None of the Above."

I answered with "Hi Richie!", and I chuckled a bit when he seemed surprised that I knew who was calling. Richie is an old-school, flip-phone kind of guy, and I regularly remind him that the Smithsonian wants his phone.

Richie asked me if I could meet up at our favorite café to "discuss a project." My curiosity piqued, I said I could, and we agreed that we would meet in a couple of hours. As I drove to meet him, I wondered what kind of project he wanted to discuss, and my mind wandered back over the course of our 35 year friendship…

In 1981, I was a 25 year-old single guy, working for Cornell Athletics, fresh off a 2-year adventure in Santa Cruz, California, where I had picked up a certification in Massage Therapy and lived the West Coast lifestyle I had longed for since I was old enough to listen to the Beach Boys.

I always knew I wanted to someday buy a chunk of property and build a cabin, and I accepted the fact that such a plan would not be possible in Santa Cruz (unless I somehow climbed a few rungs up the tax bracket ladder), so I headed back east. Given I was very close to my family (30 miles from Ithaca), I also knew I would want to raise any future children near my hometown, so I packed up and relocated to Ithaca, accepting a temporary job with the Cornell Summer Sports School. I was by no measure an Ivy League kind of guy, but I loved sports, I loved Ithaca, and I was happy.

I made the rounds every day, transporting "campers" and coaches and equipment to various sessions, and I got to meet a few of the Division 1 coaches I had read about. When one of the week-long sessions ended, the kids went home and the next day a new group of parents would bring their kids for the next session. At the drop-off and registration, the kids looked at the coaches like they were NBA or NFL players, and the parents would say hello to the coaches and staff and drive off. Then came the week of lacrosse camp...

The kids were excited, as usual, but I noticed that a lot more parents were sticking around (good lacrosse metaphor, don't you think?) to be there when the coaches dropped by. Richie Moran came in to say hello, and it was clear that many of the parents wanted to meet the legendary coach. I had read enough to know that over the course of the past decade, he had won three Division 1 national titles, and that he was held in very high esteem in the world of intercollegiate athletics.

There was something about Richie's electric personality that drew parents in, and he made them feel special. They wanted to tell their friends that their young lacrosse player was at a camp run by the sport's preeminent mentor, and Richie treated all of them with grace and gratitude. Yes, he was one of lacrosse's iconic figures, but he seemed like a regular guy to me.

I was soon offered a full-time job, and thus began a 10-year affiliation with Cornell Athletics that would see me go from Material Handler (I took I.D. cards and handed out equipment to those visiting the athletic facilities) to a Physical Education instructor to an Event Management Coordinator to an Associate Director of Tickets and Marketing to a Wellness Program Associate. I saw Richie virtually every day, and I saw him treat the towel guys and the University President with equal respect, and his "people skills" served him well. I had no formal sales training at that point, but I often told friends unaffiliated with Cornell that Richie was a guy who approached recruits with an offer that went something like this: "I know you have been recruited by esteemed colleges that offered you a full-ride athletic scholarship, but here's my proposal... I want you to come to Cornell, pay for your education, work your tail off, and develop the time management skills that will enable you to carry an Ivy League academic workload and a Division 1 athletic schedule, and you will be a part of an elite team that will compete for national championships. And, by the way, you will work in the dining halls, scrubbing pots at night." My friends thought that seemed a tall order. Good luck with that sales pitch...

Over the years, I saw Richie at Cornell Athletic Hall of Fame ceremonies, Trustee events, booster events, and I saw him having lunch with the towel guys. As the Event Management Coordinator, I hired off-season athletes to help with stadium set up, maintenance and clean up for various games, and I hired several of Richie's lacrosse players. If a football game was set for a 1:00 pm Saturday kickoff, our crew had to be there several hours ahead of time, and as one might imagine, 7:00 am on a Saturday is not usually a college student's finest hour. It was not uncommon for some crew members to be no-shows, and some coaches seemed to be less than enthusiastic about getting involved, but I remember calling Richie at 8:00 am one weekend to inform him that despite his efforts to advocate on their behalf, two of his players did not show up. 30 years later, I will never forget them reporting for duty 15 minutes later, having made the 10 minute walk in record time, half-awake, half-dressed but there nonetheless.

In 1985, I struck up a friendship with a Cornell student who had been totally blind since he was in first grade. We ran together, we worked hard, joined the U.S. Association for Blind Athletes, and with me as his "Guide Runner," Rick Holborow won his first national 10 kilometer championship in Long Beach, California the following June. Richie absolutely loved our stories, he wanted to hear about every detail of every race and training session, and he encouraged us to keep training and keep improving. The next year, Rick won national championship number two, and the following year we represented the United States at the Paralympic Games in Seoul, Korea. Again, Richie was among our biggest advocates, and he found Rick's story of perseverance and overcoming barriers deeply inspiring.

In 1986, I put forth an effort to devise a game plan for "Vern," a lifelong friend who was 32 years old and had been bravely struggling with a serious mental illness for half his life. This young man had worked hard to graduate from high school and had managed to earn a community college degree, but his illness was progressing and the support system in our hometown was inadequate for him to attain any real level of independence. I had earned an undergrad degree in Human Services, and I helped my friend access services to live in a supported group home and to acquire some employment supports as well.

To ready himself for a possible return to the workforce, Vern was encouraged to do some volunteer work, so I arranged for him to be a "manager" for the varsity football team, and his newfound network of friends breathed life into his daily routine. The fact that college football players and coaches – some of whom were former NFL players – would include him in their lives gave him a real sense of purpose.

After that season, the head coach left and the new coach had a different vision of who would be his managers, so Vern was left somewhat adrift. Some of the athletic trainers and staff still welcomed his (frequent) phone calls, and he would often take a bus up to visit the athletic complex, but he was clearly feeling increasingly disconnected.

As is his custom, Richie Moran saw a void and filled it. In the ensuing 30 years, Vern has called him several times a week, Richie has taken Vern for coffee or lunch many, many times, sent him dozens of cards, helped him financially, and the fact that a man held in such high regard by so many considers Vern a friend is a bright spot in a life that has seen more than its share of darkness.

When Richie and I sat down to discuss this "project," and he asked me if I would consider collaborating with him on his book, I thought back to the dozens of times Richie has reached out to me over the years to share a thought about an article I wrote. I have been the Sports Editor at the *Ithaca Times* for 24 years, I have written several thousand stories for publication, and while it is officially a "sports column," I perceive it a "people column." Readers have approached me hundreds of times and said something to the effect of, "I really care very little about sports, but I never miss your column," and I am so grateful each time such sentiments are shared. People often say, "I loved that story you wrote a while back, but I can't really remember what it was about," but not Richie. He says, "I loved that story about Bob," and he will proceed to offer feedback that makes it clear he read every word. Better still, his input conveys clearly that he really understood what I was trying to say.

During our initial meeting, we had a phone conversation with Jon Gordon, one of Richie's former players who has carved out a niche as an author, a consultant and a speaker. Richie handed me the phone and Jon said, "Richie's story is a great one, and I have long been advocating that he find someone who can help him tell it." He added, "I mean… here's a guy who met these people when they were teenagers, and now some of them are hedge fund managers and Fortune 500 guys." I replied, "I understand that, Jon, and while those connections are indeed impressive, I have seen Richie many times in a nearly empty coffee shop early in the morning, having heartfelt conversations with people who have spent a lot of time trying to convince themselves they have anything worthwhile to say." Jon paused, and said "That's why you're the right guy to help with this book."

I said, "Thank you Jon, that means a lot. If Richie feels the same way, I am honored, and I can't wait to get started."

– Steve Lawrence - May, 2016

It's Great to be Here

January 18, 1937 was a cold winter day on Long Island, and the Moran family's home was warm and cozy, but on this day, Al, Mary and Dottie Moran were asked – lovingly – to eat their lunch in the garage.

The kids were okay with that. They had been told, "When the midwife - Mrs. Biddick - comes over to help Mommy, your new brother or sister will come into this world in our living room, so if you'd please eat your lunch in the garage, Mommy would appreciate it." Shortly thereafter, Richard Michael Moran - the last of eight children – would make his appearance, and their home would once again be inhabitable to all.

Steve Lawrence: **Richie, You have told me a little about your upbringing, and I was thinking about your parents. Reflecting back on what I have heard about "psycho-social stressors" and how stressful life experiences help to shape people, I thought about your parents. I thought about the stress of packing up and coming into the U.S. as young immigrants. I thought about the stress of raising a young (and large) family during the Great Depression, and I thought about what it must have been like for them to see their new country plunged into a World War when they had sons who they knew would be called upon to be soldiers. Please tell me more about your mother and father.**

Things were not going well in Ireland, there was unrest, persecution and many homes were being foreclosed by English landowners.

My parents came to the U.S. separately. My mother arrived in 1915 and my dad in 1916. They met at an Irish-American Society dance, and married a few years later when he was 23 and she was 22. My dad had been promised a job, as he had some experience in steam lines, but being an Irish Catholic, he faced a lot of discrimination and the job never happened.

That must have been extremely frustrating for him, to come to this country with high hopes for opportunity, only to have those hopes dashed.

It was. He planned on going back to Ireland, but he got drafted. There is a plaque at Ellis Island, donated by my brothers and sisters, with their names engraved upon it. I have visited Ellis Island three times. I did 'the walk,' and I tried to visualize what it was like for the immigrants. I encourage people to do that, to try to envision what your ancestors experienced. I learned that many were given a lot of commands from inspectors, they were examined and detained for tuberculosis and other illnesses. They were often quarantined, adding to the uneasiness of these wonderful individuals looking for a better life. At that point, early in the century, x-ray machines had already been invented and they were brought to the forefront by their use at Ellis Island, and that use helped with the development of that technology.

Not exactly the type of welcome the immigrants had hoped for ...

I have thought about that often... these people were on a boat for weeks, and I can't imagine getting off and walking into the unknown... instead of being greeted with smiles and handshakes you were asked to follow regulations. Some of the immigrants were sponsored, and it was likely your sponsor was someone you knew only by name. I can't imagine the anxiety these people experienced as they went through the screening process that prepared them for a new life in a new country.

And your mother was 15 years old and on her own...

Yes. I have tried to check records, as I believe my mother may have been an orphan, having come here at such a young age. She was born in Lissey Casey, in County Clare. Like many people returning from a war, she didn't really want to talk about her previous life. She just looked forward, and worked as a 'domestic' for the Vanderbilt family. The people in the U.S. were very gracious, but they wanted you to abandon your old life and pick up the American ways, so to speak.

Did your father share much about his experience?

He shared some. I have tried to imagine what it was like for him... he had planned to go back to Ireland, he was not yet a citizen, yet he was drafted. World War 1 was underway, he was not sure what the war was about, he had heard the Star Spangled Banner maybe once... he completed his training, he was set to go in a month, but then came the Armistice. He became "Americanized,' and then became a citizen...

You seem to have a lot of respect for your parents' perseverance in facing those obstacles and uncertainties, and that seems to have shaped your own world view.

Yes. A few years ago, I was asked by Ithaca Judge Mulvey to come to his chambers and speak to twenty-seven new citizens. I told them my parents' stories, and as I stood there watching them with their hands raised, reciting the Declaration of Citizenship, in my mind I saw the faces of my parents. It made me think about how many people have gone through poverty and starvation, and I wish I could erase that. I have tried to do that through a smile, through friendship and being a Good Samaritan. People say 'Turn the other cheek,' but I was to turn a coin, if you will. I close my eyes and imagine I am in their situation, then I mentally turn the coin and I am back where I am. It makes me very grateful.

You mentioned the 'Melting Pot' that was Ellis Island. A century later, people who look like you and me experience very little discrimination in our society, but that was not the case for your parents.

They set a wonderful example for all of us. In the 1920's they moved from New York City to Long Island and bought a house. That was unheard of, for immigrants to move to the suburbs and buy a house. Long Island was still mostly farmland, the L.I. Railroad was still the main mode of transportation, and we lived in a large ethnic neighborhood. We were the smallest family on the block, with eight children. There were Italian, Polish, German, Jewish and Scottish families and the beauty of it was that our family got to know a lot about the others. My parents were very caring, sharing, religious people, as were a lot of the others, and there were a lot of small community laundries. The one in our neighborhood burned down, and the community came together. The women provided meals and housing to the Chinese family, and given there was no insurance to speak of then, the men rebuilt the laundry. What a beautiful thing that was to see, how all these people from all those different backgrounds, stepping up to show how they felt about their fellow man."

What was the lesson you learned from that experience?

I learned that the heart of every individual is the same color. The color of a person's skin is not important. I look at people's eyes and I try to visualize what their heart looks like.

You were 4 years old when Pearl Harbor was attacked, but you have said you have some clear memories.

I remember sitting near the radio when President Roosevelt came on and declared war on Japan. I vividly remember that broadcast. My brothers were listening to a Giants game when the President came on the air. There was total silence and I could feel something was different. My mother started crying, I could see that my dad had tears, they were clearly very upset. My oldest brother had graduated from West Point 6 months earlier, and four of my brothers had graduated from high school. Two were working for my dad – he was a steam fitter – and they had planned on going to college. My oldest sister had graduated from high school in June, and my other sister was in the eighth grade. As I said, my oldest brother, John, was already in the Army, and the other four – Eddie, Bill, Al and Ambrose, whom we called "Bob," enlisted. I think about the fact that their youth was spent during the Depression, and their young adulthood was spent on the battlefield. Many windows in our neighborhood had a banner with stars signifying that the family had a son or daughter serving in the war. Our window had five, and I remember that one family had seven. I remember seeing that a window had a gold star, and the heartbreak I felt when I asked my mother what that meant and she told me that a gold star meant the family had lost a son.

It must have been difficult to have all of your brothers go off to serve during war time. I can't even imagine what that was like for your mother.

It was a tough time for many families. In our block and a half, twenty-five young men went off to war. Three did not return, and one of them was my brother, John. He was a Captain and a pilot who originally flew B-17's, and then he came back to the U.S. to train on the new P-38 Lightning. In fact, I still have a letter John sent home – with a 3-cent Air Mail stamp - telling me about the design of the P-38, and I would guess it would be illegal now to share that information. John went back to England, where he was a Squadron Commander in reconnaissance. I will never forget the day – June 17, 1944 - the telegram came telling us he was missing in action. It wasn't until a year later that we learned we would have a Gold Star on our banner.

I thought it was military protocol to send soldiers to deliver such devastating news.

At that time, there were so many losses, too many for them to make the personal visits. My father went to the door, took the telegram and then we all sat on the couch. For my parents, it was a shock, and I remember sitting there thinking about the time my brother had been home on leave and he put me on his lap and we pretended I was driving a car.

My father was also gone for 6 months at a time. His skills were needed, and he was sent to work in Tennessee. The coastal harbors were vulnerable to sabotage, so they did a lot of their work inland. I remember when thirteen German saboteurs came in a submarine onto Long Island near Jones Beach. Anyway, my dad was away for 6 months at a time, and he would come home by train, stay a week, and those were the happiest weeks for me. I would be reminded that every day was a day to celebrate and be thankful to God for what we had. When he would leave to get back on the train, it was the saddest time. I knew I wouldn't see him for 6 months.

I would imagine that along with your sense of loneliness, you were proud of your family.

The term "The Greatest Generation" wasn't really coined until Tom Brokaw wrote his book, and I cherish that book because the term means a lot to me. There is no doubt that my siblings played a major role in keeping our country free.

What other memories do you have of the war years?

Since I was the last of eight children, people would say, "You must have been really spoiled." I'll tell you, my family didn't have time to spoil me. It was right after the Depression, and my parents were too busy trying to provide for us. We had a rotary push mower, and I was pushing it at age 6 to make some money, and I would shine a dozen pairs of shoes on a Saturday. We had a '37 Buick, and I learned how to wash, dry and polish it, and I did that once a week. I also knew the schedule of the trash pickup, and that was one of my chores. I wanted to be responsible, and do the things my dad would do if he was there. I would go shopping for my mother. I knew in her heart she loved her family so much, and she had so much strain on her heart, and I saw it as my job to assist her and take some of that strain off. I would do the edging, and whatever I could to beautify the garden and lawn. While helping my mother fold sheets, we would walk toward one another and I'd give her a kiss.

I will never forget, she would get up at 1 AM, and listen to Walter Winchell and Gabriel Heatter on the radio. They would read the list of the Missing in Action, and she would listen every night. I woke up one night and I could hear her sobbing.

As I said, my mother worked for the Vanderbilts until she got married, and she stayed very locally active in the community, and when my dad was around he volunteered for many things that helped the community as well.

I also remember when the war broke out, all the rubber and aluminum and metal went to that effort, so I never learned to ride a bike. My dad made me a box scooter, and I thought it was my first Cadillac.

When your brothers were away, you must have spent a lot of time with your sisters. Please tell me about them.

My sisters were very good athletes, and they were my coaches. They taught me Bocci, boxball, handball, stoopball and of course, stickball. Stickball was my first 'organized' sport, and I still remember the great hits, the fantastic catches, the unusual bounces of the Spaulding balls. We got some t-shirts, sewed some numbers onto them, and walked around like we were the New York Yankees.

Each day, we hoped for letters from my brothers, and if we didn't get one, we knew they were most likely on some battlefield, or on the move with their regiments.

Your memories of your family are really vivid. You must be grateful for that.

I am. I can even remember raking leaves, and the aroma when we burned them. Each season was important to us, and my parents would make efforts to mark the changes. We would come home from school, and the curtains would be changed... I remember the Irish lace ... the chandeliers would be cleaned... the significance of the changing seasons was memorable.

I will also never forget that many young Italian and Irish boys had long ringlets, and when I was little, I started to go into the boy's room, and someone said, 'You can't go in there little girl." I will tell you, I was in Sam's Barber Shop that afternoon, and I told my parents that if they didn't take me to get a haircut, I was packing up and leaving!

So, that was a precursor to the debate over gender identity and which bathroom to use...

Yes! Seriously, I cherish my memories of my family. I once coached a young man who said, "I wish I was born into another family...I don't have what others have." I told him, "What makes you think that being born into another family would bring you the luxuries you desire and the attention you seek?" I told him that not everyone is born with a deck of cards with 4 aces, and that a lot of people didn't have what he had.

The Reluctant Altar Boy

Richie, with his brothers and dad gone for such extended periods, a young boy might be forgiven for seeking attention. Were you a model student, or were you sometimes looking for ways to draw that much desired attention in other ways?

I was in parochial school from kindergarten through eighth grade, and when I was in first grade I was reprimanded for drinking other kids' milk. I told the teacher to "Go to Hell," and I will remember that day for a long time. My mother made sure I understood the error of my ways, and she did so mentally, emotionally and physically.

After first grade, my reputation was an issue with the nuns, and from that point on I was watched very closely... in the classroom, on the playground... I did a lot of repenting and soul searching for a first grader, I felt like that character Linus, the one with Charlie Brown, like I was doing a lot of good things. My teachers thought otherwise.

It seems that ultimately, someone figured out how to help you turn the corner.

Well, I was very fortunate – due to my 'unusual' conduct – to be put in the first seat in the classroom - right next to the teacher's desk.

The teacher had four or five erasers, which at any given time might be sent like missiles. Most of the nuns could have been pitching for the N.Y. Giants!

By the third grade, I was finally let out of "solitary confinement," and a new nun had been assigned to our school who did not know about my inappropriate use of the word 'Hell' in first grade. Outside of realizing I was wrong, I came to enjoy sitting in the first row. It got me engaged. I had nobody in front of me to distract me, unlike the other boys in the class. They were always pulling the girls' hair.

From 3rd through 8th grade, I became extremely active in recess. We played such games as Ringolevio, Dodgeball and "horse battles," where you had a guy on your shoulders. Of course, a shirt and tie were required at Holy Ghost school, and I ripped a lot of white shirts.After a while, my mother realized that I wasn't really getting my shirts caught on a hook, as I claimed.

When did you take your games to "the next level," so to speak?

As the years went by, I got into the 'official' sports, like baseball and basketball, and I will never forget when we students organized a 7th and 8th grade basketball team. We had no gym, and we played in a shed with a 7-foot peach basket and an 8-foot ceiling. Of course, we had all road games, and I was shocked when we played Lady of Victory and walked into their gym. It was packed with their fans – a record crowd - and I was convinced we were in Madison Square Garden. They had custom-made uniforms and we had t-shirts with ironed-on numbers and an assortment of shorts. I was the third guy out of the locker room, and the first two stopped in their tracks and said, "We're not going out there!" All their students were there, we had two priests for referees, and we had no coach.

The tip-off was very exciting, since we had a low ceiling and we had never practiced it. At the first tip, they had a designed play and we were a bunch of spectators. I think they passed three times and scored before we moved our feet.

As the game went on, it was obvious that we were overmatched. We shot "line drives," because of course, with a low ceiling in our shed we never learned to shoot properly. We were really clumsy by comparison, and when halftime came, we looked up at that beautiful scoreboard and the other team had scored 32 points... We had made three foul shots.

How many of those foul shots were yours?

I was held scoreless! A priest realized we needed some help, and he was kind enough to set things up so we could work on two separate half-court drills so we could actually learn something. We never played the second half.

So… that was the original utilization of the "Mercy Rule?"

Yes… it was merciful all right… It was Divine Intervention! Looking back, even though we were so overmatched as a basketball team, I still consider us very fortunate to have developed those friendships. In the classroom, in the church and in our athletic endeavors.

Did sports keep you on the straight and narrow?

Well, there were a few diversions… During my 6th grade year, all of the boys in my class were required to take Latin in order to become Altar Boys. When it came time for me to go through the training, my mother and father were very proud that I was keeping the tradition going, that all of their boys would be Altar Boys. Little did they know that I had other interests, and instead of completing the training I was sneaking out the side door to go to another school to play baseball and football.

Of course, when the Sunday came along to announce the new Altar Boys, I was sitting between my mother and father in church, and it became obvious that my name was not being called. I was looking for spiritual guidance, because my mother and father were looking straight at me! I knew that day was coming, and it wasn't proper to speak in church, but there was no doubt in my mind that my mother and father would have a lot to say after the announcement. Every Sunday, my mother would walk home and my father and I would walk to a bakery to get fresh rolls and crumb buns – they were our favorites – and on that day, my father did not say a word until we got to a bench. He said "Sit down," and he conveyed his disappointment with my decision, and that it was a decision I would have to live with.

I eventually did make amends, as I served as an Altar Boy for four of my brothers' weddings. Each time, I looked down and saw the joy in the eyes of my mother and father. I didn't get a chance to serve on the "Big Stage," but serving at the weddings was very special. Afterward, people would look at the photos of the bride and groom, and there I was, in the background. They would always say, 'What great photographs! And I must say, that has to be the best looking Altar Boy I have ever seen!'

Lacrosse Sticks and Politics

3

Richie, we were talking about the altar boy years, during which you got your redemption from serving in the weddings...that was around what grade?

It would have been in the 8th and 9th grade.

That was the point where the decision had to be made to go to public school or remain in private school?

Right.

There were some aptitude tests?

Yes, we had to take tests to get into the Parochial High School because there was such a demand for admissions.

Was it really competitive?

Yes, I remember going to Bishop Loughlan and taking the tests, and also on Long Island going to Chaminade High School and taking the tests. It's obvious that I did OK to be accepted but my dream was to go to the local high school where all my brothers and sisters went and that was Sewanhaka High School. I was probably inspired by the head football coach from Sewanhaka High School because he made the rounds of all the elementary schools to tell us a little bit about football and athletics at Sewanhaka. He had played at the University of Illinois.

What was his name?

Bob Thomas. I really got to like him during that period of time that he came to visit us at school and he sort of inspired me to continue my schooling at Sewanhaka. So when the test results came back, it appeared that my parents had a strong desire for me to go to Chaminade, and my brothers were kind enough to convince them that it would be better for me to be able to go to Sewanhaka to keep on a family tradition. Having Irish parents, tradition was very, very important.

"Tradition" was the key word for them?

Exactly...So I had about a week and a half where I was really on edge, thinking that I was going to wind up at an all boys school - Chaminade High School, which is a great school. And then one weekend my parents told me that they thought that it would be fine if I went to Sewanhaka. So that was the beginning of my journey.

It must have been a big relief for you, to hear that.

In a way it was, but you know Chaminade had great sports, it was a great school, taught by Christian brothers and you know it was an opportunity every young man would enjoy. I felt it would be a good match, but I also felt that going to Sewanhaka High School would be good too. The building had three stories, and when you went there they sold you tickets to the swimming pool, which was non-existent, so that was a big prank. The juniors and seniors would catch all the ninth graders and convince them to buy tickets.

So... there's a little glimpse into why pranks are so much fun for you.

That's right... it's interesting, we all fell for it. Having been in a one room classroom, and then going through a building where you change classes every 35-40 minutes, was a little confusing. In fact, we had orientation for one day. We were in the building by ourselves, and of course we thought we were probably related to King Tut and that we knew everything, and that we're going to read out of Hamlet without any problems.

Well, the next day when school opened, it was like being in an envelope and someone sealing the envelope because the hallways were wall to wall people. Lots of big people, and ninth graders were not very big, and if you looked up you probably ran into somebody.

For the first couple days you went to the wrong lockers, you didn't memorize your numbers on the lockers and sometimes when you were trying to open your lockers you got nervous and didn't get the combination right, and of course the upper classmen loved that. You know it wasn't hazing, but you definitely knew you were a freshman.

About a month into the school year, actually less than a month, three weeks into the school year, we were sort of involved in a lot of things, freshmen football, they had a 'Freshmen Frolic," they had a freshmen festival, and it was then that you started to meet your classmates.

Did you know any of the other kids going in?

The majority of my graduating class from Holy Ghost pretty much went to Parochial High Schools. I think there were about eight of us in the class that went to Sewanhaka. So we branched out and started getting new friends, and those new friends were really remarkable.

At the festival I was asked to dance. I think my knees were knocking and my feet weren't moving, because we were not really dancing, it was more like we were hopping around. My parents did have me take parish tap dancing and I think my brother started flirting with the teacher and my lessons went by the wayside. So my dancing ability was very questionable, in fact it still is. But I figured that was my opportunity as a ninth grader to be about a foot and a half from the girl I was dancing with. Her name was Janet Riley. The word filtered back to my parents that I danced with Janet Riley, so this was a match made in heaven. Our dancing would have made the colonial people – the Puritans - very happy, because we never really got close, but Janet and I became friends.

Was she a fellow ninth grader?

Yes. Then I found out Janet was in a stronger friendship with a freshman football player from Chaminade. So it was clear that we were going to play against each other so I decided not to be attached. Not that I was thinking about school. You know, when you're a ninth grader, you do see young ladies at school that you become attracted to. So I became a rover. I got interested in sports, and I got interested in young ladies that were in my class.

The Irish Rover!

Yep, people tell me I concentrated too much on athletics and not enough on academics, and I have to admit they were probably right because the teachers at Sewanhaka High School were fantastic. It was a great school district. Five towns fit into that one school district. So you had some people that were very wealthy, middle income people, and some people who had both parents working. You had areas where no one ever heard of food stamps, never heard of homelessness, but you had some people that definitely had hard times. And that high school was the melting pot because we all mixed, we all went to classes together, went to activities together, and played sports together.

You mentioned politics at Sewanhaka High School...

One of the great attributes of Sewanhaka High School was the fact that you could get involved in many activities, like athletics, clubs, charitable organizations, helping in the community. It was really a well-rounded program from the standpoint of the classroom, athletic fields, community, school spirit, and teaching us all how to be caregivers and how to share. That was a wonderful experience for all of us. I gained a lot from it because it enabled me to carry that on with me throughout my career.

My parents started what I would call "the foundation," and Sewanhaka High School continued to "add bricks" to it every year I was in school. During this period of time we had two political parties at the high school; one was Coalition and one was Student United. It was really a wonderful situation for all of us. We had primaries, we had rallies, and we had the chance to get together and speak to the student body over the P.A. system early in the morning and state what your platform was going to be.

The seniors were the people that really put this all together. This was their senior project. We had an election day and that was outstanding. To perform before an auditorium filled with freshmen, sophomores, juniors and seniors was quite exciting. One side of the auditorium was Student United, the other was Coalition. Student United's colors were blue and white, Coalition was green and white, and of course all the students wore those colors.

I was asked to run for Treasurer of Student United for the Student Council. Student Council was very active in school, so it was quite a thrill. The most unfortunate thing was, I was asked to run against one of my teammates, Don Kaley. Don and I played lacrosse together, we played freshman football together, and it was really difficult competing against a friend. However, my committee -which consisted of a lot of active seniors - felt that I had a pretty good chance to win.

You were a junior at this point?

Yes. I was a junior. Student United had not won in recent years, and we hoped to take three of the key spots, so our efforts were to overcome this losing streak. The day of the election, I voted early in the morning and that afternoon we were playing our rival in lacrosse (Garden City) and of course Don and I were on the bus, though we didn't sit together. Our thoughts quickly shifted from Election Day to prepare for the game against Garden City.

During the warm-ups, I was playing in the second midfield and there was a collision with two of our players and one of them happened to be an outstanding midfielder, John Stawecki. John got a concussion and an abrasion on his head, so I got moved up to the first midfield to start that game, and it was one of my better days. I had two goals and an assist and we beat Garden City.

Our schools were about 6 miles apart, and as we were ready to board the bus, I could see a number of Student United kids coming toward the bus in their blue and white sweaters, carrying banners. They informed me that I had won, and that was quite thrilling. I was still in the game mode and very happy about the game and really happy that we had won. Some people from Coalition came to tell Don Kaley that it didn't work out for them, and I went over and told him "Don, one of the great things is that we won the game today, and this election was wonderful. A lot of great things were said about both of us, and that will continue forever." Unfortunately, Don passed away at an early age from cancer, and that was very hard losing a teammate and friend, but that Election Day and game day were quite exciting.

Do you know the origin of the school name Sewanhaka; it sounds like a Native American name?

Yes, it was an Indian reservation at one time. It was part of the Chenecock tribe. They always told us that the football field we were playing on was an area where the Sewanhaka braves had their reservation. We were known as the Shinnecock Indians, and the freshmen program was the Sewanhaka Braves.

Freshmen football was pretty interesting, having never played with a coach. In grammar school, we had three coaches and fundamentals were something I never quite understood, but working with these coaches you started to realize what an advantage it was if you were fundamentally sound and paid attention to their instruction and what you do to make yourself better. It was a wonderful experience. I remember having study hall before school ended and it gave me a chance to do my homework and then I could go out and concentrate on my athletic endeavors. So I had some wonderful guidance both in the classroom and on the athletic field.

The school was so popular that we had a number of men and women on the faculty that actually had their doctorates. Number one, it was a very, very high salary district so teachers were compensated quite well. The school had its own radio station. Grumman Aircraft - in conjunction with the high school - had an aeronautics program, its own building. We had an agricultural program, and we had auto mechanics, so if students wanted to go in different directions they could very easily.

Do you remember the size of the student body?

My graduating class, I think, was 875.

875 kids times 4 grades… that's a big school.

Yes, very much so.

Like its own community.

Yes, and it could handle the student body very nicely. And the teacher-to-student ratio in the classroom was quite interesting, as I don't think we had more than 20 students in the class. In my sophomore year the school continued to expand unbelievably, so we had double sessions. Juniors and seniors went in the morning, because a lot of the seniors had jobs in the afternoon, and then freshmen and sophomores went in the afternoon. So it was a split session.

It was really interesting. We probably had 150 boys come out for freshmen football, and the same numbers would come out for lacrosse and baseball, so there were a lot to choose from. I actually wanted to be a baseball player. I was a catcher. At the tryouts there were 9 catchers and they kept three and I was fortunate to be one of them.

My freshmen football coach was also the lacrosse coach, Mr. Bill Ritch. Mr Ritch was one of those people you wanted to work very hard for. I was very fortunate, all of the coaches I ever had really treated me like their son, and they did that to all the players.And they knew that some of those players came from very, very, different backgrounds. Some had some hardships but these coaches were in place and gave those students a welcoming, and a feeling that they were important, and that they were definitely a major part in the program.

There was never a roster posted, you made the team every day. They didn't look at statistics, they tried people in different positions. So that was very rewarding because it gave us all an opportunity to really look at where we might be playing as sophomores, juniors and seniors.

So is this specifically lacrosse that you're talking about now?

Actually all sports. So after freshmen football season, a good percentage of the freshmen players were playing baseball and lacrosse, and I went in to speak to Mr. Ritch and I said, "Would you mind if I tried lacrosse?" He said "Well you catch on the baseball team, and we don't particularly like to take players from another sport because you know, you're sort of committed." I understood that, but I think I was envious of guys playing lacrosse going up and down the field. Catching was an exciting position, but I just felt that possibly my greatest ability would be playing lacrosse, and I wanted to use that to the fullest. But they did have a winter program for lacrosse. They played box lacrosse in the tennis courts. So I asked him if I could play outdoor lacrosse. We used to shovel the tennis courts off, and I asked him if I could give lacrosse a try. He said "Well, I really think you ought to stay with baseball." So I left his office, and started walking into the hallway and he came up behind me and said "I'll tell you what, if you'd like to try lacrosse, and it's not going to interfere with baseball, here's your stick." So he gave me my first stick.

You seem to remember that first stick very clearly.

After Mr. Ritch came up to me in the hallway and gave me my first stick, I cradled that stick like it was a newborn baby. It was a wooden stick, made out of hickory. The sidewall was gut, the stringing was leather, and to me it was a Rembrandt, it was like a work of art.

Did it belong to the team?

Yes. Mr. Ritch had gone to Syracuse where he knew a gentleman from the Onondaga Reservation, and that's where these sticks were made. He used to send down some of the finest made sticks. A wooden stick had to be balanced, it had to have a pocket in it that could be adjusted, and you pulled the strings in the leather, and like any leather product you had to take good care of it. If you played in the rain the sidewall, which is made out of gut, would become very flimsy and meshy, so you had to put tongue depressors in the side of it until it dried out. Getting checked by the wood side of the stick definitely left some bruises on your hands, because it would go through the gloves.

The stick was a work of art, and knowing that it came from the Indian Reservation to Sewanhaka High School really made it very special. It was going to be about a month before box lacrosse started, in February. I remember walking home from school with this stick and I held it in my right hand, my left hand, in those days you didn't have a book bag. I probably should have invented those. And then I wondered if I should bring this stick into the house, because then I'm going to have to tell my father and my brothers that I'm playing lacrosse. I put the stick in the garage and it took me about two days to get the courage up to tell them. Dinner at our house was wonderful, we all sat down, nobody sat down until my mother sat down, the youngest always sat to the right of my father and we always started the conversation with what went on during that day. When it was my turn to answer, I took a deep breath and said, "Two days ago I had a chance to speak to Mr. Bill Ritch." My parents said "Oh your football coach?" I replied, "Yes... he's also a lacrosse coach and I asked him if I could play winter lacrosse." My dad said, "What about baseball?" My reply was "Well, if I do make the team, which could be very tough because I've never played, I can always play baseball in the summers, American Legion." One of them said, "Well, all your brothers play baseball." I said, "Well, I think I'd like to give it a shot, because I think it would really help my football skills."

Apparently, my answers made sense, and sure enough that February I got out there and shoveled the tennis courts, had my first taste of box lacrosse, and it was scary. It was like being caught in a revolving door, and you're not too sure you are going to get out of the right side. So the experienced players taught me very quickly how to do things. Lacrosse is a game where you can practice an awful lot on your own. Get against a wall… and by the way, I wouldn't recommend that you get near a garage that had windows or a house with windows.

Especially when you're learning, right? Is this the voice of experience speaking?

Right… I was fortunate in that there was a handball court wall nearby. I went to that handball court and I used to bring some tape to mark what the goal would be like, and after a while I became fairly accurate and my stick work got better. And of course, we played box lacrosse 3 days a week and believe it or not, we used to play it on our own. And that sort of caused a little problem for me… it happened to be Washington's birthday, and school was closed, and a group of about fifteen of us met to go up and play box lacrosse on the tennis courts. The school was not open so we couldn't get gloves and helmets, shoulder pads or arm pads, but we proceeded to play. As I was getting ready to shoot, a player went to check my stick, missed my stick, and gave me a cut over my right eye, which I immediately put my handkerchief on. Everybody recommended that I go to the doctor and get that stitched. Well I'm thinking, after only a couple weeks of lacrosse, I'm going to be coming home with stitches, this will not make for a happy household. So, on my way home with my friends we stopped at the doctor's office and made an appointment, and at that stage I was a little woozy. I knew I definitely didn't want to look at the cut.

Woozy due to blood loss or concussion symptoms?

I think both. I went in and the doctor was kind enough to take me immediately. That's when I learned to never open your eyes when you're getting stitched up, or when you're getting needles. I carried that all the way through my life. To this day, I have no idea what a needle looks like, and I definitely have no idea what the sewing up with stitches process looks like! Sure enough I got the stitches, and I had a big lump over my eyebrow.

Did you guys have helmets or eye protection then?

Yes, but school was closed so we couldn't get the equipment, but we played anyway. I had about a quarter of a mile walk to think about what I was going to say to my mother, and I wasn't sure if I should try to hide it somehow. My hair wasn't long enough, and I couldn't hide it with a book, because you would never be able to keep a book up there that long. So I walked in and said "Mom, I got hit, but everything's fine. I went to the doctor." As soon as I said "doctor," all the alarms went off and it was assumed it must be really serious. I said "No, the doctor was really nice." I wasn't even sure about payment in those days, he just stitched me up, took my name and address and I left. She said, "Who did this?" I forgot the doctor's name, and she asked. "On Covert Avenue?", and I said "Yes." She said "I hear he's very nice," and I said he was. She said, "Well, did you run into something, did you bump into somebody?" And I said "No… I got hit by a stick." She said "A stick???" I confirmed that. "Yes… a lacrosse stick." She shook her head and said "You should be playing baseball!"

Everything was fine. My Dad was home that evening and my mother told him the story. I think he thought I was an Irish warrior because he put his arm around me and he said "Sorry that happened," and he added, "You gotta be careful in the future." I never told them I didn't have a helmet on, because I think if I had told them I didn't have a helmet on it could have been a different story. So that was really the beginning of my desire to play lacrosse.

What had drawn you initially, the fact that the game was so active and fast?

All of my teammates on the football team were playing because they had it in their grade schools. And all we had was an 80-foot shed and fields, and really no equipment. It really drew me to think that this would be a great combination, football and lacrosse. I continued to play baseball in the summer, and I still have a great affection for baseball. But after two summers, I started playing summer league lacrosse, and really got involved in it. I was really fortunate - my high school coach was unbelievable. He would have articles on the lacrosse bulletin board, of all the players that he had coached recently. They were at RPI, Cornell, Syracuse, US Military Academy, US Naval Academy, Penn State, every popular school in the country. Amherst, Williams, young men from his program were playing for many excellent programs. That was really an incentive for all of us to do well in lacrosse. My freshmen year, I was very fortunate. I was brought up to varsity, and varsity at that time had a 27 game winning streak. I did more observing than I did playing, but I did get in a couple games. You could call it a thirst, and my thirst to get better increased tremendously. So much so that I would go out and cut the lawn at top speed - we did not have a power mower - shine my brothers' shoes, wash two cars and do some raking and edging around the property, so I could speed off to lacrosse in the afternoon. So lacrosse really helped my work ethic. It really made me a much better person. I started to encourage younger boys in my neighborhood to start playing. By that time, lacrosse sticks, believe it or not, were $10. So I would save my money up and try to buy some extra sticks and we would always carry them around. And people thought that I was crabbing, and the sticks were used for crabbing, and few had any idea what a lacrosse stick was. Then, our team started to get local headlines.

And you're watching some of your teammates go on to play in college?

Yes, and then we started this winning streak, which eventually ended at 91. I was there for 58 straight wins. People came from all over to watch us play.

Were you a midfielder?

Yes, I was. The biggest test we had was when I was a junior. I was elected captain along with Hank Goetz, and what an unbelievable honor that was. Our third game of the year was going to be an intersectional game against St. Paul's School from Baltimore, Maryland. Mr. Ritch would always have information about all these schools, and if you looked at the St. Paul's roster and their accomplishments, it looked like the "Who's Who" of lacrosse. We had a long winning streak, and they had a 29-game winning streak. It was the first time ever in high school that two teams were going to meet with such long winning streaks, and the buildup all week was unbelievable.

Was it a home game for you?

Yes, this was a home game for us. We had a home-and-away scheduled with them, and it was the first time it was ever being done. We had a pep rally, and each day practice was very intense and that's where pranks came in, because we were trying to loosen each other up. We were juniors and sophomores. The seniors, of course, had more experience. We would try to do things that would make people enjoy being at practice. On the Friday before the game we had the top official for lacrosse, Joseph "Frenchie" Julian, an outstanding player at Rutgers. He was at that time a headmaster at a private school on Long Island and an unbelievable official. He did many Army/Navy games, and the Maryland/Hopkins game, so he came over to give us a little instruction on what would likely be called, because we were going to have top-flight officials, and in those days you only had two officials. It was imperative that as a high school player you really knew the rules, and there was no doubt that the Baltimore group were well-schooled ever since they were 4-year-old players, and we were pretty much neophytes. So they gave us a great spiel on the rules and regulations.

That night we all met at a place called The Nassau Inn, and it was one of the first places on Long Island that had pizza. The whole team got together, had pizza, and talked about the game and how important it was going to be to Long Island and to New York State. We were really carrying the flag for our school. We had no idea what the attendance was going to be that day. It was a beautiful April Saturday, the recorded attendance was 7,500, but I'm sure other people came in through other ways. When we came out of the locker room, which was probably 300 yards from the field, people formed a line on both sides of the sidewalk. I can still feel the chills.

The interesting thing is, you see it now on television, you see smoke, you see guys going through signs, you see bands playing, and you see what is called the victory walk. We had no idea what this was all about. First of all, we got to the locker room about 10:30. We did some pre-stretching, we got everything taped, and in those days there was not a lot of film. But we had a scouting report that was written up on the board.

I think to this day all of us could probably recite the scouting report backwards. The board was huge, and at that time it was a football/lacrosse locker room. The board was covered with various things that we were going to do, and things that we were going to prevent them from doing. It was so detailed that after you memorized it, your reactions were fluid.

As we walked through these lines of people, I don't think there was a player that was relaxed… I know I was so tense it was unbelievable, my arms felt like they were 100 pounds apiece. I tried to move my stick and it was like my body really wasn't functioning too well. We got onto the field, and we always ran on the field in pairs. We ran on the field, bands playing, people cheering and when I looked up to the end of the field, there was our opponent.

Sometimes you look at an opponent and think "God, he's big." I don't know if it was our vision playing tricks on us that day, but I think all of us had the same feeling. Wow, what are we in for? They looked strong, they looked big. We couldn't tell much about their speed because it was just warm-ups, but every once in a while I would glance down and see their goalie warming up. I don't know if their shooter intentionally did it, but I didn't see any balls go into the goal.

I was saying, "Dear Lord, please don't let us get shut out." So, for the coin toss they brought out Hank and me, and two players from St. Paul's, Stu Carlisle and Ernie Betz, both of whom I later played with at Maryland. Our coach said, "Always look your opponent in the eye," and there's a picture of Hank and me looking straight ahead at these two guys and they're looking down at the ground. I looked at Hank, he looked at me, and we kept looking at the referees.

The game started. I looked up at the scoreboard, the clock was moving, we got possession of the ball, they took it away from us, and in 45 seconds they went down and scored. We got the next face-off, went down, and scored. We stole a ball from them and at half time we were ahead 3-1. It was still a very tight game. The stick work was very good by both teams, the fans enjoyed the game, there was a lot of press coverage, and there were numerous reporters there. Baltimore even had a reporter from the *Baltimore Sun*. So it was more than just a game, it was an intersectional competition between two very good programs.

At half time, our coaches told us what we could do in the second half. We didn't reflect on some of the errors that we made in the first half. We talked about what we had to do for the next 24 minutes. Quarters were 12 minutes at the time. And they said "In the next 24 minutes, you can accomplish something that no team in the State of New York has ever accomplished in lacrosse." Our coach said, "Think about that." He had us all stand up, we put our arms around each other, and not a word was said.

We went on the field and scored the first two goals to go ahead 5-1. They came back and scored the next 3, making it 5-4. We called a time out, and at that time I think there was probably 11 minutes left in the game. I remember the coach saying, "Does anybody in this huddle want to be denied an opportunity to win an intersectional game against a great opponent?" I don't think anybody was breathing. I think we were all realizing we didn't want to be denied. We went out and scored the next goal to go up 6-4. They got desperate and we stole the ball, and went ahead 7-5. That was the final score.

Given the respect we had for our opponent, we didn't jump up and down, we didn't jump on each other. We had athletic maturity, and that was established from the first day we got together as players. We always respected our opponent. Believe it or not, we never shook hands with our opponents until that day. Both teams formed a line automatically. In some sports it's a given, they do it all the time. We had played two games previous to that and we never had an after game ceremony. I remember we not only just shook hands with them, we actually hugged our opponent and they hugged us.

At the end of the game, the fans were still there. I think the fans were astonished at the attitude of high school athletes, at the end of that game. We looked around, and I don't think anybody left the stadium. The band played, and they were an unbelievable band that used to lead the Macy's Thanksgiving Day Parade. There were broadcasters, cheerleaders, twirlers, and the band.

What we did that day reminds me of the Army/Navy game - both military academies get together and stand for the Alma Mater of each school. The band played, and I remember we all stood next to a player from St. Paul's. It was a wonderful tribute. It was an experience that none of us ever forgot.

Do you remember the names of some of your teammates?

Yes. Bobby Naso, John Krupa had a goal, John Howland had a goal, that was our seven goals. Jimmy Badami, our goalie, had seventeen saves, because we were playing against a team that could really shoot. Our value was, we had an unbelievable defense. Paul Rochester - who eventually went on to play for the Jets, and played for Michigan State - was a defenseman. He and Hank Getz were just unbelievable defensemen. They controlled a great attack, St. Paul's eventually went on to win for the next 3 years, so their winning streak could have been very similar to ours. We eventually went on to win 58 in a row. Theirs was stopped at 29. It was an experience I will never forget. I never thought I would go on to coaching, but that was an experience that I really carried into my coaching career.

Because you saw what a collective belief can do for people?

Exactly, and what teamwork can do. We knew we were going to play St. Paul's in the third game. We conditioned the month before that game harder than we ever conditioned. We stayed on the field after practice, and the coaches - who had gone into the locker room - would have to come out and get us off the field. We just felt that we were carrying the tradition and the success of the players that were there before us, the people we saw in our program that were playing at those colleges. And everybody was tuned in. There was no TV, there were no cell phones. I don't know if people rushed to the payphone, but the word got out quickly and it was a magnificent time. School spirit, in my opinion, is extremely important. It can be school spirit in academics, in plays, in shows, in sports or in proms. It's very vital, and I think it really helped all of us become better people.

I'm also going to guess – and I say this as a parent - that getting attention is something that all kids crave, and when you get attention for something you really worked for, it means a lot more.

Exactly... very true ... It creates an inner sense of achievement and self-respect to work that hard and be recognized for it instead of just being recognized because you sought attention somehow.

The following Monday, we never wore letter sweaters. We never walked around like we were the big men on campus. Looking back, our school probably led the high schools on Long Island in trend-setting. In those days you had pegged pants, you had DA haircuts - which were better known as duck's ass haircuts -you had long side burns.

That Monday, a diverse group of people that normally looked at you like they were looking through you were smiling, because collectively, they were part of the success that we had on Saturday. I thought it really brought a sense of harmony to the school. There were people who felt they weren't recognized, but after that game, they all felt that something special had happened.

I never missed a day of school. I remember sneaking out the back door and I wasn't sure if I had the flu or the mumps, whatever. My mother called the office, and wanted me to come home and she said I was contagious. So of course they drove me home. School was very important to me. I still recall every teacher I had, and everything they did for me. The high school experience is something you should really cherish; it only lasts four years.

A lot of people find fault with going to school. Well, I saw what my brothers went through. They went through school, then they went to war. Unfortunately, the Korean War had kicked up during that period of time. I was really concerned about a repeat of many men and women having to go to war. I was too young to go to Korea, but some of those players that were on our bulletin board did, and some died. Our senior year we probably should have worn patches with the number of the three men that died in Korea that played lacrosse and football but in those days patches were not an item.

So this is round two for you because you lost your brother, and so you knew exactly what those families were dealing with. There were probably a lot of people your age that suffered losses like that, uncles, or cousins, or dads.

Yes, and it was the first time that we really had a "television war," and it was scary because by that time I was reading a lot of books about the Second World War, about these soldiers being surrounded, being ambushed, being shot down, and then you heard about the Chosin Reservoir. All these Marines were surrounded, and the temperatures were in the minus 20's. They were starving, they were freezing, they had frostbite, they were running out of ammunition, and hordes of enemy soldiers were coming towards them on an hourly basis.

Here I was, getting ready for my senior year, and they gave me hope, and a lift. I remember thinking a lot about that in the classroom. I remember going through our hallways, seeing the names of all the students that were in the Second World War, and now we had a wall with Korean War veterans' names on it, and some had Gold Stars next to their names.

Fast-forward 60-some years. There are actually two heroes here in Ithaca that were in the Chosin Reservoir. On the Marine Corps birthday, the VFW has a very nice program. Having been in the Marines, it's an unbelievable feeling to be in that room. The Marine Corps ROTC comes down from Cornell, and when I look at the men that were in the Chosin Reservoir, I think to myself, these men were over there and they were probably not really sure why they were there. To their everlasting credit, their loyalty to our country outweighed any uncertainty they were experiencing.

I still go back to that high school. It draws me back. I walk in the main lobby, and the school was beautifully designed. It was built in the 1930's with marble floors, hand carved wood etching on the walls, and it is still immaculate. I look at that wall, and there are more Gold Stars up there than were there when I was in high school. It's extremely difficult. Students, athletes, young ladies that might have been cheerleaders or Rockettes, people who played in the band, guys who were in machine shop, guys who were in aeronautics.

In fact some of my players at Cornell were in that program, and when they came to Cornell, they almost had sophomore status because it was so advanced. It's a trip I have to take every time I'm on Long Island. The football field just recently was changed to artificial turf, but I used to walk that grass field and think of my teammates. Some have passed away, some are not in good health, and it's sort of like a tabernacle; it opens for me, and I want to reach out and thank them for being great friends, great team mates. It's a beautiful journey.

That's great, that's a perfect choice for this chapter. I see the importance of revisiting these areas in your life, and the people, and the roles they played, and how team sports shaped you. I just keep hearing this recurrent theme of gratitude... that you're grateful to be able to be in a position to share these stories, grateful that you have the ability to recall all of these details. To be honest, a lot of people half your age can't remember half this stuff, and too many people wait too long to tell their story.

It's interesting. I go back on that field, and I remember a goal line stand against Hempstead High School. I remember the opening kick-off against Mineola. We ran a reverse, and Jim Mason threw a block on a player by the name of Jergens, who was a 6'5" tackle for Mineola, and while it unfortunately broke his leg, it was a legal block. I remember that poor young man being in such pain that I looked up to Heaven and I sort of prayed that it wouldn't be serious.

I remember blocking a punt in the Chaminade High School game. We were down 13-0, we were very dormant, and they were very good. It was the opening game of the year. It was played at Sewanhaka High School. We had worked all summer to beat Chaminade, and their guys used to date the girls from Sewanhaka High School, and that used to upset some of my teammates. Some guys from Chaminade had cars. Most of us were lucky if we had roller skates.

That summer we'd work out and a young lady in town had a swimming pool, and she invited us over for a little swimming after our workout. She was dating a guy by the name of Red Quinn, who was a Center on the Chaminade football team. Red Quinn left his playbook by the pool, and in those days you didn't have carbon paper. We took the playbook - we probably shouldn't have done it - but we thought he left it there intentionally. We took the playbook, and that night we copied down everything that Chaminade had in their playbook, including a pass play where the quarterback would fake a hand-off, put the ball near his groin area, walk back, and nobody would know where the ball was, thinking the guy was running with it. Well we knew that play, so the first time they ran it, it was 3rd and 14 and I was playing defense then with Ernie Fiero. We knew it was going to be called, so Ernie and I called it the "Red Special." We were thinking he was going to call it, and sure as hell, we knocked them for about a 16-yard loss. Brian Dennehy was on that team, and he played opposite of me.

Who?

Brian Dennehy, the actor.

Are you in his book?

I don't think so... Eventually he went on to Columbia, where he was Captain of the team, but he decided to give up football his senior year to concentrate on acting. Their lineup was like a Who's Who. They were heavily recruited, and we called it "the best team money can buy." I blocked the punt and we went down and scored to make it 13-7, and boy, that gave us a shot. We eventually won 27-13, I think.

You know, you don't forget those days. When I'm on Long Island, I always visit my football coach, Mark Martone, who's probably approaching his 90's. God bless him, his health is good, but he has a hearing deficiency. There's fourteen of us, and we try to meet him every time we're on Long Island. We organize it, we meet at a special diner in Commack. If you ever want to do a story about a famous diner, that's it. Contracts have been signed there, pro football players have quit there. It's a celebrity hangout, and we're just high school guys - high school guys who are just 60 or 70 years older.

The joy is unbelievable. The coach hugs and kisses everybody, we hug and kiss each other. Ernie Schwasnick comes to it. Ernie moved from Austria with his parents, and I think it was at a time of extreme turmoil. Ernie didn't speak very good English, in fact he didn't speak English at all. He went through the 8th grade, learned a little English and played freshmen football with me. Eventually he became our quarterback. It was difficult for Ernie to decipher play calls, so we had our halfback give us the calls in the huddle and Ernie ran them. Seeing him is like turning pages back.

I remember the first time I met him. His locker was four away from mine, and I remember some kids were making fun of him, and I think one guy slammed his hand in the freaking locker. I think I was a nice guy in high school, but I think I was, I guess, outspoken if the situation called for it. We never tolerated bullies, rednecks, and we never tolerated guys using the "n" word. We tried to bring some civility and acceptance to our team.

It sounds like you would tolerate all but intolerance.

Yes. My spiritual background has been a great help to me throughout my life. Believe it or not, I would go to Synagogue with some of my teammates, to the Lutheran Church, Presbyterian Church, and it was such a wonderful experience, because I was learning about other people, other religions. I personally believe it really helped our teams be successful. We knew about each other's families. In those days you didn't come for tailgates. Parents sometimes couldn't come to games because they had to work or they had other children at home, so you brought your experience home. And they relished in that experience even though they couldn't be there.

When I return to Long Island for get-togethers with my high school coach and former teammates, everybody embellishes their version of the story. And sometimes you think that story is a little bit different than how it happened, but guys tell the story just the way they remember it. He didn't run 50 yards he ran 47, he didn't score 6 goals, he scored 4 and had two assists, so it's close to being accurate.

We were thrilled in 2015 when the NFL awarded each high school that had turned out a player who played in the Super Bowl a golden football to commemorate the 50th anniversary of the big game. We all went back to see Paul Rochester, a Sewanhaka teammate, who played in Super Bowl III with the Jets. Paul is still a giant, 6'4", probably weighs about 260, and in high school he was probably about 220. To be back there together, and be able to touch that ball with him was an experience I will never forget.

I can imagine what that was like for him that you guys came back to share that with him.

It felt like we never left the huddle. My high school coach actually raised Paul. Paul's father died when Paul was a sophomore. They had moved from Michigan, and his mother died about a year later, partly from being heart-broken. Mark Martone was able to become a guardian, so Paul lived in Mark's house. Mark renovated the basement, and the story goes that Paul used to sneak out of the basement window to hook up with his buddies.

He was a remarkable athlete. He won a Thorp Award, which goes to the outstanding football player on Long Island. While at Michigan State, he played in the famous 0-0 tie against Notre Dame. He made the last 3 stops on the goal line. You can go on and on about what these players did, and what they did in their lives. The thing that hurt me was we didn't have any junior colleges on Long Island at that time, because a lot of these players couldn't afford to go to college. Some were recruited to play football and lacrosse, but they had to work to help support their families, because some of them were the oldest boy in the family and they might have had four or five siblings. That was really tough, and I'm grateful that I was given the opportunity, but the love we had for one another wasn't based on the material things we had, it was based on what you kept in your heart.

When we get together as a group, it adds years to my high school coach's life. We go out in the parking lot, we form a circle, we put our arms around each other and we sing the Sewanhaka fight song, and that we put in the book. Singing it gives us the chance to think back to those days in the locker room, before practice, after a win, after a loss. The saddest day of my life was graduation day. It's a happy occasion for a lot of people, and I know my family and my parents were happy, but I was sad that I wasn't going to be in that building anymore as a student.

You have spent a lifetime helping other people try to have that experience.

That's so important to me, because my parents expressed this, as did my brothers and sisters, my teachers, my coaches and my neighbors. When I speak at schools and clinics, I try to bring out some points about the athletic and academic experience. As I look out into the audience, I feel like some of them just drift, but I try to engage them and get them to consider a few points. What if an illness came upon you tomorrow and you could never go to school again? How tough that would be? Now you have a golden opportunity, to be in school, to have the very best provided for you, and you'd be very wise to embrace it. As I've said often, I see this cloud hanging over some people's lives, and I wish that one day I could have the opportunity to cure people that are ill and disabled. Someday it may happen.

You're lucky that you realized that, a lot of people don't understand how magical those years are until much later, if ever.

It was a beautiful experience. I never miss reunions. In fact, I'm going to a 60 -year reunion of the class of 1956, because a lot of my teammates and friends were in that class.

Does your saintly wife go with you to all of these gatherings?

She's been to a couple of them. It's sometimes hard. I know a lot about her high school and she knows a lot about mine. We both had different feelings. I'm sure she has some sentiment for her high school. I'm a very sentimental guy, and I will never forget putting on that purple and white uniform, doing my very best for Sewanhaka High School. It was something special.

A Title, a Frat and a Girl Named Pat

Moving on from high school, I have a few questions: How did you decide to go to the University of Maryland?

What other schools were you looking at? What was the recruiting process like? How many visits did you do? How did that experience impact how you recruited later?

As I mentioned, one of the saddest days of my life was graduation day from Sewanhaka High School, but now we were moving on. I graduated in January. Parochial schools in those days had mid-year graduation, and by graduating in January, it was probably not the best time to start college. The schools I was very interested in were West Point, Maryland and Syracuse. I was advised to start school in January and then transfer to one of those schools.

The West Point dream was not realistic for me. My brother, John, went to West Point, and was in the class of 1941. My nephew, Michael – John's son –was a member of the class of 1964. My dream was to go there because I really enjoyed that combination of education and discipline, and I was very interested in the military. I came to realize that West Point would not be the best match for me, so my focus turned to Syracuse, Hofstra and Maryland.

What made Hofstra enter into the equation? Was it the fact that it was local?

Yes, it was a local school. Howdy Myers was the football and lacrosse coach there. He was a remarkable guy who is now in the

National Lacrosse Hall of Fame. It would have given me the opportunity to play both football and lacrosse.

I definitely wasn't big enough to play football at Syracuse or Maryland, but I admired all of the coaches at those schools. I drove up to Syracuse. In those days, the recruiting process was much different. You didn't have official visitations. You might have gone to campus with your parents but it wasn't like it became later on.

Did they have any film to look at, or had they seen you play?

They pretty much were going on the advice of the player's high school coach or alumni in the area. My high school coach, Bill Ritch, played at Syracuse, so he had some insight into that program, and he was great friends with Dr. Jack Faber and Al Heagy, who were coaches at Maryland.

I drove up to Syracuse with two of my friends. One was a football candidate, and my friend and I were lacrosse players. I was really reluctant and a little nervous about going in to see Roy Simmons Sr., the lacrosse coach, so we looked around campus first, and really enjoyed it. Some of my former teammates from Sewanhaka were enrolled at Syracuse and were playing lacrosse there. They were all playing on the same team as Jimmy Brown, and that was a great team at Syracuse at the time.

You went to school with the legendary Jim Brown?

I played at Sewanhaka and he played at Manhasset. He was a junior when I was a freshman. It's ironic, he and I both got inducted into the United States Lacrosse Hall of Fame at the same time. But during the Syracuse visit, I was really shy. I didn't know what steps to take. I did see Mr. Simmons in the hallway and said hello to him but I didn't acknowledge my interest in lacrosse to him.

I came home and I was advised to think about going to college in January, and then transfer on to other schools. People thought that if I sat around for six months, I would get involved in an activity I really enjoyed and never go to college, which is what a lot of young people did at that time. So, I went to Cortland for six months. It was a great experience, and then my high school coach called me and told me there was an opportunity for me to go to Maryland.

What kind of courses did you take at Maryland?

I took Physical Education and Education courses. It was a wonderful program and a great group of people. We had excellent professors. I was home during the Spring Break from Cortland, and the coaches from Maryland called and talked to me about possibly transferring there. That was a great relief to me because that was one of the schools that I really wanted to go to.

Mr. Ritch contacted me, and he was kind enough to set up an opportunity for me to meet with both of the coaches in New York City. Their headquarters for recruiting was at the NY Athletic Club, and there was a gentleman there by the name of Jack Kelly, who went to Maryland. He was a lacrosse player, and he resided in New York City for a period of about 32 years, and he had a penthouse at the NY Athletic Club. His business was in New York and he had a great love for Maryland lacrosse. So I went in to meet these two gentlemen, and I guess they were impressed with my interview because 2 days later they called me and offered me a scholarship to go to Maryland.

In September, I started at Maryland. I didn't know a lot about the players, but I knew some things about the program. I knew I wanted to go to Maryland. No one from our area in recent years had gone there, and Maryland had a very good lacrosse program and it was a very good school academically, so it was really a boost for me to get this opportunity.

A friend of mine was going to Maryland, but he was not an athlete. We drove down to Maryland together in his convertible. We arrived on campus with the top down. Two Northerners at what might be called a "border school..." When I say border school, I wasn't sure if they favored the Civil War from the south side or the north side, and here we were, two Northerners with unbelievable Long Island accents, which created somewhat of a language barrier. We had to repeat some of our words a few times because some of the people from Maryland thought that it sounded like a foreign language.

I didn't live in the dorms the first year – I lived in a private home that rented out rooms, and I walked to classes and walked to practices. We did not have full practice, so my concentration was getting in shape, getting organized academically, and every once in a while there would be a team lacrosse meeting. There is no question, I felt like Jackie Robinson. I was the only Northerner on the team, and they never heard of Sewanhaka High School. 70% of the team was comprised of prep school players, and the other players were from exclusive high schools in and around the Maryland area, and it was very obvious it was going to be a great experience for me in many ways

So, you felt like an outsider in many different ways?

Yes, I did. It was a wonderful experience in the beginning. I had to adjust to a totally new culture, which was good for me. I missed the hands-on approach that was at Cortland and at Sewanhaka High School, and I found myself feeling like I was in a foreign country, even though the state of Maryland is a beautiful state. I just felt that it's nice to be here, but do I really belong here? I had to adjust to a new culture and environment. Being a member of a team really helped with this transition.

I went home for Christmas, and I was proud to wear my University of Maryland blazer. When I got back in January, we had a meeting and practice started. We were given an unbelievable amount of equipment - two or three pairs of shoes, and sweatpants that were sort of designed by a fashion designer. I was used to the baggy sweatpants.

How had Maryland been faring nationally up to that point?

They had won a national championship in '55, so a lot of veterans were coming back. We went into the locker room, and there were name tags on the lockers. It was very professionally done, with our game number and name tag. One interesting thing about my locker was, it was within 3 feet of the urinal, and I sort of got the message very quickly.

It was extremely interesting, the first day of practice my style (Long Island style) was aggressive, and it was very obvious that I upset a few people. In fact, my first experience was similar to Rudy, the main character in the movie made about Notre Dame. When he went out for the football team and decided he was going to make the team by being overly aggressive. I guess my aggressiveness upset so many young men that were not used to getting knocked down. So, not only did I have the locker room experience of my locker location, but I was sort of in a situation where not too many players talked to me and that was kind of difficult. It was so different than my experience in high school. I also played one year at Cortland, so my teammates at both places were a little bit more congenial.

How did that affect your eligibility to play?

I was eligible at Cortland and then eligible at Maryland the following year. Eligibility was a little different then.

As practice went on, coaches had me face off, which I had not done in high school. They had me doing things that sort of made me fit in. I played extra-man defense, and I was always instructed to play the best scorer in practice. I think the coaches liked my style of play, but the players were not accustomed to it, so I had a decision to make. Do I become a pretty mild-mannered athlete or do I continue my style of play? I continued my style of play.

We were getting ready to open the first game of the season with a game against Mt. Washington Lacrosse Club - which was and still is one of the top lacrosse clubs in the country. Every person on that club was an All American from the various Baltimore schools and academies. They were very good. Maryland had not beat Mt. Washington in about 10 years.

They played at Mt. Washington's Norris Field, which is off the major highway going into Baltimore, and the attendance was great. They could seat probably a thousand people. That was a large and vocal crowd. Of course they favored the southern players at Mt. Washington, and there is this kid, Richie Moran, being introduced from New Hyde Park, NY - Sewanhaka High School, and there was complete silence…at least I thought it was complete silence. I think one or two friends of mine were at the game, and they clapped and whistled, but it was definitely not the uproar that others got, but it was fine.

We faced off, and I was very fortunate to have the ball in my stick. I was driving to the cage when two very athletic gentlemen from Mt. Washington decided they were going to knock me down, and they hit me with a tremendous impact. As I was going down, I threw the ball into the lower corner of the goal to score, and to some in the audience, that was astonishing. How can this little runt get knocked down and still put the ball in the cage? I think I had my eyes closed, I think my heart was beating fast, and it was just instinct.

Divine Intervention on behalf of the altar boy?

Yes, very much so. When I scored that goal and came off the

field, it was the first time the players seemed excited about me being their teammate, and it was wonderful.

The following year, we had a new president at Maryland – Dr. Wilson Homer "Bull" Elkins. He was actually an outstanding football player and scholar athlete in Texas. He came in and enforced the rule that today would probably be pretty interesting... The rule was that you had to have a 2.5 average in order to compete in athletics the semester before your season. I'm not too sure what that status would be today in college athletics, but we lost about six players that didn't have a 2.5 average. Some of them were double athletes, so it was tough for them because some played football and lacrosse, or soccer and lacrosse.

Six players from a roster of what size?

Twenty-five. So it was difficult because we had to make up for lack of the depth and talent, and that following year we beat some good teams, like Army and Navy.

What year was this for you, eligibility-wise?

It was my junior year. We were having an undefeated season and, unfortunately, we took a tail spin and lost to Johns Hopkins in the final game of the season before a huge crowd at home – it was very disappointing. I felt really bad because the two coaches were unbelievable men. Jack Faber - who was head of the Microbiology Department at Maryland, and Al Heagy, who was involved with the Chemistry Department. Both were outstanding athletes at Maryland in the early 1930's, and then they decided that in addition to their faculty duties they wanted to coach lacrosse, which they had played. I felt bad for them because during my junior year my dad passed away and they really picked up the role my father would have played during my time in college. I will never forget how nice they were and the things they did for me that helped me recover from a very difficult time in my life. I remember they took me to the airport and I had not known that my dad had passed away. I got home and my brother-in-law, Jim Costello, met me at the airport. As we were driving from LaGuardia to my home, he told me my father had passed away the night before, and it was very tough for me.

Was this unexpected? Had your dad been ill?

My dad was diagnosed with cancer, and I remember being with

him at Christmas. I would give him massages. He was a very strong guy but I felt the deterioration in his back muscles. I didn't know a lot about cancer, and how it had progressed. It was a very difficult time for me. My teammates and coaches were really outstanding people, and I can never thank those two men for what they did for me.

It was around that time I met my wife - and not to confuse lacrosse with romance - but I was walking up one staircase in the Biology building and she was coming down the other. I had a roommate by the name of Charlie Wright. Charlie was a Korean War veteran. He came from the southern shore of Maryland, and I loved him. He was a baseball catcher, a much older guy because he had spent 3 years in Korea. I think he started his baseball career at age 24. I was a young 20, and I had a tremendous roommate in Charlie.

I was walking up the stairs and this young lady was coming down the other side and I said to Charlie, "I'm going to marry that girl." I had no idea who she was, or anything about her. Charlie said, in his Southern drawl, "You are crazy Richie." A couple of days later I pledged a fraternity, and I was accepted to Phi Kappa Sigma, which was at 5 Fraternity Row.

One of my friends in the fraternity had a girlfriend who was a sorority sister of this unknown individual that I saw on the staircase. I happened to see the girls in a college pharmacy in town - which was great for lemonades and milk shakes - and I happened to see them together. Now again, this lady is totally unknown to me and I was thinking 'My god she is beautiful,' so I asked my frat brother, "Can you ask your girlfriend to introduce me to the girl she was with the other day?" He asked who, and I confessed that I really didn't know who she was, and he too said "You are crazy." I said "Not really… I would like to know who she is."

He went down the list of all of the sorority girls. He happened to have a picture of all the girls that his girlfriend had given to him, because he was a bus boy at that sorority. Sure enough, I picked her out and it was a young lady by the name of Patricia Jean Smith. I asked if he could fix me up and he said, "Okay, I'll try."

Sure enough, we had a blind date. Once again, my "foreign accent" created a bit of a problem. We went to Glen Echo Park on our first date, and I don't know if we had dinner or if it was a hamburger, but the four of us got along really well. It was very obvious that I didn't hit a home run on the first date with this lady from Washington, D.C. – in fact, I don't think I even got out of the dugout.

Being persistent, I let a week go by and I called her and asked her if she wanted to go out for lunch. I almost fell off the chair when she said "Yes, I'd like to." We went to lunch and I told her we had a frat party coming up on Saturday night, and asked if she would like to go. She said "Yes, I would like to go."

Apparently, my accent wasn't an issue, and I didn't need a translator. We had a very good time at the fraternity party. From that period on things worked out beautifully. She is now my wife and I am glad I walked up those stairs that day.

I would like to point out the profound irony that Pat could have married "Mr. Wright," but instead she got you!

That is truly ironic.

Were you and Pat classmates in school?

She was 6 months ahead of me. Pat was great at typing reports and various papers that I submitted. I used to walk by a number of private homes with beautiful rose bushes in front and I would bring her a couple of roses every day. Someone asked "Where did you get the money to buy those roses?" I'd say "I pinched them as I was walking along." That was a big hit with the sorority sisters, because some of their boyfriends were slugs and didn't bring them anything. I became a very, very charming suitor of a sorority girl.

Despite your tendencies toward thievery?

Right… The nice thing about the Maryland situation was, I was on scholarship and my job was to clean the floors in Washington Hall. I lived in Washington Hall 2 years before I became president of my fraternity. Washington Hall was four stories tall, and Sunday morning was the best time to do it. Maryland was a school where at that time, a lot of students went home on the weekends. I had a roommate who was a chemical engineer. He was about 6'5" and 150 pounds, and he slept on the top bunk because there was no way I was going on the top bunk. He would help me do the floors. He eventually because a top scientist. Anyway, we roomed together that year and then I got a single room, but the beauty of it was he took glass blowing at 8 am on Saturday mornings and had to get off the top bunk early. He would wake me up periodically. In those days I dreamt a lot, and every once in a while I thought it was Dracula coming out of the pillows.

Most students lived in the area, so Sunday morning was the best time to wash and wax floors. It was a great experience, a great job. That provided me the opportunity to do things at Maryland – it helped to alleviate the burden on my parents financially, and then when I became president of the fraternity my senior year, I got free room and board. I also had my scholarship, so I was living high on the hog. In those days I got what was called "laundry money." Every 2 weeks we got $15 from the athletic department for incidentals. I think it's something we should do today, but $15 would not go as far as it did back in the 50's. But it was an opportunity for us to take a date out, or go to White Castle, which was famous for tiny hamburgers. You would get twelve in a bag, and that was definitely a great place to go after a heavy night of dancing.

Did you have some pretty good moves?

No, I was terrible. I was also a busboy, because it gave me the opportunity to meet some of the ladies on campus. The house mother was remarkable. In those days, every girl smoked, and they would take their cigarettes and put them out in their coffee cups and saucers. Just try to get ashes out of a coffee cup... The house mother would come in and yell at us for not doing a good job. So one day I decided to take all the ashes and put them in a canister, and when we were going to have ice cream, I'd put the ashes on top. I didn't tell anyone for 3 weeks, and that prank is still talked about at the Kappa Delta house.

The summer of my senior year, I stayed at the University of Maryland and got some jobs. I took kinesiology during the summer. I loved history – I took a history course, it was Civil War History. And of course, it allowed me to court Pat. I went to her house for dinner on the weekends and I would stay in her brother's room and once again, I'd hear "You're from Long Island? Where is Long Island? New York? Are you from New York City?"

My religion is Catholic, I'm a Democrat, and I don't like the "N word." The reason I'm saying this is, my mother-in-law grew up in the south, in Roanoke, which was not the heart of the Confederacy, but pretty close to it. All of the things I mentioned, she was not in favor of, so there definitely was a barrier. I wondered, how do I convince Pat's mother that I'm a nice guy who is worthy of her daughter?

We would go out to parties on the weekends in Georgetown – it was extremely lively with college students from all over Washington and Maryland, and it was a very exciting time of my life. We'd go to these parties and get home late. I was never a guy with a watch, but it was probably 2:30-3:00 am, and it was very obvious that Pat's mother knew when we came home. I would go in her brother's room, take a shower, put on my suit and tie, and sit in a chair with an alarm clock. The alarm would go off at 6:15, and I would go to a 7:00 am Mass. I would use their car because I didn't have a car, and I would come back, stopping at the bakery on the way. For years, Pat's mother talked about this to her friends. On Pat's block there were probably 7 or 8 doctors, and they all belonged to the same country club, same church, swimming pool and tennis courts – they all did things together. It was very obvious that she would tell people about this Catholic guy that would come in at 3:00 a.m. and go to 7:00 church. That was a very smart move on my part.

It showed that you were sincere?

Apparently. On Friday, we would have early practice and I would always like to go to a movie, so once in a while we would go back to her house. It was a fairly easy drive from Maryland to Washington, D.C., so we would go there for Friday night dinner. Pat would pick me up, and the evening would start with a cocktail party that I wasn't a part of, as we didn't get there until dinner. She would have guests there – the dining room table setting was fit for a king or queen, and I would sit down and they would have the greatest steaks that you would ever see. In the Catholic Church during that time, you had to abstain from meat on Friday. Hilda the maid would make me the nicest, most elegant tuna salad you'd ever seen. She dressed it up, and in fact they should have taken pictures of it, because in any food magazine you would see today it would have been a highlight. And then I remember cutting it and everyone was cutting their steak and bringing it up to their mouth and looking at me with tuna fish, and of course for a college guy to see a steak is like looking at an expensive car, something you will never have, but boy, I loved that tuna fish.

That's nice they respected you and accommodated you, and apparently felt you were holding up your end of the bargain.

Ha, ha… I was a freaking outcast.

You had a lot of the good things going for you, right? Smart college guy, good athlete, right ethnicity…

Yes, definitely, although my ethnicity was in question because I was Irish. Our courtship continued and it was a wonderful time in my life. Having lost my dad, it really hurt that I couldn't do more for him.

Please tell me about your final year at the University of Maryland.

The final year we caught up with what I would call the "academic index." We were required to have 2.5 grade point average, and the majority of our players were in Liberal Arts programs. Some were in Physical Education, Physical Therapy, and we had some Engineers on our team. My major was Physical Education, Safety Education, and I really thought about Physical Therapy because I was encouraged by what I had seen. It was a new field, but so was Safety Education.

With the loss of some players, we now had to take on different roles. We were national runners-up the year before. It worked out well. Everyone played hard and I think we lost two games that year. We beat Army and Navy, which were big games, and we lost to Hopkins again. It was a great year. It was sad like high school, because when you come into your last game you say to yourself "Wow, I'm never going to have this experience again." The friendships that you make are enduring. I am still very attached to my teammates from Maryland. I visit with my friend Fred Kern in Florida when we are there. He was a football and a lacrosse player. That, to me, is what it's all about. We all experienced the same thing. The attachment is very important. I always advise people that you are going to move to different parts of the country, you are going to get different friends, but don't forget the people that helped get you up those steps to the different environment, different culture. A phone call, a card, a note… To me these are all extremely important.

Tell me about how the National Champions were determined in your senior year.

There were no tournaments. The national champions were picked by a board of coaches. If you look at the national champions, it's very obvious that outside of Army and RPI, no one else was declared champion. It was Southern based. That all changed in 1971, the first year of the National Championship.

Did you have any post-college plans at that time?

My dream was to finish college, get a good job, and be able to send my parents back to visit Ireland. They had never been back since they came to the U.S., with the Depression, the birth of eight children, the Second World War. It just wasn't realistic for them to make that trip. In college, my mind floated in a lot of different directions. Why not join the military, why not defend your country? It crossed my mind to forego college, but Pat encouraged me to finish what I had started: To finish college.

I was in Air Force ROTC at the University of Maryland, and I really enjoyed it. ROTC was compulsory for the first 2 years at UMD, and the Air Force was the only ROTC option. During my junior year, you had to make a firm commitment to the Air Force. At that stage it was a 3-year commitment, and I felt I could accomplish my military goals by graduating ROTC, taking the 3-year assignment, and come back and work in the real world. Midway through the year, the U.S. Air Force decided to increase the obligation to 5 years, and I withdrew. When I did so, I got notification that my draft status went from "Ineligible/College ROTC" to "Eligible." With that change, the local Draft Board determined that I would be #7, and I would have been drafted in January.

I wanted to finish college, so I was in somewhat of a panic mode. I got some great advice from my coaches, and also the people in ROTC. They said go back home and check to see if there was an opportunity to sign up for a Reserve group. I tried them all… Coast Guard, Army, Navy, Merchant Marine, and the only one that had an opening was the Marine Corps. That resonated with me. I enlisted in the Marine Corps, which prevented me from being taken out of college. I never realized how important the Marine Corps was going to be in my life.

After graduation from Maryland, I went to Parris Island. Everything I had read about Parris Island was true, and you could add a lot more to it. I remember getting on the train in NY with all of the recruits. We were going to Yemassee, South Carolina. Of the recruits on that train, about 80% were from NYC – tight pants, DA haircuts, mustaches, side burns, constant smokers and drinkers. I said to myself, from what I hear about Parris Island, you better be A J squared away when you get off the train. Of course, I've never been a smoker, and I never drank on the train. I read while I was on the train, and no one else wanted to read. They just wanted to have a good time.

We pulled into Yemassee, NC about 5:30 in the morning, and for some of these guys on the train it would be about the time they were getting home from a night out. We got off the train, and they were so nice to us. They lined us up and we were only allowed to bring a small bag – the small bag went to your right and you lined up on the white line. There was space between the first line, second line and third line, and they ask you to take your jacket off if you had one and put it on top of your bag. For a half hour they fired off the coarsest, sternest words I had ever heard. We had two guys get off the train smoking, and they were still smoking in line. The drill instructor went up to them and took the cigarette, put it out, and went back to the guys and told them to eat it. I knew they meant business. Plus, they made them go down and pick the ashes up. We turned to our right and it was like you were assembling an automobile. You went into a room, and all your stuff was placed in one area. You walked in – there were 20 barbers. They were tougher than the drill instructors. They took off all of your hair, and likely left some scarring on some of the recruits that is with them today. I think they were intentionally trying to find out who were the wise guys. The side burns would come off and some guys have markings from the shaving, so either the razors were not sharp or those Barbarian barbers put on a special device to make sure you were maimed. From there, you went into a shower area and from there, you went on to get your uniform. They were definitely not tailor made. You got your uniform, put it on, walked through another door, took an oath of allegiance, and went through another area. That area was sort of like a storage depot or a supply area, and you picked up all the essential things you needed. They handed me a rifle for the first time, and I think I reached for it improperly. The butt of the rife came up to my freaking chest, and they said "Don't ever grab a rifle that way!"

So, here's the Long Island guy, holding it like a lacrosse stick –

not the right way. From that day on, I learned a lot, and we did a lot. My platoon was close to forty college graduates that probably had the same situation that I had. Pete Brennan, who had played basketball at North Carolina, was 6'5 ¾", and if you were 6'6" you didn't get drafted. Pete was actually drafted by the Knicks, and we had a couple football players from the Big 10, athletes from the Ivy League, and a couple of guys that boxed in college. Boxing was big in the 40's and 50's in college. We had a few wrestlers, so our platoon was very athletic. In the morning they would wake us up at 5:00, and by 5:20 you were outside the barracks, wearing your sneakers, shorts, Marine Corps hat, a PT (physical training) jersey, and you would have to run a mile. The drill instructors were not like your mother. They were very tough, and for a reason. I shouldn't say they weren't nice – we just didn't understand them the first couple of weeks. After the first couple of weeks, we understood that they had been at war, understood the dangers of war, and wanted to make sure we were going to survive if ever we had to go to war.

So, the first time out we ran a mile. I think we were upset because we were setting some kind of record for the mile because we were all athletes and were accustomed to running the mile. The drill instructors were upset – so we had to do pushups and sit ups before breakfast. They wanted us to do 50 of each – we did 75 - and they realized they had a little problem. The next day we ran 2 miles instead of one.

That night, they played a game called "Hide the Bunny." Hide the Bunny is a game during which you stand in front of your bunk – there is a top bunk, lower bunk - and you had a trunk in front that had to be neat in alphabetical order: toothpaste toothbrush, which would you put first? Toothbrush because it has a "b" in it... Everything was folded neatly, and in Hide the Bunny – you get underneath your bed in t-shirts and undershorts. In the center of the squad bay was a place you hung your uniforms in a neat and orderly fashion. If the drill instructors looked down the rack and someone's pants were a little bit longer – everyone was in trouble. This is a way of teaching discipline and regimentation. So we all got on our stomachs and we had no idea what Hide the Bunny was. So the instructor said "When I blow the whistle, you guys start moving to your right – when I blow the whistle again, you go left, when I blow the whistle again, you get up and get back into your bunk." Very simple, right?

No problem. The bay floor was wood. He blew the whistle, we went to the right, went to the left, and on the next whistle we knew where to find our bed.

The only problem was the lights were out, and have you ever tried to find your bed in the dark? This, of course, resulted in total chaos as we scrambled to find our bunks. You don't know where you are after crawling around, and we had a few guys that nearly got decapitated by the clothing bar down the middle. A couple of guys cut their head, some guys ran into each other. They turned the lights on and it looked like we had just had an indoor battle. The building sort of engulfed a bunch of bodies. At the end of the squad bay, the drill instructors had their arms folded and miles the size of the Mississippi River. They said "Now you have 15 minutes to straighten up all of this stuff in the bay, and if you don't straighten this up, we have another game that is better than Hide the Bunny.

It is difficult to imagine a better game…

Exactly… You can't believe how quickly forty-some guys cleaned up that squad bay.

So the purpose of that was to get people adjusted to unexpected outcomes?

Yes, and also to listen to the drill instructors. By doing 2 miles, seventy-five push- ups, and seventy-five sit-ups, we were not following instructions, we were trying to be smart asses. And it was very obvious they were going to put a stop to it, and plus they didn't want to run 2 miles themselves.

Semper Fidelis 5

I'd like to hear more about how your years in the Marine Corps influenced you.

The Marine Corps was a wonderful experience for me. The training was outstanding.

It taught me a lot about discipline in life, and it taught me about my fellow man.

We have all seen or heard the term "Semper Fidelis," which means "Always Faithful." I say "Semper Fidelis" when I exchange greetings with Marine Corps personnel. It's a motto that I have lived by through many years of my life.

After Parris Island we went to Camp Lejeune, in North Carolina. That was quite an experience, a lot of field work. We had wonderful instruction. They made us a force that could contend with the enemy, and they also taught us survival. That was extremely important if we had to go to battle. I remember our field programs, when we went out in the field to take our training and put it to good use, going under barbed wire, getting into fox holes – this story about a fox hole is pretty good…

We had been out in the field for about 3 days, and it was obvious that we were going to have a simulation of battle at night. Fox holes were dug and it was obvious that the fresh soil attracted snakes. I was in a fox hole in about the second row. It was just getting dark and we were getting into our fox holes, and tracers were coming in. I look ahead of me and saw two of the Marines doing the greatest vertical jump you have ever seen. There was a snake in the boot of one of the Marines, and both of them jumped completely out of the fox hole! It was obvious that their fox hole was more attractive to the snakes than ours.

At the end of the 3 days and 2 nights out in the field, we got into formation. I was in the 2nd row, and in front of me was a young man by the name of Don McAllister. He had played at Chaminade High School, and of course, that was our rival, so I always played some jokes on him. Number one, there was a company known as McAllister Tugboats, but the whole time we were together he thought I was an heir to the Moran Tugboats in NYC. So of course I always had the upper hand. The only tugboat I had was probably the one I had in the bathtub when I was a baby.

So, people treat you nicely when they think you have a lot of money?

Exactly... So Don was standing in formation, and standing in front of us was this remarkable Sergeant. He looked a lot like Louie Armstrong. In fact, we used to call him Louie behind his back. He had a great smile, a great feeling for people, but he was tough as hell. So, Louie was in front of us and telling us how poorly we did, even though we got A's throughout the period. But he was always the type of guy that would take the positive and put some negative in it to make you want to work harder, which I thought was a great move in the service. So, Don was standing at attention, and right above his boot was his calf, of course. I reached down in the semi-darkness and pinched his calf. He thought he got bit by a snake! That prompted him to jump on Louie Armstrong the Sergeant, and they both fell down. Louie got up and thought McAllister was crazy, that something had happened to him out in the field. It sort of loosened up those 3 days that we were out there, because when we were marching the 4 miles back, I could hear people laughing under their breath. Had Louie detected this humor, we would have been running back, which wouldn't have been too bad except for the fact that we were carrying about 45 pound packs on our back.

So, we put in a little bit of humor, but we understood what our role would be if we got into a battle.

Yet another good story about the snakes and the Irish...

Correct ... It's interesting, St. Patrick supposedly got all the snakes out of Ireland, and I got all the snakes out of North Carolina!

You talk about the discipline in the Marine Corps, and how to contend with the enemy, and you clearly took this with you into your career. Based on our many conversations and interviews over the past 30-some years, I would gather that you somehow came to believe there can be internal as well as external enemies. Would you say that a primary enemy can be one's self, and when you gain mastery over yourself you are then prepared to deal with outside enemies?

Yes, and that applies to a team as well as to individuals. The Marine Corps is a team. Coaching is working with a team. Education is working with a team. There are very few things in life that don't rely on teamwork. Psychiatrists work with a team, doctors work with a team, musicians work with a team, so the team aspect is very important.

In the Marine Corps, we would have field days on Sunday, and it would be one platoon against another. That's where you really saw the teamwork. We would carry heavy poles in a relay. We would do crawls, rope climbing, relays, and other demanding physical activities. All of this was designed to bring us together as a team. They talk about never leaving a child behind in education. Well, one of the attributes of the military, one that was a theme we were taught from the first week in the Marines, is that if someone was injured or shot, they were never to be left behind. You can look at some of the film that shows some very tragic scenes in the military, and they were always helping their comrades. That goes with the theme: Always faithful. That principle has always been a part of my desire to help people.

Understood... I was thinking about that time frame... Your commanding officers probably had an eye looking at what was unfolding in Southeast Asia in the early 60's. I am sure their mindset was to be ready at any given time, but they likely knew the training might well be for practical use in the very near future.

Correct – The vast majority of the instructors fought in Korea, and they saw some very terrible things. Earlier, I pointed out the battle at Chosin Reservoir, and some of the other battles where they were overwhelmed by huge forces but still held together. Their experiences cemented their ability to train us to accept any hardships, to adapt to any unusual situations. We were trained to be prepared, and to remember that you are always to be there for your comrades, your fellow Marines, and that was remarkable training.

So, your Marine Corps chapter came to an end (although you're a Marine for life)...

Yes. Since we were in the reserves, our time was up after Camp Lejeune. We did take tests for what was then known as "Candidate School." I had the opportunity to go to Quantico, but again, it would have been an extensive period of time. I felt that it didn't fit in with what I wanted to do in life. Every once in a while, I think how great it would have been to make a career in the Marine Corps. I had some friends do it, and it was a great experience for them. It was sort of a hardship on their family, given how much time they spent away, but they certainly served the Marine Corps well.

I always thought that was a direction that I wanted to go. I think more of it now than I did then, but when I came out of the Marine Corp I had some time before I had to get a "real job." I was staying at home, and my mother was definitely a saint. I became a social butterfly. I was single, I'd put a tux on and go into New York City with some of my buddies and we'd wine and dine with the rich and famous – the celebrity-type people, the people that thought they owned NYC. I would get back home at 3 am, and quietly go to bed.

How did you get your foot in the door with that group? Charm? Wit? Good looks?

Thank you. I did this for about 6 or 7 days - probably wearing out a white dinner jacket and the tux - and one morning my mother woke me up and said "Why don't you come down to breakfast early?" Having been coming in so late, my early was about 1pm, but not on that day.

Were any siblings in the house at that time? Your mom was widowed, correct?

Yes, my sister Dorothy, and my brother Hal, were home. I got up and went down, and my mother said "You are really wasting your time. You have 4 or 5 months before you get into the workforce, and you have an education degree, so you should think about substitute teaching."

I thought about that for a moment, as my mother always gave me great advice. She was actually the glue that kept Pat and I together, because we had a long distance relationship. My mother was in her corner. I felt like I was in the boxing ring sometimes, and she was the referee. Every shot Pat took was a good one, and every one I took was a foul, so it really made our relationship strong. The beauty is that my mother's comments really woke me up.

I took a shower, put on a suit, and went over to the high school that I attended - that I loved and still love to this day - and I spoke to Howard Nordahl. He was Dean of boys, and a great friend. He helped establish lacrosse at Sewanhaka in 1938. I asked Mr. Nordahl if there was a chance for me to do some substitute teaching, and he said "Yes". So I filled out all of the material that he requested, and he said that he would call me in the morning. He told me they would call me about 6:30 am on the days I was needed. I stood there for a moment and realized that my nightlife was going to disintegrate quickly.

Within a day I got a phone call to sub in History, and I was thrilled. I loved History, and I had taken a number of History courses at Maryland, so it was right up my alley. I did this for about 3 days, and then the fourth and fifth day I subbed in Physical Education. Then I got a phone call from Mr. Nordahl on a Saturday, and he said "Are you free anytime today"?

We met at the school and he told me that they had a teacher that was going to be gone for about 2 months, and he asked if I'd like to substitute for 2 months. I thought, That's wonderful. He said, "I'm going to take you up to the classroom," It was a room on the third floor next to the elevator. In all the years I was there, I never knew we had a program for children with disabilities. I always thought they were home-schooled, and here at Sewanhaka High School, this program had been in place since 1947. I was a student in this school for 4 years, and we never saw this room or the students. We thought it was an administrative area, as we never went into this part of the building. I sat down and he explained that I would have two assistants to help out with the children. They came in at 9:15 am, everyone else came at 8, so they didn't see these students come in. They would take the elevator up to their classroom, eat their lunch in the classroom, and they worked in the classroom. I said "Can I think about this, and get back to you tomorrow night?" He said I could.

So, I went home and told my mother what was involved. She advised me to go to Hofstra Library and pick up any books I could find about education for children with disabilities, which was a great idea. I wasn't a student at Hofstra, so I explained to the woman what I was doing - and she was very kind. She took me to a section that dealt with mental illness. I said that wasn't really what I was looking for, but she said that there was a manual that dealt with education for children with disabilities. I went to the section, and found the manual, which was less than an inch thick – maybe 14 pages. It did help me somewhat, but then I continued to look around, and asked her if there was more material. That was 1961 – and there was no other material. I asked if I could take it and return it on Monday, and she said that would be fine. She knew what I was thinking about doing. I went home and read it cover to cover, and read it again. I didn't think I was prepared, from the standpoint of working with students with such special needs. I didn't want to be there for a couple of months and not be able to do the right things to meet those needs.

My mother convinced me that this would be a great challenge, and that if Mr. Nordahl didn't think I was qualified, he wouldn't have asked. I called him back to tell him I would do it. We met on Monday morning to talk about the students and the plan, and at 8:45 we walked up to the classroom. The first students arrived at 9 am, and by 9:15 all of the students were in the classroom. There were 22 students, with a wide array of disabilities. Some used a wheelchair, some had difficulty controlling their hands, and there were students with various developmental, physical, and emotional disabilities. I looked at the curriculum, and I stayed with it that day. I went home that night and did a lot of praying, because I wanted to do the right thing.

The next day we went to the next phase, which was English class, which turned out to be the staff reading to the students, and having them look at the book. The assistants would go up and down the aisle, and do the same thing. I thought we should teach them how to write a letter to someone that they really admired.

Sure enough, I put it on the board, pointing out the various components of the letter. With the help of the assistants, the students wrote some very nice letters. I wanted them to get to know each other better, so I would have them read their letters aloud.

After school, I went to every barber shop and doctor's office that was still open, and I collected every magazine they didn't want. I went to Woolworths for some safety scissors, and picked up some books that we could use to make scrapbooks, and brought them to the school the next day. We had a period of time that the students could contribute to the class, and during this period I decided that I would hand out all of the magazines (two or three for each person). I put on the board the categories: Cars, Fashion, Movies, Boats and Sports - I think there were five categories. I told them to cut out pictures from their magazines, then we would give them to people that were interested in that category. They cut them out and pasted them in a scrapbook. I wanted to do something for them that nobody was doing.

Was this something you learned while student teaching?

No, it just came to me. One of the things I felt strongly about was that I wanted the other students in this school to know that these students were there. I was in great physical condition from the Marine Corp, and you don't turn on and off your aggressiveness, but my aggressiveness switched from the military to education.

I went to speak to Howard that afternoon after school, and I asked him if he minded if I took the students to lunch in the cafeteria. I wanted some inclusion. He said that he thought the students would laugh at them, and I said, "I don't think so." My idea was to get some of the leaders in this school - athletes, twirlers, people in the band, Student Council - and assign three people to every child. He said I would have to clear this with the superintendent and our principal. He wondered about the parents. I shared that I thought the parents would appreciate it because the students were going to be in that classroom from 9:15-1:30, and I thought getting them out would be beneficial. He said he would think it over and let me know the next week.

We continued our work in the classroom, and I got a note asking me to go to the office after school. I did so. By that time I had contacted the various captains of the teams, and they were stunned.

They had no idea that these students were even in the building.

I had a meeting in the classroom, and forty-one students showed up. I told them exactly what was going on and they stepped forward impressively. Mr. Nordahl said I could try it, but if there was any uproar he wondered how I was going to handle it. I said "That's very easy. We are going to tell everyone to sit down and I'm going to put our people in one section, and I will come up with a song that will be good for everyone. If there is an uproar, we are going to sing God Bless America." He said, "You know, you aren't at Camp Lejeune." I said "We can make it Camp Lejeune for an hour."

He laughed. It took me 2 days to get this all organized. All of the students that volunteered during their lunch hour showed up, and they knew a lot of people. I know the word got out. Nervously, we got everyone down to the cafeteria which was on the 2nd floor. Some came on the elevator, some came in walking with their fellow students. We walked into the cafeteria. I looked to my right, and there was the Superintendent of the school. All the principals from the area district were there, and it was like I was looking at a stone wall. No expressions. They were looking directly at me. It was like dodging arrows. They were looking at me like I was the worst thing that happened to this program.

As the students started walking in, every student got up and applauded. I'll tell you... talk about a lump in your throat. Every person in that room had a lump in their throat

Where did this empathy come from? Did you have kids in your neighborhood that had disabilities?

When I was about 11, I had a friend that had a disability. His name is Joe McClosky, and he was born unable to hear. In those days, they used a derogatory term - "Deaf and Dumb" - and Joe was not dumb. I loved him like a brother. He became a very strong guy. He went on to play football in high school and college. He was a middle guard. He would go on a "snap count" so he didn't' have to worry about hearing the signals.

Joe went on to play 4 years of football at Gallaudet University, in Washington, D.C. (a college specializing in providing educational services for the deaf and hard of hearing). I've really lost track of him. Thinking about him right now, I'm going to find how his life is going for him. He's the first person with a disability that I ever played with or socialized with. He lived on the other side of the Jericho Turnpike, and we would always meet downtown. One of our first stops was always an ice cream bar, and Joe and I loved Breyers ice cream. We were served by a Mrs. Hayes, who had great admiration for Joe.

While Joe was the first person I knew that had a disability, there was another young man who was the son of Mike Lee, who was a famous writer for the *Long Island Press*. Mike's son was in a wheelchair, and he was a manager for our football team. I didn't think about him being incapacitated. I just thought, this young man uses a wheelchair, and he was something special. He was just another hard-working guy who always had a smile, raised the spirits of everyone on the team, and was included in everything we did as a team.

Getting back to that cafeteria scene, it was unreal. Now, my next wish was to have them participate in physical education classes. I spoke to the PE teachers, 90% of whom were there when I was a student, and they looked at me and thought I was wacky. I thought that being involved in physical activities would be a great boost to these students. Maybe do some weight lifting, throw a ball from the sitting position, climb some ropes. They bought into it. We went from the cafeteria to Physical Education.

My next goal was to do something for the girls in the class. We had a great program known as Home Economics, and it was big at the time in the U.S. It was designed to teach young women how to cook, take care of a house, be a beautician, and I thought it would be wonderful for these young ladies to learn these things. The two women who were teaching the class were single, they were around my age, and they thought my interest had more to do with flirting with them than with asking if these girls could be in their class. I think my curly hair attracted them. It worked out well.

So, my 2 months assignment was coming to an end, and the original teacher was planning to return. My hope was that they would continue with the revised curriculum. The students still got strong educational values in the classroom, and it really helped me decide that my future would be in education. I never took the job in Industrial Safety, and instead I took a teaching job that paid about $7,500 per year, which was far less than the $30,000 I could have made in

Industrial Safety. I never told my wife-to-be. I thought I was going to be extremely happy teaching, and I think the teachers' salaries were a little bit higher in Washington DC than in New York State, so she bought into it. Teachers in those days could survive pretty nicely on $7500 per year. We ate a lot of tuna fish, Spam and bread, but we survived. Pat was hired by Sperry Gyroscope because of her background with the National Science Foundation. We were very fortunate. We had two salaries, and we didn't have children at the time, and it worked out beautifully.

That experience stays with me to this day. In fact Jack Murphy, God rest his soul, encouraged me to be a member of the Board of Directors at the Franziska Racker Centers, an Ithaca-based agency that serves people with disabilities. I went from a Board member to President of the Board, to Benefactor, to Fund Raiser. The Racker Centers is a very important part of my life. Dr. Franziska Racker lived a block from me on West Hill. Once I got involved with the Racker Centers, I found out what a wonderful woman Franziska Racker was.

She left Austria in the 1940's. The Nazis took over Austria and they killed all the young Jewish people that were going to medical school or law school. She was in medical school. Luckily, she and her family left for the U.S. where she finished medical school. In 1947 she came up with this program for children with disabilities. It was a wonderful program for a number of reasons. It was a great help for the parents of these children, and it put the counties of Tioga, Cortland, and Tompkins closer together to come up with solutions, ideas, and improved facilities. Of course, I started my educational career in the same kind of atmosphere, and I feel very blessed to have had this opportunity.

Having been friends with you for 35 years, I have seen your interactions with our mutual friend that has been struggling with a mental illness for his entire adult life, and it is clear that your empathy runs deep. When I used to run with that young man who was blind, and we were raising money to train for, and compete in, the Paralympic Games, you were among our most vocal supporters. It seems like there are a lot of people who need to be convinced that a disability is not an inability, and you are clearly able to look past a person's disability and focus on their abilities, and now I understand how that is a longstanding, internally held value.

When I was recruiting while at Cornell, I visited many high schools and I passed many classrooms. One day, I looked into one of those classrooms, and there were two children sitting in the front of the room, in wheelchairs. This was the late 60's and early 70's, before mainstreaming. We've come a long way. I always worried about what it was like before this occurred. Many of these kids were home-schooled, they didn't have a lot of friends, and that's part of the reason inclusion is so important.

I assume you and Pat raised your own children with a lot of exposure to young people who were receiving services from the Racker Centers and other such agencies...

Yes, we did. The Racker Centers has helped my grandson greatly. Ryan was not speaking at the age of 3 or 4. He wasn't saying anything. I would play ball with him all the time. We would be in his living room, and I would roll the ball to him with his legs spread out. My words to him were "keep your eye on the ball," and he loved catching and diving for something. So I would have this little rubber ball, and I would throw it and he would dive into the couch but I always told him keep his eye on the ball.

The speech therapist from the Racker Centers visited Ryan twice a week, and he started to speak. The first words he said were "eye ball." The speech therapist couldn't figure out why he was saying "eye ball." Jennifer called me up and said "Dad, Ryan is starting to speak but the therapist can't figure out why he's constantly saying 'eye ball.' I said, "Jennifer, remember when we played and I would tell him keep your eye on the ball? That's what he is saying!" Everything worked out wonderfully after that.

We now have services available to help these people become included in everyday life. It is so important to me, because in my coaching I dealt with young men that were extremely healthy. Physically strong, mentally strong, they had so much going for them, and anytime I feel down, I think about people with disabilities, and the hardships that they are going through, and it's tough. We will get more into this when we talk about depression in a later chapter.

It seems that a significant piece of your spirituality and your identity in general is rooted in gratitude. You really appreciate all of the opportunities that you had - your physical health, all these opportunities - and a way to pay forward that gratitude is

to try to enable people to live to the peak of their own potential, whatever that is. I've seen you interact with a lot of people - from university presidents to people who don't think anybody knows who they are - and I can honestly say without being gratuitous, that you make them all feel that they matter. I can tell that's important to you. You value people equally.

My next question… after that 2 month assignment, were you bitten with the education bug, and did you know that this was going to be your path?

After that 2 month assignment, they retained me in the Physical Education department. That's where I got to meet a tremendous number of coaches that I had admired when I was there as a player. Jim Fraley was an outstanding coach of the track and cross country teams, and he was a tremendous football player. If I'm not mistaken, he may have played with the Giants. Ironically, a close friend of mine, Jim Shreve who lived here in Ithaca and coached football at Cornell, played for him in high school when they had an undefeated football team. Coach Fraley decided he would rather be involved with track, and in fact, he and his assistant coach developed Al Oerter, who was a four-time gold medal winner in the Olympic discus throw. Al was also a teammate of mine of the football team until it was detected that he had a kidney defect that made contact sports too risky. Sadly, Al passed away in 2007.

Coach Fraley also had great sprinters and distance runners. Many of them went to Kansas (where Coach Fraley was from) and ran with the great Kansas teams that had Wes Santee, Artie Dunn and Vinny Hill. Our cross country team was always rated in the top three in the U.S. It was remarkable to be associated with these men, including Bill Ritch, my high school lacrosse coach. It was a magnificent time for me to get this type of assignment, and it made me feel more that I wanted to coach than I wanted to teach. I was hoping for a full-time job at that school, and we were just getting a new football coach. His name was Bill Brown. He is deceased now, but he had played at Syracuse, and was an outstanding high school football coach. I was going to be his assistant. There was supposed to be a vacancy, but the gentleman that was going to leave decided not to do so. So I was moved to Elmont High School, which was in the Central school district, and that was quite an experience.

In that district, a lot of teachers who were at the end of their careers were relocated to Elmont, and a lot of them were outstanding teachers. We had five schools in one district, so there was a lot of shuffling of staff. The Elmont facilities were still going through a lot of transition. The cafeteria and the library weren't completed and the athletic fields weren't in great shape. There was a lot of ill feeling because the students that were juniors at Sewanhaka were then transferred to Elmont. You'd have students that were involved in athletics and were now going to a new school, and they may have been unsure of the current status of the athletic programs. It was a place where there weren't many smiles because a lot of these students had adjusted to Sewanhaka, and they felt they were now outcasts, they were shipped out. They wanted to stay with their Utopia, and that wasn't the case, as they had to go to a satellite school. At age 22, I was the youngest man on the staff, and I had no coaching assignment there because all the coaches that were sent there all had jobs that were given to them by the school. My first year, my school day was over at 2:00 pm, and I was really anxious to coach. If I was going to teach, I wanted to coach. I heard of a freshman lacrosse job opening at Manhasset High School. Now remember, I was in New York State, I was teaching at Elmont High School, and I was going to apply for a job after school at Manhasset after hours, and it was about 15 miles away. Pat and I were living in an apartment at this time, and she had a great job with Sperry Gyroscope. I applied for the job and I asked one of my high school coaches - Bill Ritch - what he thought. He said I would probably get fired from Elmont if I accepted the coaching job. I said "I'm going to test this. I can't believe that. I'm finished with duties at 2 pm, I can be a gas station attendant, work in a bar, I can take any other job but I can't take one in coaching? I don't think that's right so don't tell anyone but I'm going to apply for the job."

So I applied for the position. I went for an interview with Dr. Ed Walsh, who is a remarkable individual, skilled in leadership and organization. He was fantastic. Dr. Walsh coached football at Manhasset, and Jimmy Brown played for him. After the NY Giants played on Sundays, they would send the films to Dr. Walsh's home, and he would break the films down for his friend Steve Owen, who was a coach for the Giants at the time. They wanted him to come to coach for the Giants very badly but Dr. Walsh had children, he loved being a high school football coach and athletic director, so he never went in that direction.

I went over for the interview, and having been in the Marine Corps, my shoes were always shined. I had a suit and a tie. In fact my tie was the color of the school colors: blue and orange. I had a great talk with him. He said, "You know, you may lose your teaching job." I said "Dr. Walsh, what grounds would they have?" He said, "Well, you are in one district and you're representing that district. What if Manhasset competes against Elmont and you are coaching?" I said, "Well, that could happen but since we are in different sections of Long Island, it's not likely to happen. I really want to start my career in coaching, and if it doesn't work out, I have the flexibility to do something else". He said he understood.

I thought after that, there was no way he was going to give me the job because of district conflict. I went home and I said to Pat, "If I get the job in Manhasset and I get fired, what are you going to think?" She said, "I will make sure you get another job someplace."

So, it was very obvious that I had my wife's vote of confidence. Finally, a week later, I got a call from Dr. Walsh. He wanted me to meet with him and Dr. Collins, the superintendent. I met with them, and Dr. Collins said, "You are taking a big chance. Do you still want your application retained here for the job?" I said "Yes, I do." I went back the next day and talked with my high school principal, Frank Driscoll and told him that I had applied for a coaching job at another school. There was total silence.

He said, "That's never been done." I said "With all due respect, if you were finished with your assignment at 2:00 in the afternoon, and you want to be beneficial to yourself, your career, and hopefully to the students you are working with, would you want to be denied?" Well, that was a pretty good approach, but he said "I will have to report this to the Superintendent." He reported it to the Superintendent. I got a call from the secretary that night, informing me that I was going to meet with the Superintendent at 7a.m. He was about 6'4," a former Colonel in the Army, here I was a corporal in the Marines. I went in there and I was standing at his desk at attention. Never once did he ask me to sit down. I know he wanted to be on the offensive. In the Marine Corps, you brace up and stand at attention.

He said, "Were you in the Military?" I replied, "Yes, sir." "What branch"? I said "United States Marine Corps, sir." "What's this thing that you want to take a job at another school?" I said, "I have a choice. I could be working as a sanitation engineer." He asked, "What's a sanitation engineer?" I said, it's a garbage man. Or I can be a bartender, better known as a mixologist. Or I could find other employment. But since I'm in education, I want to continue to educate after school." He replied, "It can't be done. It's NYS law." I said, "With all due respect sir, I have not seen that NYS law." "Well, it's a NYS law." I stayed on point. "I told you what I could do after school. I just don't see why it's so objectionable that I want to go into coaching." He said, "We'll see. Our meeting is over." I thanked him and said "Yes sir."

I walked out realizing he was a pompous ass. I went to teach that day, and of course the word was out to everybody. The coaches said "You can't do that." I said "Why not?" I didn't know a lot about NYS school law, but I sure as hell dove into it. There was nothing written about working at another school. It was just that you couldn't work at a school that would be competing against the school that you received your main salary from. The Superintendent called me back on three occasions, and it was very obvious they knew when my lunch hour was. It was my lunch hour, not his. Sometimes he made me sit by the office receptionist waiting room and then call me in, and I'd have 10 minutes to get back to school. He'd say, "Have you changed your mind?" "No sir," So the meeting was over.

By the third time, I brought my lunch with me and ate it in the waiting room. In fact, I even offered some fruit to his secretary. She was as stone-faced as he was. I went in and he said "Well, I understand you have sought some legal assistance." I had just passed the word around to some other coaches, and if you want to get word out, you just tell certain people and it will definitely get around. "Yes sir, I have gotten some legal advice." He said, "This can possibly hurt your future in our district." I replied, "I sure hope not, because I have great respect for this district and I love Sewanhaka High School. I think this will be a great opportunity in developing my educational values." With that, the meeting was over.

In February, I received a call from Manhasset High School, and I met with their Superintendent, Dr. Collins, and a Dr. Walsh, who was the Athletic Director. I was not aware that all three lacrosse jobs at the school had vacancies. I had only applied for the Freshman job. I was also introduced to two other gentlemen in the room - Luke Belsito and Mark Fingerhut. I thought that since Luke was older than me, he would get the head job. Mark would get the JV job, and I would get the Freshman job.

After the meeting, we went into the hallway and Dr. Walsh said "I'm going to take you gentlemen to meet your teams." They had them in different classrooms. We walked down the hallway and Dr. Walsh said, "Mr. Belsito, here is your JV team. I'm going to go in and introduce you. You two others wait here in the hall." He came out and said we would go to the next classroom. He stopped at the classroom and said "Mr. Fingerhut, this is your freshman team," and with that my knees were knocking – I was having difficulty breathing. As we walked down the hallway, I said, "Dr. Walsh, I'm going to be Varsity coach?" He said, "You are going to be Varsity coach." I thanked him. He opened the door and we walked into the classroom.

It was obvious that a lot of these young men were specialists in Aeronautics because they had paper planes all over the place. They had scribbled on the blackboard in code known only to savages, the blinds were in disarray, and the windows were out of whack. It was obvious that they tried to play bumper cars with the desks, and there was a lot of noise. It was also very obvious that someone was smoking.

I walked in and said to Dr. Walsh, "Before you say anything, can you step out for a minute?" He did so, and I said to the group, "Get up on your feet. I am going to leave this room for about a minute and 30 seconds. I want the windows taken care of. Whoever is smoking cigarettes - you better eat them because if you throw them out the window of the second floor, I'm going to throw you out to get them. You guys have no idea who I am. I want those boards cleaned, the desks cleaned, and when I turn the handle to that door to come in with Dr. Walsh, every one of you'd better be standing at attention and looking straight ahead."

To this day, Joey Capela says he almost wet his pants. He said "We had no idea what the hell just hit us!"

You were just a few years older than these guys?

Yes... I was best man at Joe's wedding a few weeks ago. He's 71 – I'm 79. I walked in with Dr. Walsh, and everyone was at attention. Dr. Walsh introduced me and he said "Coach, I'm going to have the other coaches stop in on their way out if they have any questions. You know if my door is open, please come in. If my door is closed,

I'm talking with someone." I said "Thank you sir, and what a great honor this is going to be."

It was ironic that I was hired at Manhasset High School, given I had disliked them so much. When I was in high school, their players used to drive to practice in convertibles, and their parties were elegant. That's where I learned to keep my pinkie out. They kept their pinkies out when they were drinking. The girls had their noses in the air so high that they could probably goose butterflies, they were so stuck up. There was the assumption that someday we Sewanhaka guys would be working for them. It was the rich guys against the poor... the Golden Spoons against the Trench Diggers. So when we played them there was no love.

To whom did you relate?

The Trench Diggers... So, after the meeting, I told them we would start conditioning in February, and that was very unusual to them. In the past, they had not started focusing on lacrosse until March. I went back to Dr. Walsh's office, and I reminded him I had never coached a varsity sport. He said, "I know but you were recommended by the coaches you played for - and all those recommendations were outstanding."

It seems you brought in some credibility. You played collegiate lacrosse, and you knew what it took to balance the work on the field and in the classroom. You came in with earned credibility.

Apparently! I went home, and Pat and I had bought a brand new car, a 1961 Chevy Impala convertible. I loved that car, and I wish I had it today. We probably put 300,000 miles on it. It was a great car. It was February, and believe it or not, I wanted to put the top down because I wanted to yell all the way home. I was so delighted!! I didn't even ask what the salary was going to be. I got home and told Pat, and in fact, I stopped at the Lotus Chinese Restaurant. They were beautiful people, and they made the best shrimp chow mien and I wanted to bring some home to celebrate. We were both extremely happy. Sitting on the couch, the fireplace was going, and Pat said "What happens if Elmont fires you tomorrow?" I said, "I will definitely be unemployed, and I will find another job."

A few days later, the announcement of my coaching assignment hit the paper, and the School Board of Elmont was up in arms. Some of the people in the community thought I was Benedict Arnold. Elmont had to drop their lacrosse program after the first year due to a lack of interest. All the programs were in disarray, but the coaches worked hard to put them back together.

I accepted the job on Friday in Manhasset, and on Saturday and Sunday the phones were buzzing. Some people were calling me up and saying, "Dude, how the hell can you do that?" I said the answer was very easy, I wanted to coach. They said, "What about loyalty." I said, "I am loyal... to every young man in the country. I want to be as loyal as possible, but I also want to advance my career if I can, and that's not being selfish." I would have had a lot of problems going home at 2:00 in the afternoon and doing nothing. You can only shovel the snow so much in the winter, and cut the grass in the spring, and I was enthused about coaching. Originally, if I was going to stay at Sewanhaka, I was going to be the assistant lacrosse coach under Bill Ritch, and assistant football coach under Bill Brown. That would have been a tremendous opportunity for me, but it never materialized because my teaching assignment was at Elmont High School.

We got underway at Manhasset in March, and we needed a place to practice. I asked Dr. Walsh, "Do you think there is a possibility that we can practice in the back parking lot?" And he said sure, on Saturdays it will be open. I said "No, how about during the week." He said. "That's where the teachers park." I said "Boy, it would be nice if we could move the cars after 3:30 to the front parking lot."

Great idea... He called Dr. Collins' (the Superintendent) office and he sent a memo telling the teachers, "To the teachers staying after school on Monday-Friday, we would like you to move your cars at 3:15." Oh baby, my picture was on every dart board in that high school, because the teachers now had to put their coats on to go out and move their cars and walk back in the cold. I was definitely on the hit list. Luckily I was not at that school.

The players realized that we were going all out, and we were going to be serious about practicing. In the past, when practicing in the gym they wouldn't even break a sweat. The equipment guy passed out hoods, sweatpants, and a little flannel shirt to be used in inclement weather. We took tape and taped their earlobes so the wind wouldn't blow through their helmets, and we went to the parking lot in February. The first day in the parking lot when people had to move their cars, two protestors said they weren't moving their cars, so we practiced around them. I wrote something down: "We are not responsible for any dents that may be left on your car." That was apparently the language they understood, and the cars were moved.

We had great workouts in that parking lot. It was very obvious to the players that with me having been in the Marine Corps, everything had to be just right. We had 5 or 6 players come out with their shorts on the outside of their sweats. I never liked that style, so of course they would say "Coach, that's how we always wear them!" My response was "That's why you haven't won a game in the last couple of years. Shorts are to be worn on the inside." That's the story these guys still talk about – I don't even remember this happening.

We got ready to scrimmage against other schools, and I felt it was imperative for us to go against teams that would help us get ready for the season. Hempstead High School, where John Mackey, the All-Pro NFL player went to school, had a lot of exceptional athletes. Ollie was the head coach, and he said, "Richie – I'm so happy you got the coaching job. You are the talk of Long Island! Man, my buddy Jackie Robinson broke into the Dodgers, and you broke into Manhasset High School. What a remarkable thing. How about scrimmaging?" I said. "Ollie, I would love it. I'll give you a call."

Ollie's team was approximately 70% Black, and they were great athletes. They played other sports, and Ollie was an outstanding coach. In fact, he was also the basketball coach. We scrimmaged and it really helped us. We had referees, and the contact was very intense. In those days, more so than now, you could throw blocks. Some were questionable, depending on the vision of the referees, but it was physical, and it really helped me evaluate my players.

We had that scrimmage, and then another, and then we opened up against Freeport. Freeport High School had a very sound football program.

Our first game was a nail biter, in the rain, on a grass field, which kind of became a quagmire as the game progressed. We lost the game 3-2, and I realized that we were going to have to change some players' positions. We had a player on the team by the name of Joe Capela who was a midfielder. I felt we needed more speed on defense, and a little bit more tenacity and aggressiveness. He was 5'6", and it was unheard of to have a defenseman under 6 feet. Joey had hands just as quick as Muhammad Ali, and he had feet as quick as a sprinter. We had wooden sticks in those days, and his stick was the closest thing I've ever seen to a hatchet. He could take your freaking hand off! I think he played the way he did because he had that "Napoleon Complex," you know... I may not be able to look you in the eye but I'm surely going to kick the shit out of your belly button! So he moved over to defense. We moved Gerry Gschwind to midfield, and Gerry was very unhappy because he was a defenseman, but I told him that his excellent stick work would result in greater scoring potential as a midfielder.

After the Freeport game, we never lost another game. We played Garden City, a team Manhasset hadn't beaten in a long time, and that was the rich against the rich. It was very obvious that a lot of the fathers worked on Wall Street. They probably had some side bets, and for years, Manhasset had been eating crow. The Wall Street guys went on the train together, got off the train together, they went to lunch together, but once they got off the train they decided they didn't like each other! So, they went in opposite directions – one to Garden City – one to Manhassett.

We played Garden City in an unbelievable game. The score was tied numerous times, and with about a minute and half to go, a player from Garden City took a shot and hit our goalie right in the chin, and split his chin open. The field was jammed with people. We had stands that would seat about 300 people, but they were about three-deep around the field that day. Our benches were right in front of the stands, but that would be changed very quickly after this game because we had too many comments coming from the stands... "My boy's not playing enough!" So we had moved to the other side of the field. After that shot to the chin, our goalie Buddy De Houst went down on one knee and the referees called us over. I went over and I could see the blood coming out. In the Marine Corps, you have a Corpsman. I had my assistant Luke Belsito. We opened Buddy's chin strap, and you could probably put a half a dollar into the slice he had in his chin. I had a clean handkerchief in my jacket, and Luke said "He needs stitches." I said, "Luke let me ask you a question... are you going to be the goalie? Our backup goalie isn't ready." I asked Buddy if he felt dizzy, and he said "No, I feel great!" I said,

"If we take care of this, do you think you can play?" He said "I'm not going out of the game! I thought you were coming out just to look at me."

Believe it or not Buddy would go on to Maryland, and he became a helicopter pilot in the Marine Corps. He was one of the pilots involved in the historic hostage rescue mission in Iran. Anyway, I took the handkerchief and asked Luke to get me a cup chin strap to put the handkerchief in. I put the cup on tight, and he made two unbelievable saves. The score was still 5-5, and Garden City was attempting to clear the ball but it was stolen by Steve LaVaute. We called a timeout and set up a play for Jack Heim. He made an excellent dodge, causing his defender to stumble. Jack took a big hit coming around the crease, and still put it in the cage, making it 6-5.

Garden City had like the Who's Who of Long Island athletics... they had Frank Quayle who went on to play football at the University of Virginia and for the Denver Broncos. They had Todd Middleton, who was 6'4" and built like a tank. They, like us, had great athletes. Garden City came down with a barrage of shots, and they fouled us. We had the opportunity to go up 7-5 to seal the win.

Everyone was excited, including the benefactors that may have had a wager on the game. They were jumping up and down, and I was, of course, pretty happy that we had recovered, especially after losing to Freeport. That's when we started to come of age as a team.

As I was walking off the field, I saw a local judge by the name of Ken Molloy, who had played at Syracuse and was a PT Commander in the 2nd World War. I did not know Ken Molloy, but this distinguished white-haired gentleman approached me and said, "Coach you have a lot of work ahead of you." I said "Yes sir, I know that." He said, "You have to work on your extra man a little bit." I said, "That sounds good... you know we were 2 for 2 today." He said, "Yes I know, but the next time the team will stop what you did today." I said, "Okay...by the way, what do you do in the afternoon?" He said, "Well, I have my law practice." I said "Here is a whistle. If you have nothing to do, why don't you come over and work with us in the afternoon?" He looked at me with amazement. He walked away, and I walked away.

I got home that night and got a phone call from Bill O'Connell – a friend of Ken Molloy. Bill said, "Richie – who did you talk to after the game?" I said "I didn't talk to any parents… I talked to some players, and congratulated the team from Garden City." He said "Did you talk to Ken Molloy?" I said "What does Ken Molloy look like? Describe him to me." He did so, and I said "Yes." Bill said "I think you just got fired!" I replied, "Fired? I just got hired." He responded, "Yeah, but Kenny was really upset you offered him a whistle." I said, "Well, he was telling me what I should be doing at practice, so I told him if he could come and help coach, he should come." He said, "Well, let me tell you, he didn't' take it that way!"

I kept my job. I never had to make any appearances in Ken Molloy's courtroom, so everything turned out fine."

Return to Long Island

6

You have mentioned that you spent some time coaching the Long Island Athletic Club. Please share more about that experience.

When I came out of the Marine Corps, I was enthused about continuing to play lacrosse. There were a number of club teams throughout New York State and in Baltimore, and there was a club league which was divided into North and South divisions. This was a competitive arrangement and it meant that we would play teams in Baltimore, New Jersey, and Washington, D.C. It was very well organized.

What was the age group of these players?

There were high school graduates, college graduates, veterans from the military. There was a lot of diversity in terms of age and playing experience.

Players in their twenties, mostly?

Yes, many of these players had played in college. In fact, the roster was probably comprised of 90 percent former college players.

Was this the precursor to Major League Lacrosse?

That's correct. The selection process was very competitive and very demanding. We did not have a coach, and when you have 30 players trying to coach at the same time, it does cause some confusion. In fact, our selections were often like alphabet soup... everybody had an idea but it really wasn't cohesive.

What we decided to do was to have a coach for each position - mid-field, defense, attack, goalies - and that worked out fairly well. Our first year was 1961. We played well, and we won some big games, but we lost some that we should have won.

The following year it was decided that we should select a coach, a full-time coach, and we'd all chip in to give the coach an honorarium. That gave us better organization. We did select a coach, and after he found out that everybody on the field was also going to be a coach, it was very uncomfortable for him.

When we got started, I tore the ligaments in my ankle playing softball, so that put me on the sidelines with crutches and a cast. We were getting ready for the club season the following year, and we were still playing softball in the late fall. That's when I tore the ligaments in my ankle. The coach had departed 2 weeks before this happened to me, so they looked at me as a possible coach with the ability to keep everybody contained. There's no doubt about it, I wanted to come back and play in the future. I did play that summer, as we had a great league at Jones Beach. Sixteen teams tried out for eight spots, so it made for competitive try-outs.

Jones Beach had a very unique situation. We played in the stadium on the beach. Robert Moses—a fantastic visionary—was the one that helped design and create Jones Beach. In fact, he built a parkway called Meadowbrook Parkway which was built in the '30s and, to this day, it's still one of the best parkways on Long Island. It takes you directly to the beach, which is a magnificent setting.

Our team was fortunate to be picked. We were known as Mayfair; as we were sponsored by a real estate agency.

The coach had departed and they asked me if I'd coach. The honorarium was not bad; I think it was close to $800. I thought about it and I said, "I'll tell you what. I don't want to accept any payment. I'll be happy to coach but we're going to change our methods of getting ready for the season. We're going to practice two nights every other week. We're going to be indoors in the gym at Elmont High School. We're going to go through various conditioning programs, fundamentals, team sequences, team strategy, defense and offense."

I was determined that we would really be prepared when the season started.

I had no idea that that change would increase our number of players. We had 75 players come to the opening night. Just picture it - the Knickerbockers having 75 players come out, competing for 32 roster spots.

With a group that size, it would have been extremely difficult to trim the roster effectively, so we put a couple of policies in. They were: if you intended to make the squad, you had to have good attendance at all these early season work-outs. That did not eliminate anybody because everybody was sincerely interested in playing and they all showed up.

So then I had a dilemma as I called myself "The Coach in the Cast." I was hobbling around in that cast, and we were going through a lot of physical training, very similar to Parris Island. I could not find too many faults with any of the players. Their stick work was excellent, with the background that they had, both in high school and college. We wanted to try to get the squads to about 32 players, and I knew that it was going to be a very difficult task to determine the final player selection.

I decided we were going to have two teams, and that worked out really well. Around March, we finally selected the final rosters. We had captains for the various positions. They were veteran players that had proven themselves. We put a list of players together and then categorized them as A Team, B Team. The reason why we had A Team, B Team was that I didn't really want to cut anybody. All these men had come out with a lot of enthusiasm, and they came religiously every Tuesday and Thursday night, and worked hard.

So we set up a schedule, and we were going to have scrimmages—B Team, A Team—against teams like New Hampshire - who had lacrosse at the time - Brown, Massachusetts, and Hofstra. These scrimmages enabled us to evaluate our players further. It was very obvious we were going to have two sets of schedules, a schedule for each team.

Was there much of a discrepancy between the A and the B teams?

Not much, really. Some of those men had been college All-Americans, had played in the North-South All-Star game, so they came with some outstanding credentials. That said, they had to prove it on the field.

We went down the line, putting everything together, making sure each team was well-oiled, and we got into our scrimmage phase of the season. I considered myself a volunteer coach; the financing was not there so it wasn't important. Probably to my wife it would have been important, but it wasn't important to me.

Eight hundred dollars is a couple of months' salary for a school teacher, isn't it?

That's right. So after one of the scrimmages, two of the players that weren't on the extra man unit stormed off the field. They felt they weren't getting a lot of playing time. They came up to me, one on each side, and said, "We quit!" And I said, "It's hard for me to accept that" because we were working in units. "Well, we're not getting enough playing time."

That's when I first heard the word "playing time," which is now known as PT. I always thought "PT" stood for physical therapy or physical training. But the lack of PT was their objection. So I said, "Fine. Turn your equipment in." Of course they stood there in front of their teammates, threw their helmets down, threw their shoulder pads down, threw their gloves down. They kept their sticks, which were, in their mind, their own—and continued to walk out to the parking lot. When they got to the parking lot, they realized that the equipment they threw down was their own. They had to come back in front of the whole team and pick their equipment up. I think as they walked back they realized, number one, how ridiculous it was for them to quit the team. And number two, the fact that they were so frustrated that they didn't realize it was their own equipment. So that joke stayed on for years and years. In fact, it's still talked about in a lot of the local pubs on Long Island—about the famous "Turn your equipment in" incident.

Well, we built a really good team that year, and we played Mt. Washington, which was the club lacrosse team from Baltimore, which had its own field and locker rooms, and had the longest history of any club team in the country. They were outstanding athletes and outstanding players. They had a coaching staff of five former college coaches and All-Americans. We lost to them in a very tight game – it was 11-9 - in Baltimore that year. The winner of that game would represent the U.S. in what would be the beginning of the World Games in Canada.

The objective the following year, of course, was to continue our training program and get better. I was then a player-coach, and while I did more coaching than playing, I wanted to stay active. I also had a lot of opportunities to play in the summer at Jones Beach, so that's when the coaching bug really set in. It was developed at Manhasset, continued at Elmont, and when I was home from Maryland—I didn't go back to school in Maryland until the beginning of September - and I actually helped Leon Cohen at New Hyde Park Memorial High School. He was the football coach. I lived in that town, and the foundation of my coaching career began to take shape and solidify.

Of course, when we were growing up, we didn't have our fathers to coach our teams. We coached our own teams. We went out and raised money for uniforms and equipment. Our first baseball team was known as the New Hyde Park Jays. We had pinstriped uniforms, and to get them, we sold raffle tickets. We also played sandlot football, and unlike the more properly-run leagues of today – like Pop Warner for example - it was organized by us. We were sponsored by the Nassau Inn (which was the first establishment in our area to make "pizza pie") and our first objective when we went to our home field was to walk the field with buckets, pick up rocks and glass, and then line the field ourselves.

All those experiences helped me think a lot more about coaching, and would eventually lead to my journey from Sewanhaka, to Maryland, to Manhasset, to Elmont, to the Long Island Athletic Club, to Cornell, and eventually on to the Irish National Lacrosse Program.

The following year, we played Mt. Washington at Hofstra before a huge crowd. Mt. Washington had a tremendous following. Everybody loved club lacrosse. People watched games after the college games, or watched club lacrosse in the evenings. We beat Mt. Washington, and that was their first loss in about 40 games. It was a remarkable win. We had a local tavern where we used to go and have dinner or have some libations, and of course, the celebration was unbelievable that night.

We actually won the club championship. It was the first time a northern team had ever done so. It was quite a victory. The spirit on our team was a combination of high school and college traditions, because we were developing a new tradition on Long Island that had never been there before. For a club team to win a championship was a new and very exciting development.

In 1968, the North-South game was played on Long Island. Ned Harkness was coaching Cornell lacrosse at the time. He had some players in the North-South game, so he was in attendance, along with a friend by the name of Jimmy Bishop who was very involved with lacrosse in Canada, and with a radio station that was affiliated with the Detroit Red Wings.

I met these men at lunch before the North-South game and we talked about lacrosse. Ned had some players that actually had played on the Long Island Athletic Club, and he also had some players from Manhasset that played for me. He wanted a chance to really get to know me better, and during the conversation, we talked about a lot of things dealing with lacrosse, education, and how it all fit together. After that meeting, I got a call from Bob Kane who was Director of Athletics at Cornell. They had an opening for an assistant freshman football coach and assistant lacrosse coach at Cornell. He asked if I would like to come up for an interview. At that time, I was not really enthused by the idea.

You were firmly entrenched in Long Island, right?

Yes. I thought I was in paradise. I was a high school Athletic Director, I was coaching the club team, playing for a club team, and enjoying my summers playing softball and lacrosse.

No children yet?

Kevin was on his way. I thought I was on Golden Pond. I couldn't do anything wrong. Everything was coming up roses. My wife said, "You know, this might be your last chance to get into college coaching." She said, "It may not happen again." As always, Pat's advice helped me make the right decision.

I thought about it, and a day later, I called back Mr. Kane and said, "Yes, I'd like to come up for an interview, and I'm really honored that you'd consider me for those positions."

I went and spoke to Dr. Walsh, who knew Bob Kane, and he said, "Make sure your shoes are shined." I looked at him and I said, "Dr.

Walsh, I was in the Marine Corps. My shoes are always shined." He said, "I'll tell you why. This man is very dapper and he's a fashion plate. He's going to look at your shoes first." I said, "My God. This is going to be some interview."

I flew up to Ithaca, and I was met by Frank Kavanaugh, who was a trainer. This was well-planned because Frank came from Ireland. He was an unbelievable trainer. He had worked in the All-Star college football games where the College All-Stars used to play against the pros. He was very well known throughout the world with his training techniques. He also designed a helmet for MacGregor, which was ahead of its time. A lot of teams across the country used his helmet.

Frank took me to The Station Restaurant, which was very unique. I never thought about railroad cars being turned into dining cars. We walked in and three or four people came up and greeted me. I had no idea why they knew me or why they should know me, but it was very obvious that Frank had sent the word out that he was bringing this Long Island guy with a funny accent to the restaurant, and they were to make him feel welcome.

Mr. Joe Ciaschi was the owner of The Station Restaurant, and we became very close friends. He was also involved in a number of real estate holdings in Ithaca.

That night I stayed at the Statler Hotel, and I couldn't sleep very well. The next morning, I was going to have a professor taking me to breakfast for an informal interview. That was really thrilling because he was a history professor, and I talked about my enthusiasm for history. We had a great breakfast.

The next person I met was Assistant Athletic Director Pat Filley. Pat was an outstanding football player at Notre Dame. In fact, he was the first—and maybe the only—two-time captain at Notre Dame, so that's a little trivia for you. Pat was a remarkable man. He was a state champion wrestler in Indiana. He had hands on him the size of Virginia hams. I think when he shook hands with me, his fingers reached up to my elbow. Pat took me around the campus on a tour, and he was clearly very enthusiastic about Cornell.

Believe it or not, in 1949, my mother decided I needed some fresh air and a change of environment. My brother Bob – whose real name was Ambrose -was finishing college; as he had come out of the Navy and he was on the GI Bill. He was married, and he finished his education at Ithaca College. I got on the train in 1949 to come to Ithaca, New York, and I arrived at the same station where I would - in 1969 - have dinner, at the Station Restaurant! It was quite a coincidence. I am proud to say that Bob is now a member of the Ithaca College Athletic Hall of Fame.

I stayed there a month. I played a lot of baseball and softball. My brother lived in Titus Flats which was veterans' housing. They had a name for it: Vetville. My brother would take me up to Cornell in the evenings when he didn't have to work. He was going to summer school, working, and had a baby boy named Robbie. He and his wife Gloria were just unbelievable hosts, and I was always very grateful.

At that time, I was drinking four quarts of milk a day and eating everything in sight. They had a little garden out in the back, where they were growing corn. Before the corn developed, I was eating some of the kernels. So, a lot of S-O-S signals went out to my mother to send up some more money to feed this baby gorilla.

I will never forget stepping on that field at Schoellkopf Stadium… it was as nice as a golf course green. I got to meet Norm Padulla a few years later. People claimed he cut that grass with a scissors. It was so manicured, so beautiful. What a delight it was for me to go out there and run pass patterns with my brother, catch the ball, kick the ball, and be on that field—just my brother and myself.

One evening we were up there, and there were a lot of Cornell football players from the class of '49 staying in and around campus - working, going to summer school - and a group of about 25 came out to work out. Little did I know that I was watching a team that eventually would beat Michigan that year. That game was played at Cornell, and remains one of the biggest wins in Cornell football history.

I've always been a West Point Army fan, given my brother John went to West Point. Every time I played a game, I made believe I was a West Point player. And there I was at Cornell, watching those men work out and get ready for the season. Little did I know that 20 years later, I'd be stepping on that field and spending a major part of my life in Schoellkopf Stadium. That, to me, has been an unbelievable journey.

Getting back to 1969 and my coming to Cornell. After Pat Filley took me around, I went in and visited with Bob Kane. His office at the time was in Teagle Hall, and the secretary welcomed me. I sat there for a few minutes, and Mr. Kane came to his door, welcomed me to Cornell and invited me in. Sure enough, he looked right at my shoes.

I sat down and he had received my resume. He looked at it and he was delighted about all the coaching experience I had. Our JV football team had been undefeated three years in a row, and he felt that I could make a great adjustment to working with the freshman program as an assistant.

A lot of young men have dreams about coaching football on Saturdays, and even though I put more time into lacrosse coaching, one of my dreams was to get back into football. The opportunity to do so really increased my enthusiasm for the position at Cornell.

We had lunch together, and we talked a lot about the students, including Bruce Cohen, who had been an All-American lacrosse player and also a top soccer player at Cornell. Bruce was an outstanding player, and he's in the Hall of Fame. Bruce played for me with the Long Island Athletic Club, and Bob Kane mentioned that Bruce had talked about my technique, my strategies, my philosophy, and my policies. I talked to Mr. Kane about this over lunch. I think lunch had started about 12:15. I guess I talked a little too much because at 2:15 he looked at his watch and said, "This conversation has been remarkable. I just missed a meeting with the Vice President." So kiddingly, I said, "You want me to write you a note?" and we laughed about it.

There were no cell phones, so he went out to a desk phone in the Statler. Believe it or not, the Vice President came over from Day Hall to meet me. So that was quite thrilling. And then the afternoon was spent meeting and talking to other coaches.

Were you still on the fence at this point?

I was definitely on the fence. Meeting the other coaches made me realize something. Some of them had been in coaching for 10 or 20 years. I think some of them had a feeling that they were not sure they wanted to take another rookie onto the staff. It was fine. I enjoyed the conversations with them. I had a light dinner with a group of people and then got back on the plane and went home.

Two days later, I had an assignment with the United States Marine Corps. Our reserve unit went to Norfolk, Virginia, for rubber boat training reconnaissance. I was going to be there for 2 weeks.

The Cornell search committee asked my wife to come up for a visit and look at houses. Now, I wasn't available by phone while I was going through training, so we didn't connect for about six days. By this time, she had already been up to Ithaca and looked at houses. She was ready to accept the job for me. When I got on the phone with her, I was quite surprised. I was really overwhelmed that they thought that highly of me, that they might take a chance on a high school JV football coach and high school lacrosse coach.

When you're on reserve duty, you don't have a lot of time to soul search. So luckily, I carried out my assignments with the Marine Corps because a lot of it consisted of live fire, and your concentration better be at its best.

On the way back from Virginia, I started writing down pros and cons of job selection. We came back by train, and everybody was happy that reserve duty was over. All my friends were asking me "What are you writing down?" They thought I was writing about the camp that we were just at.

I started to look at this very seriously, very carefully. It seemed that the cons were really starting to outnumber the pros. Like leaving Long Island and taking a salary which was much less than I was making, and the challenge of taking a new family to a new area. By that time, Kevin and Jennifer were just babies. I really was looking at more reasons for not going than going.

Then I looked back at that month that I was in Ithaca in 1949, and I felt that this might be a golden opportunity. I said that it might be a stepping stone, football-wise, from college to the pros. And I sort of laugh when I think about that, but when you're in coaching, you always want to reach for the next rung of that ladder. I found myself always reaching: as a player, as a coach, as an educator. I always found myself reaching for the next phase of my career ladder, and as I mentioned, that golden ring.

I arrived back home. We were living in Manhasset at the time. The people that were there before us had built a small baby pool out of cinderblocks, and I always used to tell everybody I had a house with a pool. In fact, my little nephew came over on Sunday, and it was the first time he'd seen that house. He didn't even say "hello." He sprinted right out, figuring he was going to jump in the pool. It was about three feet high and about maybe twenty feet square, but it was great for our little babies.

Anyhow, that Sunday, Pat and I took a ride with the kids and went out to the beach. I walked the boardwalk. She told me that this could be the last chance—not that I was getting that old, but when you're in your 20s, you think 30 is old. When you're in your 30s, you think 40 is old. So I was in my late 20s and she said, "I found a great house. The area is beautiful." And she said, "I think we ought to give it a shot." As I said, she thought I could do the job, and do a great job at that. I accepted the job, although I wasn't quite sure if they offered it to me or to Pat!

I accepted the position in late August, however, I had a commitment to Elmont High School as the Athletic Director. We were in the process of redoing our stadium field, and doing some other improvements to our athletic facilities. I had a great allegiance to that school. I remember the slogan "I Love Elmont." Leaving Elmont was one of the hardest decisions I've ever had to make.

I met with Frank Driscoll, the principal, told him about my job offer from Cornell, and then I met with the superintendent. This thing happened so quickly. I went up for an interview in early August. My wife had accepted the job on my behalf toward the end of August, and before I even accepted it, I talked to the principal and superintendent. I told them that ideally, Cornell would like me to be there September 1, but I was planning to try to convince them that I really couldn't come up until October. That meant the football season at Cornell was going to pass me by.

But I also thought I could do some recruiting for Cornell, in multiple sports on Long Island during that two month period. I could also scout if they wanted me to scout. But I was really committed to seeing all those projects finalized and making sure that I was leaving Elmont in a good position for the next person to come in. I had a strong dedication to the student athletes at that school.

So, I made the move up here in October, and Pat came about 3 weeks later. I never did anything with football because of the time factor, but I did recruit some football players and some soccer players from Long Island, to help out in what I considered a Cornell assignment.

The following February, Ned Harkness decided to give up lacrosse. I was on the team bus going to the Colgate-Cornell hockey game, and we had a reporter by the name of Jerry Langdon, who was a top reporter for the *Ithaca Journal*. Jerry sat next to me and he said, "Congratulations." I thought he was congratulating me for accepting the job at Cornell. I wasn't sure why else he would be congratulating me. I really didn't know. And I said, "Thank you."

The next day at 7:30 in the morning, I got a phone call to meet with Mr. Kane at 8:30. It was February, and I was having a tough time adjusting. I can thank my wife; she got involved with a bridge club, and immediately we had downtown friends.

The climate in Ithaca, as we all know, can be a little cold from time to time. And the coaches...sometimes they were even colder. It was not easy to make friends, and I consider myself pretty outgoing. So I looked for other avenues of friendship. I came from Long Island where everyone's your friend. I really didn't have any enemies. When I got here, I found out that November, December, and January can start getting pretty cold. And February set the record.

So I was bundling up while my wife was discovering new friends. And in February, we went to some "game dinners." Now, on Long Island, a game dinner was a card game. Up here, it was pheasant, duck, deer, you name it. And having come from a steak, and chicken, and pot roast family, the event was nice—but I think I had more salad than I had anything else. To this day, I'm still not a "game guy."

But the beauty was, that February morning, when Bob Kane called me in, he said, "We'd like you to be the varsity lacrosse coach." I was saying to myself: Well, what happened to Coach Harkness? Mr. Kane saw my look of confusion and stated, "Well, he's going to taper down and just work with hockey. I want you to think about it." I said, "Mr. Kane, if you feel it's the right thing for the program and for Cornell University, I'm all set."

I knew I was going to face some obstacles. Here I was, a new guy, who only worked with the team for about 5 days during fall practice.

I was in limbo about football, and there I was being presented as the head coach.

So, you were 32 years old and you had no head coaching experience. Did you feel any skepticism from people, or did Bob Kane's vote of confidence make you immune to any such negativity?

His confidence in me was tremendous because he had done so much. He was involved with the U.S. Olympic program. He eventually became President of the United States Olympic Committee. He made great decisions for Cornell. During his tenure, several buildings and facilities were built that made Cornell's athletic facilities a showcase that rivaled any other university. He worked under James Lynah (for whom Lynah Rink is named), and Mr. Kane also had a law degree. He was quite a man to work for. I really idolized him. Not because he hired me, but because of what he stood for.

I'm sure the recommendation that came from Ned Harkness also bolstered your confidence. Having those two men on your side had to be a major up-side for a new coach.

It definitely was. They didn't leave anything uncovered. They contacted Bruce Cohen, a former All-American player at Cornell who hailed from Long Island. They contacted my high school coach, Bill Ritch. They contacted Dr. Ed Walsh, Manhasset High School's A.D. They contacted Kenny Molloy, who was a judge in my hometown and was the President of the Long Island Athletic Club. Bruno Mazza was a lawyer in Ithaca. He had been a roommate of Ken Molloy in law school, and he was also a friend of Bob Kane, so that was a nice connection.

It all makes sense. It sounds like they were really doing their due diligence without you knowing about it. Getting information from the Long Island Athletic Club was a wise move, because if you were indeed the right match, you could build a great recruiting pipeline. Given Long Island is such a hotbed of talent in several sports, it sounds like this was a match on many levels. It was well played by all, and it's safe to say at this point that it worked out pretty well.

It did. It definitely did.

Unknown Journey

Richie, I'd like to talk about that season of '69, when you had players on the field that were, obviously recruited by another coach with another philosophy, and the challenges you faced while transitioning into being the head coach.

You clearly had to earn some credibility from many people - given your relative youth and the fact that you had not yet been a head coach.

I would also like to talk about the fact that there is a recurrent theme that I have heard many times over the 35 years of our friendship. Many people have shared how much it means to them that, even after many years, you remember their uniform number, their position, where they were from, and quite often, their family members' names. It is tempting, but unfair in a sense to say that your ability to recall those things is a real gift, as the term "gift" implies that it was just handed to you. I'm sure that a lot of mental work goes into remembering these things about people, knowing that it means something to them.

Thank you for that... When I was young, I had a problem with reading, and I had to memorize paragraphs. I remember going to bed at night, taking a flashlight and a book up to bed, and trying to read the paragraphs over and over to memorize them. And at an early age, that really helped my ability to recall events and situations in my life. It enabled me to remember certain features of people, and that would help me recognize them when I saw them in person, or when we spoke. It was sort of a technique that I used to make people feel comfortable, like when you go up to shake hands and you're not sure who you're shaking hands with. I would start out "It's great to see you and I hope things are going well for you." And then I'd start recalling who they were. It is a wonderful gift for me, because it enables me to have stronger relationships with people.

That brings to mind the beautiful Maya Angelou quote. She said, "I've learned that people will forget what you said, people will forget what you did, but people will never forget how you made them feel." It makes people feel valued when you remember their names. I'm sure that has been helpful throughout your coaching career and the rest of your life, to be able to make people feel that you value them. That is a gift, for sure, but it's also something that at which you work diligently. That said, I'd like to hear about the first year when you came in and you were coaching a whole roster of players brought in by someone else.

The 1969 season was very interesting. I got the job in February; and practice was starting in a week so I really didn't have a lot of time to prepare as the head coach. I knew we had to take care of a budget deficit, but we had to get some new equipment, and we had to start planning travel. I was pretty much by myself, so my wife became my administrative assistant. She did a lot for me, organizational details, setting up schedules for team travel, and arranging accommodations. And I did get a lot of help from Pat Fillie, who was a remarkable man. I think I might have mentioned he was a two-time captain at Notre Dame in the 1940's. In fact, last night I sat and watched "Rudy"—probably for the 10th time—and for my grandson Chase, it was his first time. Chase just turned 12, and he was amazed at that movie. There are movies I'm going to recommend further in this book that parents should have their children see, to give them a real concept of the role that athletics play in life.

In 1969, the facilities at Cornell were not like they are today. We had Barton Hall, which was really stressed from a usage standpoint. Part of the hall was in use from 7 o'clock in the morning, with ROTC, all the way to midnight with intramurals. So Barton Hall would be unavailable as a place to practice. In the past, the team had worked out in the Livestock Pavilion, but I felt it was a little too narrow and it was not long enough.

I went over to Oxley Arena, which is where the polo team practiced and played. Oxley Arena was built before World War I, and Mr. Oxley was extremely generous to Cornell. Polo, as we all know, is quite a sport. A lot of people said it's a rich man's sport, but there sure were a lot of farm boys who were tremendous polo players. Believe it or not, my father, when he came from Ireland and then resettled on Long Island, would take the family to watch the Boswick brothers play in Westbury, on the beautiful polo fields out on Long Island. And when I was a little boy, I went to their polo matches. Little did I know that Oxley Arena and the polo arena were going to be great locations for me to work our team into condition and get them ready for the season.

To describe Oxley Arena to you; they took care of cavalry horses there during World War I. The surface was semi-hard, and as you got into Oxley Arena, you walked past at least fourteen stalls. The horses would usually be out on the edge of these stalls, and when I went in for the first time, I sort of chuckled because I was going to try to ask the facility manager if I could use it in the evenings. Also, the chuckle came from imagining the reactions of some of these players that were accustomed to playing on high school fields that were sometimes better than golf course greens. And here we were in February, and the temperatures were going to be in single digits, even minus digits, and we were going to be in a polo barn. Number one, it was going to be pretty cold. Number two, it had some leaks in the ceiling. And the first thing these young men were going to see was a shovel and a broom, and we were going to clean the surface off so that it would be playable for us to really go up and down the field.

It was a dirt surface, an inch or two deep, right?

Yes. It was great conditioning. Butch Hilliard was my assistant, and he and I went in to inspect the facility. I thought it was going to be ideal. The ball could carom off the wooden walls, and we could put goals in there. The lighting was not the greatest so we didn't really put goalies in the goal. We had shooting boards with hooks that were fastened on the goals, with the corners and the lower part of the board cut out, so it gave players the opportunity to shoot at the corners, shoot at the lower areas, and the board would rebound the ball if they weren't accurate.

So the first night of practice, all our freshmen thought when we mentioned the word "arena" it was gonna be a little bit like Madison Square Garden or one of the other fine arenas throughout the country. We dressed in Schoellkopf Hall, and when they came over to the polo barn, their amazement was something to see. Our practices started at 11 o'clock at night, and we had a routine. One group would be in the polo barn; the other group would be lifting, doing some stretching and looking at lacrosse film. So we rotated the groups every 45 minutes. The first group came at 11:15, and then we had another group come in after them. When the first group came in, of course, they were going to be the sweepers and the shovelers. The shock on some of the freshmen's faces was visible! Here they were, coming into a facility that was a very cultivating location - if you're a rosebush - but not the greatest if you're going to be running in it.

Personally, I felt it helped our conditioning tremendously. I can never recall an ankle injury, so it's obvious we did strengthen our legs and our ability to play, because when you were running on that surface, it really made you push off harder, run harder, and it made you dig in. Going after ground balls was definitely not a luxury. When you went after a ground ball, frequently a player would check your stick and you might not be just picking up a ball. As you picked the ball up, there would probably be some soil picked up at the same time, and if he checked your stick, sometimes that soil would come right back in your face, so it really made us execute much better. We got to the ground balls a lot quicker. We picked the ball up and protected the stick better. So there were some great things that helped us with our fundamentals, and I really attribute that to the Oxley Arena surface.

When we played in there, we played a version of box lacrosse, without goalies. We had different methods of keeping score and we would chart the winners after every night. The winning team would get a spray-painted jock and it was called the "Golden Jock Award." We sprayed it with gold paint. The team that finished second would get the "Holy T-shirt," and that was a t-shirt that was no longer useable, as it had multiple holes in it. So that made it exciting.

I'm going to guess that had these young men accepted full-ride scholarships to Virginia or Maryland or elsewhere, they wouldn't be shoveling out a horse barn...

That's correct. Our wrists were strong, and our technique of shoveling and sweeping built up the shoulders.

Those were some transferable skills?

Very much so.

I'm also going to guess that if they knew that whenever they picked up a ground ball they might get a face full of whatever was in that stick, they were going to be a little bit more thorough when shoveling it out.

No doubt! Some of the stories are astonishing. We always told the players: "Do not run into the arena because people were giving riding lessons there." Well, one night we had a young man who was really very interested in working on his skills to make the team. I couldn't have had a more dedicated group of people that first year, and this young man, Donald Dworsky, who grew up in town, took it upon himself to run over to Oxley Arena early, and when I say "early," we started at 11 pm. He probably went over about 10:45. I had just arrived after having the luxury of driving over. The players jogged over. So I opened the door, and Donald had already gone through the door. I didn't see him. He ran past the horses and started to run into the arena. And there was someone that was coming out of the arena and he spooked the horse she was riding. The horse and rider both went down. And I was saying to myself, "God, no..."

So... a serious incident might have spelled the end of your polo barn arrangement, and the future of the Cornell lacrosse program was laying on the ground with that horse. And you were hoping that they both got up.

Exactly... I was trying to figure out what the big wigs would say the next day. The *Ithaca Journal* headline would have been "Horse Has To Be Shot Because He Got Spooked By a Lacrosse Player." I didn't know a lot about horses. I knew a lot about merry-go-round horses, and they don't move too much. As I got there, of course, Donald was in shock. The girl was in shock. Luckily, she had a helmet on. And I was praying, "Please, horse. Get up. Get up." Because I was thinking we're going to have to shoot the horse. Sure enough, the horse got up and jogged around the arena. And there's no doubt in my mind..: I think the good Lord got that horse up because I'm not sure what happens when horses fall. I've never seen any. I never

maging. What a difference that made! There we were on a regular full-size football field in the open spaces. The temperatures were in the 80's. It was exciting.

The first couple of days we were there, we also practiced in Gainesville, Florida, at the University of Florida. We would practice three sessions, and we ate in the dining hall. I tried to caution the players, telling them, "You're gonna go pretty hard this morning. Eat a good breakfast but don't overdo it." And that was like talking to the wall. Some of those guys didn't believe in that and, sure enough, paid the price at our 8 a.m. practice. So we went from 8 a.m. to 10. We had a rest, had lunch, and we came back out at 1:30 and went until 3:00. We let the players go in the pool and relax. We had dinner at 5:30, and after dinner we had a brief meeting, and then we went out at 7:00 and worked out from 7:00 to 9:00.

We did this for two days. During the second day, members of the football staff from Florida came out. They were laughing, and Ray Graves, the head coach, came over to me. He says, "Coach," in his southern accent, "We're looking at you for the last day and a half. You guys from the north are nuts!" He said, "It's anywhere from 80 to 90 degrees out here. We never practice as much as you guys practice. Are you trying to include these boys in the program, or are you trying to run them off the program?" I said, "Believe it or not, Coach, we're trying to make a program. In order to make a program, we've got to put some time in." He said, "I'm a little concerned. Are they going to be able to hold up?" And I said, "Well, the north has held up in other areas and I sure believe they can hold up again!" He laughed, and we shook hands and we kept going.

On our second day, we were practicing right near the tennis courts. We were working a lot on shooting, and we had a real fine shooter by the name of Al Rimmer, who hailed from Canada. Al had a different technique than I was accustomed to seeing, and sometimes he was extremely accurate. But sometimes his shots were over the top of the cage. I decided to look at his stick, and take a shot with it. I was going to tell him that if he came a little bit more overhand, he'd have much more accuracy. I said, "I don't want to discourage you, Al, as I know you've got some accurate shooting ability." I took his stick, and I was not accustomed to it. They were wooden sticks in those days. I took a shot, and the ball went about 40 feet in the air, over the top of the tennis courts. Two young women were playing tennis, and one said "I'll get the ball for you." She went to hit the ball, and being a lacrosse ball, it was about two pounds heavier than a tennis ball! It knocked her right on her tail! With that, I ran over and apologized. All the players were turned the opposite way. They were all laughing. So we bought a little humor into the Sunshine State. I apologized to her and she asked, in that nice southern accent, "What is that ball that I just hit?" I said, "That is a lacrosse ball." She had no idea what I was talking about.

We took care of the southern gentlemen, we took care of the southern socialites, and then we continued to practice. The next day, we scrimmaged Duke, and I liked what I saw. Next up was Virginia, and that went very well, and when I say "very well," I will add that the score was not important. What mattered was that we were seeing definite improvement. It was a scrimmage, and we wanted to play every player that made that trip.

The trip home was memorable. The bus trip was 24½ hours, and we had two bus drivers. We left Boca Raton after dinner, and when we got to the Carolinas it was snowing. And we just kept chugging along, taking periodic breaks. We would stop at various rest stops—and there weren't a lot in those days. We would stop, get out, and stretch. We had fluid on the bus and it was not Gator-Aid, but Coca Cola (as water was not a big thing in those days). We had an assortment of beverages, so we kept everybody happy. There were a lot of card games. Some players brought a lot of books with them because we were going to be away for 9 days of spring travel. It was a great opportunity to catch up on a lot of studying and reading. We had some guys that were pretty talented, some comedians, which was good. So before we knew it, the trip was not as long as we thought it would be. Plus, I told everybody to leave their watches in their traveling bags because I didn't want someone looking at their watch every hour, "We're an hour closer." It's like that old thing: Are we there yet? Are we there yet? And I definitely didn't want to hear that.

Did your administrative assistant make this trip as well? Otherwise known as Pat?

No, no. We had babies at the time. It really was great, and the Florida trip was a big help to us. On our way back; our opening game was against Baltimore University, in Baltimore. We beat them, so that was my first win. It was our team's first win under a new head coach.

So you started off 1 – 0.

Yes.

Did you contemplate retirement?

No, I was just getting started!

We lost our next game at Hobart; and I got my indoctrination to playing away from home. They had a ritual in Geneva when they played Cornell. Classes would end at 2:00 and the game started at 3. They celebrated from 2 to 3 outside the fence. For one dollar, you could bring a trash basket and have it filled up with beer. And they had kegs surrounding the outside. By the time the students got into the stands, we were definitely an enemy. They had some ritual where they threw fish at the opponents, and I could have opened a fish market that day. So, we definitely were facing hostile conditions.

Jerry Schmidt, who has since passed away, had taken over the Hobart job. There's no question he had a dislike for Cornell, and that's when I first realized you've got to really pep your team up to play an opponent because they were sky-high. They came out of the locker room and it seemed like they were getting to play the most important game of their lives. They weren't just getting ready to play Cornell, they wanted to beat us, badly.

They did win, and that was a very difficult game for me to swallow, but I learned some beautiful lessons.

I learned coming back on the bus that silence meant we were going to be better. We were going to work harder. I'm sure the team lost a lot of confidence in me as a coach, which is only natural. Too often in society, we're always pointing the finger. In athletics, my belief is when things don't go well, there is no need to point the finger, but the people in charge of your program have got to do a better job of preparation.

That night, I don't think I slept an hour. I took a lot of notes, writing about things that I was going to have to do better, or we were going to have to do better. I gave the players off the next day. That was a mistake because my firm belief is, after you get taken apart, you probably should get back as quickly as possible. Get back to the drawing board. Get back to the field. Get back into the team concept. Get back into the locker room. Get the smiles back on everybody's faces.

You're not going to change the scoreboard. Once the scoreboard goes out, the game's over. Start rebuilding for your next game. Start organizing for the next practice. Start becoming a better leader. Start finding the key players that are going to help other people become leaders. My belief is that a leader is an extraordinary person. I sort of sensed that people were looking at others who had made mistakes in the game, and I could constantly harp on it during my next practice: Show me a person that doesn't make a mistake and I'll show you a person who is not trying. I wanted them all to try. And they did.

Our final home game was against Princeton on Lower Alumni Field, which was our home field at the time. Schoellkopf Field, being the football stadium, was God's Little Acre. We weren't permitted to go on it. But Lower Alumni Field was a great home field. It could seat about 4,200 people on one side, opposite the bench side. On the bench side, there was roping where people could stand behind. The Cornell students and faculty were very into lacrosse, they were a big part of it. Princeton was heavily favored to win the Ivy League title outright. We had to beat them to gain a tie.

It was a sensational game. The way those players came through was magnificent. We won 13-9. We wrapped up my first season as head coach with an 11-8 win at Syracuse. We finished as Ivy League co-champs, and a tremendous amount of credit should be given to the seniors for their leadership in our six-game winning streak to end the season.

What a way to go out—to beat the heavily favored Princeton team, to grab your share of the title.

Moving on to the next season, 1970, how did you feel about your first recruiting class?

I felt I was successful at getting quality depth at all positions.

What can you tell me about the transition period of blending the players you brought in and those recruited by Ned Harkness?

In 1969, I had the luxury of running fall practice, and that was very competitive. We all practiced together, and the freshmen were very talented. The transition went very smoothly. The first year, it wasn't easy for the players who had been playing a different style under a different coach, but they adjusted well and I really admired that. I felt that I was being tested every day by the returning veterans.

One particular challenge was to make sure that everyone was on time. During that '70 season, we had a young man who didn't like the early parts of practice. Our trainer at the time was a wonderful man, Alf Eckman, and I think Alf was either from Sweden or Finland, and he was a remarkable trainer. Of course, to be hired at Cornell, you have to be really good.

This one player got tape on more body parts than any mummy I've ever seen—shoulder, wrist, ankle, knee, foot... He contributed to the team, but I think his delay tactics were starting to get to me. At that time, we were practicing a lot on Lower Alumni Field and we were dressing at Lynah Rink. Two days in a row, he was late. We were already into the second phase of practice, and if you're going to be late because of class or labs, that's not a problem. But as for taping—you should get it done early, and if it's necessary, get it done early and be out there with all your teammates.

Well, this one day he came out a little bit later than he should have, and late was late. So I went over to him and Alf. I said, "Tomorrow, if he's not on the field for the beginning of practice, he's getting cut. And you're getting fired." They looked at me like I had two heads. The kid said, "I've got to take care of these injuries." I said, "Let me ask you something... Did you go to the fraternity party last Saturday night?" "Sure." I said, "Did you dance?" He replied, "Yeah. I can dance." I said, "Do you get taped up to dance?" "No." I said, "Well, guess what? Think of this as a dance, and your ass better be out here early tomorrow."

Well, we started practice the next day; he wasn't there at the beginning. I told everybody in practice that we were practicing early, like 15-20 minutes early. Well, we were out on the field and he wasn't there. So I took the team and we went to hide behind some bushes. We saw Alf and this gentleman come running out on the field. They couldn't find the team. And Alf was thinking, "We're late! You're getting cut and I'm getting fired!" So then they ran down and they thought we're down at Hoy Field. Then they ran back up to Lower Alumni Field, and by that time, we'd come out from hiding.

So they came over and the kid was shaking. "Coach, we were here. We couldn't find the team." I said, "We were here. You guys better get your eyes examined." I said, "What do you mean, you couldn't find the team?" They were dumfounded, and he was never late again!

He probably showed up early for work every day for his whole career.

I think he became a brain surgeon!

Or an athletic trainer... Did you want to say anything else about that season?

After the '69 season, I did an extensive evaluation of myself, the program, where we were headed, how we could get national recognition, and how we could be perceived as a strong athletic component at Cornell.

Not just a good Ivy League team, but an elite team nationally, right?

Right...I felt that we were tops in the world academically, and we should want to be up in the upper echelon of schools that are similar to Cornell, like our fellow Ivy League schools. I did want to be able to bring recognition and honor to Cornell. I felt that it was within our grasp. I knew the old ladder theory—reach for one rung at a time—but I was probably stepping up two or three rungs at the same time.

So I made an appointment to see Mr. Kane. When I went in, Pat Filley was with him. And I said to Mr. Kane, "You know, I would like to change our schedule and include some non-league games against some of the top five teams in the country." And he said, "Who would those teams be?" I said, "Well, I'd like to play Virginia, Army, Johns Hopkins. I'd like to play Navy and I'd like to schedule Maryland."

He said to me, after a pause, which I thought was like five minutes, but probably was 20 seconds, "Where would you like to work next year?" I wasn't going to smile at that. I knew I had to come up with an answer. I don't think it took too long, but in my mind, it took a long time. I said, "I'm extremely content working here at Cornell University." He said, "You know, with that schedule, you may not do very well." I said, "That's a possibility. Anytime you schedule teams in advance, you're not sure what kind of talent they have.

But I think over the last couple of years we've been denied national recognition because of our schedule. According to the pollsters, the committees that picked the best teams in the country for what is considered a national championship, cannot vote for Cornell. They perceive our schedule as weak by comparison." I thought that was a great injustice, so I want our team to be the best. I think we should play the best. And with your permission, I would like to start researching some scheduling." And I looked over and Pat Filley was smiling. He was a state wrestling champion from South Bend, a two-time captain at Notre Dame. Bob Kane said, "Well, come in with some of your ideas. Write them down."

I went home that night and wrote down the beginnings of my plan. I wanted to try to start off with Virginia, Johns Hopkins, Army, and Navy, and if we could, maybe as part of our southern trip, to play Maryland. And I kept pondering this that night and the next morning. I was going to make an appointment for that afternoon to see if Mr. Kane was available.

A Title Earned

> Let's talk about the '71 season... I can imagine some of the rumblings throughout Division 1 lacrosse... Cornell hired a young guy from Long Island with no experience as a head coach at the collegiate level, and he led his Ivy League upstarts to an undefeated season in 1970.

Now, it's 1971, the Big Red are riding a 12-game winning streak, they just beat a heavily-favored Army team to make it to the championship game, and they are headed to Hofstra to play Maryland for the national championship. And, it just so happened that Cornell's coach had played on Maryland's national championship team a dozen years earlier... That is quite a story line.

There was a tremendous amount of joy in the locker room from earning the opportunity to play for the national championship. For a lot of players, the trip to Hofstra was going to be a homecoming because quite a few of our players lived in Long Island and surrounding areas, so it was going to be great.

Then, coming back, we have our traditional bus breakdown. We got halfway home on Route 17, in an area that is pretty isolated, and sure enough the bus broke down and it was a fuel injector that caused problems for us on our trip.

Did you charter the same bus for every road trip?

We tried to. It was Crispell, and is now Swarthout. With my superstition, we always had the same driver. Rick LaFrance, our trainer, and the bus driver would get out and go to the back of the bus and one of our players, Rob Wagner, a tall guy about 6' 4," got out of the bus. I did not know this, but he put on a Halloween mask! That was one of his pranks – scaring people in their hotel rooms - so he put the mask on and tapped on both the driver and Rick as they were underneath the back hood of the bus attempting to get the fuel injector functioning. Startled, both guys jumped and hit their heads on the back of the hanging bus compartment and started running in opposite directions. Of course, that prank was talked about for a while.

Eventually, the fuel injector worked fine and we got on our way back to Cornell where we had a great few days of preparation. Going down to the championship game, we invited the late Ben Mintz, our Sports Information Director, who reminded me of Peter Lorre, the actor. Ben had his own way of doing things over the years, and he was a sprinter on a great relay team at Ithaca High School back in the 30's. We were on our way to Hofstra on Route 17, and bingo, the bus breaks down, so we pull over to the side and Ben was a little shook up because he's worried about getting there on time. Luckily, it was Thursday, so we had some time even if we had to walk. They went back again to fix the fuel injector and we got on our way and I told Ben that every time we had a problem with our fuel injector, we usually win. I said don't tell anybody that, just keep it a secret. We had a great practice session on Friday, and we had a special guest from the University of Maryland there, as one of their top players had been confused about the schedule and wandered onto our practice field.

Scouting reports were very important to us. Maryland's concentration was on the number one team, and that was Army that year, and they never thought those Ivy League kids from Ithaca could outrun, outplay and stay with Army throughout a grueling four quarters.

So this is familiar territory for you, in that when you were a high school coach at Manhasset, you coached against your old team (Sewanhaka) and now you're the head coach at Cornell and you're coaching against your old team (Maryland). Although that was your alma mater, I'm sure your loyalties were in the right place.

That's true, when I was at Manhasset, we won the sectional championship (north shore) and we won the Nassau County championship and beat Sewanhaka at Hofstra.

Astrologers frequently note how the stars and various planets line up, and I believe that everything started to line up for us - from the Friday workout, to the team dinner, to the phone call from Dale Corson, to the preparation on Saturday. Everybody was really into it. You could sense it at our team breakfast, which is also our training meal before the game. Final preparation was done at the hotel, and we arrived at Hofstra to a huge welcome. It felt like a political rally. Everybody rallied around the bus. I think our players became a little nervous at that stage, because they realized how important this game was to not only them but to their supporters, parents, and friends, and of course former teammates that were from Long Island and had showed up to support us. There were banners and signs. People brought some musical instruments. This definitely made for a nice welcoming.

As I mentioned earlier, Hofstra did an incredible job in preparation for that tournament. There were a lot of people who doubted that that inaugural tournament would really be organized properly. Well, it definitely was first class. It was the first NCAA lacrosse championship, and it was definitely handled by a wonderful university and their staff.

You could sense in the locker room that there was a high level of commitment. We arrived with coats and ties. We knew we were on a business trip, and the business was about to commence. Players went out and walked around the field. I always wanted them to get off the bus and walk around and stretch their legs. Every bus trip we went on, we usually parked some distance from the locker room but in that case we couldn't. So the players went out on the field, came back in, and got all of their equipment organized. Taping was done at the hotel. Our trainer, Rick LaFrance, is a remarkable guy, and we always taped at the hotels. It was much easier, as it minimized some of the chaos in the locker room.

Everybody put on their practice jerseys and went out and threw the ball around. Then they came back in and it was time to suit up. You could sense that it was going to be a special occasion. And it definitely was. You had the whole lacrosse world looking at us because of the TV coverage, which was good, but it still wasn't nationwide. However, we didn't really care about the TV. What we cared about was our assignments, how we were going to produce on the field, and how we were going to make sure we came off that field a victor.

I'm wondering if some of the press wondered if you were there because of some sort of deficit on the part of Army. If that was indeed the perception, that probably fueled the fire even more, did it not?

Very much so... You know, all of my teams have really been underdogs. We've had winning streaks – as a matter of fact, our 42 game winning streak is still a national record, and 39 games in a row in the Ivy League is still a record. We knew what our capabilities were. We knew our strengths, we knew our weaknesses. And we also knew a lot about Maryland. We had a gentleman by the name of George Rehorn who played behind me in high school. I'm sad to say that George recently passed away. He was my idol, even though he was 4 years behind me. He always got a big kick out of that. His nickname and codename was "Hornet," and he was our chief scout. He had seen Maryland play three times, so we took his scouting report and put it into a fine game plan with excellent match-ups. Maryland was a very strong team - not just physically, but also in their transition game and their quickness, so we wanted to match our quickness against theirs. Our strength was a motion offense, and we used many sets on offense. We actually had six set plays, and we had three options off each play, so that gave us eighteen sets that we could run. We also had various offensive plays designed to be run against unusual defenses, like box-and-one, zone defenses, and an all-out press defense.

When you're in the process of completing a puzzle, you have multiple pieces left. You want to take all of those pieces and finish the puzzle. At the opening face-off, we were in the process of putting the extra pieces together to finalize that puzzle, or as I mentioned earlier, a painting. A Rembrandt. It was important for us to make sure that we had complete confidence throughout the game. And that was established by everyone realizing several things: you have an assignment, carry it out, rely on your teammates, always look ahead, and don't look behind. If you make a mistake, forget it and move on. Because as I have said, show me a player that doesn't make a mistake and I'll show you a player who isn't trying.

One great thing about Cornell teams, they would go from opening whistle to the end, no matter what the score was, and no matter what the outcome was going to be. I always wanted the players to come back into the locker room realizing that they did their very best.

So, when you had these players who have already done enough hard work to get accepted into an Ivy League school, and they're sharpening that work ethic and skill sets on an ongoing basis, you're quite confident that you can throw these complex defensive schemes and play books at them, and that they will continually evolve in that regard as well?

Absolutely. You know we had a number of engineers on our team. We had young men who were interested in pre-Vet, pre-Med, and a number who were aspiring to go to law school. Some were going to go into education or into the corporate world. Sometimes, when you have a mixture, it's like alphabet soup. When it all comes together, it makes for a wonderful flavor. Well, this team had all of the components. They had the toughness, the quickness, the intelligence, and they had the athleticism.

As I mentioned, we had given what would be considered a pep talk. It wasn't of the Knute Rockne style, but it was designed to let these players know how much they had contributed over the past year to get where they were, and that we really owed the 1970 team a chance to be recognized along with us. Everything we talked about that year was really based on the 1970 team because there were eleven players who graduated from that team, that were teammates of those players competing for the national championship.

The atmosphere was there, and our team had met challenges all year. From the cold nights in Oxley Arena, to the running (which was called a sweat hog) around the Plantations and back to Barton Hall, to the vigorous Friday afternoon trainings, to double sessions on Saturday, they had all paid their dues. We did not have an extensive weight program. We worked a great deal on agility. Every player had a jump rope, and their job was to get their feet and hands quicker. I recommend very strongly to young men and young women, if you really want to master athletics, get yourself a jump rope. It will help your vertical movement, your horizontal movement, your foot quickness, and it will coordinate your upper body/lower body very effectively. These factors all contributed to our readiness to step on the field at Hofstra. We had prepared all year for that day.

Before the game, traffic on Long Island was quite heavy. That was due to the fact that Belmont Stakes were being run, and it was probably 8 miles from where we were playing. In those days you had a police escort to the stadium, so we got to Hofstra and it was a sellout crowd. The teams were welcomed onto the field by Cornell fans and Maryland fans and as we approached game time, I looked up and noticed that the Maryland staff looked like they were about to enter a fashion show... white patent leather shoes, checkered pants... and we came out with our normal gear that we had been wearing since February. Of course, we did have it washed or dry cleaned, but they definitely won the fashion show. I remember walking through the gate and there were always a lot of people that are Doctors in Knowology – in other words, they are know-it-alls. One guy said "Hey Coach, you're not dressed as nicely as the Maryland coaching staff," and I said to him, "They won the fashion show, and we're gonna win the game." I walked toward our bench and there were three New York State refs near the gate, who I had gotten to know quite well from playing in upstate NY. It was obvious that Maryland was a little bitter that refs from upstate NY were assigned to the game, but I had nothing to do with assignments. We had Joseph Julian, a long time official, we had Jim Garvey, God rest his soul, and Bob Cooper, and as we were warming up I noticed that Bob Cooper had cleats on that were a little too high for the type of turf we were going to play on, so I went out to him and I said "Bob, we have special shoes designed for this type of turf, and if you'd like to use a pair I'll have someone go and get them. He said "No thanks," that he was accustomed to reffing on turf and didn't think anything of it. I thought the turf at Hofstra was a little different, but I respected his decision.

So, it was opening face-off time and he's in charge, and sure enough, he bent down and put the ball in place. He backed up and fell backwards. In fact, some people would say he went "ass over tea kettle." We gained possession, but they blew the whistle quickly because the official was out of position - on his butt – and we would now have a re-faceoff.

The game was televised in Baltimore, New Jersey and Connecticut, and was broadcast by WBAL in Baltimore. Bucky Gunts's father was a part owner, and in charge of all the media work at WBAL.

Would you say that Maryland was favored by a goal, or by two, or by five?

According to the Baltimore papers, Cornell was really wasting its time coming to Hofstra. All that time and expense, and many were really not in favor of the NCAA playoffs. Some of the parochial purists from down south thought it infringed on the great game. They wanted to keep control of the game, and their voting powers were becoming non-existent.

As the game proceeded, the crowd was very enthusiastic, and at half time we were leading. Mike Waldvogel, my assistant coach, went into our locker room before the team came in, and we put some strategies on the board that were really pertinent to how we would approach the second half. One of the things we wanted to do was to be more aggressive on defense. We wanted to give our goalie a lot more support than we had in the first half. We wanted to outrun Maryland. They were very athletic, very big and strong. I felt we were quicker, and our quickness prevailed in the second half. Bucky was available, and scored two goals in that game. He eventually became the Director of the Today show, and he won an Emmy for NBC's Olympic coverage. I was really considering getting Bob Rule into the game, because he had done so much for this team, and he and Bob Buhmann were just remarkable goal tenders. Given he would have to limp onto the field wearing a cast, I just didn't think it was in his best interest. Later in my career, I probably would have. There's a code that goal tenders live by - they root for each other. It's one of the most difficult positions to play, with balls coming at you from many directions and angles. Baseball pitchers are now clocked between 95 - 101 mph. A skilled player could throw the lacrosse ball about 75-80 mph, and that's from ten feet away. The speed can increase, and some players can now throw the ball 90mph with the advances in equipment. A goalie has to have unbelievable reflexes and quickness, and you definitely have to be very courageous because you do not have all the padding they have in hockey. Plus, hockey utilizes a four by four-foot goal, and a lacrosse goal is six by six, and like I said, shots come from all different directions. Most of the shots in hockey come up at you, and in lacrosse they're coming down at you, or up at you on bounce shots. I give those men a lot of credit for standing in the line of fire.

The game continued and little did I know that we had Brooks

Bradley in the stands. His son, Jim (Brooks) Bradley was on our team. The elder Bradley probably believed in our prospects of winning more than anybody else, and I say that because he had bumper stickers made up that said "Cornell Lacrosse – National Champions." I'm glad I did not know that either before the game, or while the game was being played, because it would have been a big concern to me with my superstitions. I believed that things can happen, and that a bumper sticker could somehow affect the game. It was, to me, something for people to look at and say "Those guys are pretty cocky," and one thing we never wanted to be was cocky.

The history books show that your preparation paid off, and since your one-goal loss to Virginia in the season opener, your players had run the table. Using that polo barn metaphor, your horses came out of the gate strong, went up 4-1 after one quarter, increased that to 8-3 at the half and finished strong down the homestretch for a dominating 12-6 victory. After being snubbed, even after going undefeated in 1970, and finally getting a chance to determine the national championship on the field, that "How Do You Like Us Now?" statement had to feel good.

It did, for sure. During the seasons of 1970 and '71, we were 24-1, our only loss being a 10-9 overtime loss at Virginia. That team started out on a mission in 1970, and had clearly moved into the elite ranks of collegiate lacrosse.

After the game there was a large group of people that came on the field. I spoke to WBAL for the live interview, and I commended the Maryland team. I conveyed how proud we were to win this first on-field NCAA championship, and I reminded the committee that it was unfortunate that the undefeated 1970 team didn't get a chance to share or win the championship outright, because it was a great team. I said on-air that all of us – Cornell's players and coaches – wanted to dedicate the win to those that didn't have the opportunity to play for the title in 1970. I mentioned how great these fans were, and what an honor it was to be in the first NCAA championship game representing the Ivy League. Several other radio stations – including Ithaca stations - interviewed us as well.

I got to the locker room, and saw my friend Dick Schaap who played lacrosse at Cornell in the 1950's. He was a goalie, and he grew up in Freeport, Long Island. I actually knew him as a Long

Island Press "cub reporter." He covered Saturday afternoon football games, and he wrote about a couple of our games. There were a lot of dignitaries from Cornell's history, former players from the 20's and 30's, and that was a wonderful feeling. One of our players, Harry Nicolaides - unbeknownst to me - had about 6 bottles of champagne and of course, it was taboo in the NCAA to have alcohol at your celebration. While pictures were being taken, Harry was pouring champagne over everybody and it looked a lot like World Series time. Goggles were not available in those days, so when that champagne hit their eyeballs, we definitely had some guys that looked like space cadets.

In an interview, I thanked president Corson for the phone call he made on Friday night, and a few hours later, I found out it was made by friends of ours that were celebrating in Ithaca before they were leaving to come to Long Island! It was all great - that prank phone call, the success, the chance to see what it's like to win a championship - and it was my first national championship as a coach, so it was really terrific looking around that locker room and seeing the smiles and the joy. I thought for a second, what if I had to come in here and speak to a team that had just lost?... so that went out of my mind completely once I continued to look around the room. Sadly, Harry Nicolaides passed away five years ago. We did lose quite a few players from the 1971 team - Dr. Henry Olivier, Bob Buhmann, Jim Nowak, Tom Mygatt, Bruce Teague - losing those gentlemen really hurt. Over the years we have paid great tribute to them, and we have honored all the wonderful achievements they had here at Cornell as students, athletes, teammates.

"Band of Brothers" is a remarkable book, and the 1971 team was truly a band of brothers. In the book, the priest was Father John Mahoney, and he later became a priest here at Immaculate Conception in Ithaca. I was making a trip to San Francisco, and my wife gave me the book "Band of Brothers" as a Christmas gift. I started reading it, and there was a statement about Father John Mahoney giving last rites to a young paratrooper from Iowa and immediately, I thought 'I know that name,' so I looked through the index and he was listed and mentioned at least six times, so I started to go through the book and sure enough, it was our father John Mahoney. He received the Distinguished Service Cross for his involvement in the Battle of Bastogne. He had to take up a weapon to help protect the soldiers that were surrounded, because there was tremendous fog during that period of time, and our troops could not use any air support. They could not get supplies, so these poor men were surrounded until the fog lifted. At some point, I would really like to put a plaque up in church, in his memory and I am definitely moving in that direction because I think it's things like this that our youth and our people in the community should know about, the efforts put forth and the sacrifices made by people during that generation. I feel like I'm part of the greatest generation because when I was young, I watched my brothers go into the service and watched my sisters and my parents help in many ways. I knew my dad was away helping build ships that were going to be used to help America win, so the "Band of Brothers" was and still is a very special book for me.

Like the "Band of Brothers", I allowed this team to celebrate, and I knew they had common sense and wouldn't overdo it, and I knew I had things that I had to do, like attend a friend's Bar Mitzvah. One of my good friends was Al Levine. I met Al at a lacrosse game on Long Island many years earlier, and he was from New York City. During a time out the ref came over and said "You've gotta get that guy off the field," and I didn't know what he was talking about. I looked over and there was a gentleman directly behind the goal, not out of bounds but directly behind the goal with a bag of baseball bats, a ball bag, and it was obvious he was working with youth baseball. My assistant coach went out and said 'Excuse me sir, you can't be in that area," and Al wanted my assistant coach to explain what this game was like. It was a tie game at that time, so my assistant said, diplomatically, "You're gonna have to come back another day." Well, 2 days later I'm on the practice field, and he came up and he had a little boy with him, Matt Levine, and he said "After you finish coaching could you talk to him about lacrosse?" So I did, and I got Matt a stick and he was so enthused about the goalies. He wanted to be a goalie, so I gave him a goalie stick and watched his progress in youth lacrosse with the help of Jason Stranahan, who was a remarkable educator. Jason played at Union College in the '20's. He played lacrosse and football, and in fact, he was so kind he gave me his helmet that he used in the '20's, which is all leather. It has no face mask and on the back of it is "Patent Pending."

After the championship game as I said I had some stops I had to make, and the first stop I made was to my house on Long Island. My mother was there, and she had received periodic phone calls from a pay phone to give her updates on the score. She was sharp enough to know that it was covered on a radio station from Long Island, so she also had a chance to listen. All my brothers and sisters, cousins and uncles had attended the game, so it was quite a family day. I took the NCAA trophy and gave it to my mom, she kissed the trophy and then I got a kiss. Hugging and kissing my mother was very special, and then she said "I know your dad watched this whole game, and I know that he was one of the instrumental people to help our family achieve all the wonderful things that we did over the years." The kiss meant so much to me. The memories of my dad meant a great deal as well, so after the celebration we were at my mother's house and I excused myself to go visit a friend in Manhasset whose son was celebrating his Bar Mitzvah that day. I arrived there with my wife, a contingent of Cornell fans that were with us and lifted the trophy to the people at the Bar Mitzvah! That was very likely the first time in history that an NCAA trophy ever made it to a Bar Mitzvah!

After the Bar Mitzvah, I went back and had some food with my mom and our friends and family, and then we went to meet the team at one of the players' homes for another celebration. Before we did that, I stopped at a favorite watering hole which was near the high school where we had the famous donkey race and a lot of great sessions after lacrosse and football games. It was like Cheers, a friendly neighborhood pub, and we took the trophy in there and everybody touched it. There must have been one-hundred fifty people there, and we passed it around. That trophy belonged to them as much as it belonged to me and our Cornell team, because some of those people were my teammates, some were great friends and I had wonderful relationships with all of them. It really enabled me to share with them a very special day. After that we went to Fritz Mueller's house. Fritz's son, Glenn, played on our team and he was a force. He could have been a 3-letter winner at Cornell. He played lacrosse and basketball and did not play football, but he could have been an outstanding college football player, as he was in high school. We had a great time at the Mueller house, and there were a lot of people there. One of his friends, Bob Hoffman always had a whistle with him so they played some poker and blew the whistle.

You mentioned that when you got back to Ithaca, there was a

really nice reception for you. How much time off did you take before you started thinking about the next year and how you were going to fill in some of these pieces when some of those players graduated and moved on? Was it a year 'round enterprise to be building and maintaining that program?

When we got back, there was a nice reception for the players and staff at Stewart Park. We really appreciated the turnout. The next day, Monday, my assistant coach Mike Waldvogel and I actually emptied out the players' travel bags and sorted out the equipment so it could be returned to our equipment manager, as the players had left campus. The semester had actually ended a week earlier.

The team had been dressing in a new locker room facility. In 1969 and '70, our locker room was in Lynah Rink, which we shared with the hockey team. And then Schoellkopf House was built, and we used the locker room that was on the ground floor.

The purpose of Schoellkopf House was to provide quarters for visiting teams. Most of the Ivy League schools had facilities where teams (other than football because of their numbers) could stay on campus. That saved a lot of money. We ate our meals in the dining halls at the universities and colleges where we were playing.

I remember that room, a cinder block structure with bunk beds everywhere. Not exactly the Hilton, but serviceable.

Right. As we were sorting through the equipment, Mr. Kane evidently heard us downstairs, as his office was located upstairs above our locker room. He wrote in his book ("Good Sports: A History of Cornell Athletics") that he couldn't believe that two coaches who had just won a national championship 48 hours earlier were sorting through equipment. I didn't want the equipment staff at Cornell to have to labor constantly with the teams. Our locker room was cleaner than most kitchens. Shoes were never left on the floor. In fact, we had a freezer that was not in use but was kept cold, and equipment left on the floor would be put in the freezer, which made it a little difficult to put on your body on a February day. Or, we'd put it up in the 90th row of the stadium and you'd have to go all of the way up there in the snow, which was a little tough. So after one or two infractions, the word would get out, and there would be no soap left on the floor of the showers, and the water would be turned off. We wanted the locker room cleaner than it was when we got there.

Here's an excellent example of our locker room etiquette... It was in the '70s, and we were down on Long Island, ready to play Hofstra and the Long Island Athletic Club, and we worked out at Adelphi. The custodial staff and some of the regular staff at Adelphi were on strike, so they didn't have people to take care of the locker rooms. One day, we had practice and we were on a field that was quite muddy. Players took their shoes off outside but plenty of mud found its way into the locker room. We cleaned and washed that floor. The Athletic Director of Adelphi wrote to our director saying how astonished he was that our team would take the time to do that, but that is the way you build a champion, by doing the little things. Everybody can score goals and play defense. Show me the team that picks up the debris after games, and cleans up locker rooms that they're using as a visitor. To me that's a lesson. Wherever I've been, I've always felt that these lessons would definitely make us all better people. And with that group, I'm sure it did. With their leadership, now in their communities, they're doing things that they can refer back to, like locker room cleanliness and cleaning the bus. Cleaning the bus is very important. We'd get back sometimes at two o'clock in the morning, and that driver had been driving for 7 or 8 hours. We would have him come in and we'd make hot tea or hot chocolate, let him relax, and we would clean the bus. Evidently the word got around the circuit, and then other athletic teams started to follow our example. I thought it was important that the driver shouldn't have to go back at 2 o'clock in the morning to pick up after us. It was much easier for thirty players and coaches to get that bus cleaned up for him.

It sounds like you really expanded the concept of "Team" out from players on the roster, to equipment managers, to athletic trainers, bus drivers, and athletic support staff - all of these people you perceived as important to your program's success. I would assume that fostered some loyalty throughout the whole department.

Very much so... I had no idea that the gentleman from Adelphi had written a letter. I had no idea that the Athletic Director at Hofstra did the same. To me, it was something that probably came from my youth. I remember walking around the neighborhood picking up pieces of paper, cleaning sidewalks that were covered in debris. I remember when we were involved in athletics as a young person;

we'd have to pick up rocks and glass off the fields in order to play. So I guess it was something that was innate, and I wanted it to carry over to our teams. To this day I think it's very important to do things with some kind of order, and some sense of pride.

Thinking back to the earlier chapters, I'm thinking about how much pride you had in your brothers' service to our country. When I think of the locker room that looked like an Army barracks, and your high standard of how it should be left, I agree that some of it was innate, but many of those tendencies seem to have been sharpened through yours and your family's military backgrounds.

No question. I remember when I was growing up I'd have an assignment on Saturday, and of course, I was always eager to get to the baseball field. My assignment would be something like shining fourteen pairs of shoes, wash one or two cars, and cut the grass without a power mower, because we didn't have one. I would hustle to get those tasks done so I could get involved in baseball. I loved doing it, and the compensation was the love I got from my family. Every once in a while I'd be handed some currency, but that wasn't important. The most important thing was, I was doing something for them because they did so much for me.

I remember some of it being very difficult. In 1941, I was four years old, and for the next 4 years I didn't have brothers or a father with me on a constant basis. I learned a lot from my mother and my sisters, my neighbors, and from school.

All of these pieces are like a crossword puzzle. You fill it in and you hope that you complete it. And I haven't completed it yet. I have a long way to go to complete that puzzle. And you notice I talk about puzzles, and when you plan a strategy for a team, from the first day to the last day, you're putting the pieces of the puzzle together. Each day you're filling in a crossword blank, hoping that you're doing it correctly, because if you don't, the result might not be what you want for your team. That was something that always really bothered me, and I'm sure other coaches have gone through this. I always took losses extremely hard. If it was a home game, my wife and I would always put together a non-alcoholic reception after the game. We'd have food for the players and the parents. It was held in the Hall of Fame Room. It was always a nice occasion. As I mentioned, we always had policies, one of which was that we always left the locker room together. We came in as a team, we are going out as a team. Everybody was neatly dressed, and the policy was you go up and you kiss your mother and your father, hug them, acknowledge their guests, and you introduce some of your teammates to your parents. A few words would be said, and as you know, a speech after a victory is a lot easier. A speech after a defeat is very difficult, mainly because I personally felt I'd let the team down.

After the reception, Pat would take the children home, I'd go back to my office just to cool down, to relax mentally, jot down some notes, and maybe look at a video. In those days we didn't have the luxuries that you have today, with all of the high-tech capabilities, so we had a manager do videotapes for us, and I would look at those tapes and relax. I'd go home - the scoreboard is off, the game is over - and now it's time to concentrate on my family. That worked out extremely well for me because it would give me the chance to not bring my work-related stress home. My next thoughts were, what are we doing the rest of Saturday, and what can we do with the children? Sunday was a very important day, going to church, maybe having breakfast out, which was always a treat for all of us. And then we'd do some things with the children. We loved to go to the parks. We are very fortunate to have such beautiful parks and facilities in Ithaca. It was nice to get a change of pace. On Sunday night, my thoughts would go back to what I had to do on Monday.

So you had that work/life balance they talk about now... That's not a term they were using a few decades ago but it's a very popular term now.

Another thing I'd like to revisit is that recurrent theme of manners, orderliness, and gratitude. Part of your job as a coach was to put "W's" in the column, but because of your background and experience, you believed the other part of your job was to help these young men grow into adults. You just addressed one of the most important life lessons in that process, when you talked about your post-game speeches. You said, "A speech after a victory is a lot easier." Taking that into a "real-life" context, it's easy to do things you feel like doing, things you want to do, that are fun to do, but it's not as much fun to clean up a locker room or a bus at 2 am when it's ten below zero. It sounds like all of those components were fitting into that puzzle of helping boys become men.

That was the idea. I was always concerned that these young men faced a lot of challenges on campus. They worked so hard, they played hard, I didn't want that to affect their academics. I didn't want that player - who maybe felt he let the team down on game day - carry that with him. If I sensed that, I would probably call him up on Sunday night, or meet with him. A lot of our players went to mass on Sundays, and at Cornell they had an evening mass. I went to mass with my children during the day, and if I sensed that a couple of players were taking that loss and putting it on their shoulders, I would see if they were going to church, and I'd meet them. The purpose of that was not just from the spiritual aspect, but I wanted to let them know that I was there for them.

They were obviously more than just players to you.

Yes, they were and they still are. I didn't want this to bother them on Sunday night when they had to be prepared for Monday through Friday academics. That was important, very important.

Something else you said that I think is compelling was that when you lost a game, it was important to embrace the fact that the team might have been better than you on that given day. One of the life lessons that you seem to have imparted was that if your athletes brought their best on that day, you wanted them to know that was all you could ask of them. Some days, you play like a super star, and other days you can't pick up a ground ball, but if you brought your best, you just move on.

Exactly.

You clearly had really high standards, and you conveyed that you took it really hard if the team lost, as if you had done something wrong. However, I have also heard you say that the program's winning streak was the team's, that you didn't take credit for that. So, how is it fair for you to blame yourself if they lose but not take credit if they win?

We can visit that another time. I'd have to give that a lot of thought.

Right… I don't want to get too far above my pay grade! You're paying me to emulate Mitch Albom, not Dr. Phil!

Oh, baby… It's like being the captain of a ship. You have a huge staff that works extremely hard for you, yet you're the guy who is unfortunately in charge of the shipwreck. I'm the leader, and I've developed a system, but you can't be perfect all the time.

In discussing that '71 team; in those days championship rings were not the fashion. The Super Bowl didn't come about until the 60s, and Super Bowl rings were the thing. I wanted to get rings for that team, but it wasn't in the budget and it wasn't something that Cornell had done. They gave you a varsity blanket for earning letters, and if you won an Ivy League title, then you would get a really nice watch. Believe it or not, 15 years later we got rings. That was important, mainly because it gave them the chance to realize that they were recognized as a super team.

The connotation with Super Bowl rings is that everybody wants one. When we played in 1971, we didn't even think about rings. All we thought about was winning and competing as a team. And we also thought that team could go down in history because it would be the first team to win an NCAA title by winning the tournament, and it was the first Ivy League school team to win an NCAA lacrosse title.

And earn it on the field, rather than in some conference room.

Correct. And that's something you can never take away. Someone asked me what my feeling was about that first championship. It was a remarkable feeling. Anytime I coached a Cornell team it was a memorable time. But that championship had a special meaning because we were denied any recognition the year before. We were looked at as an "Ivy League team" that was not that talented. Talent is a combination of athletic intelligence, stamina, and heart. Those three components were definitely in abundance on that team.

I can imagine what it must have felt like for the players to be perceived as Ivy Leaguers and therefore perceived as very brainy - and as you said, perceived by some outsiders as pampered - and I'm guessing that when they were cleaning out a bus at 1 o'clock in the morning, they didn't feel pampered.

They sure didn't. We got a lot of these young men summer jobs - construction jobs, working for an exterminator, working in restaurants, painting - we definitely had the blue-collar "pampered" lacrosse players. It's a beautiful combination.

You and I have talked about this, and we agree that one of the

greatest things that you can acquire and carry throughout life is self-respect. And one of the ways to foster self-respect is to take care of what needs to be done, whether you want to do it or not.

Yes, we certainly do agree on that.

It sounds like you were helping your players understand and embrace that concept as young men. I'm sure there were times they were mumbling under their breath that they were busy enough, and didn't need to be cleaning up the locker room or the bus. I've talked with many of your players years later, and looking back, they've told me that they get it now. They understand how that puzzle was being assembled.

Good. Later, we can talk about the earrings, the long hair, wearing your hat backwards, attempting to wear a hat into my office, wearing a hat on the bus, wearing a hat in the locker room, hair too long in the back. We can talk about those things at some stage. A lot of that has some humor in there.

In fact, I'll tell you the earring story… we were going up to a reception in the Hall of Fame Room, and I noticed that one of our players -who had never had this on before- had put an earring in his right ear.

His father had been a Marine officer and had about six of his closest friends there for the game. This gentleman was very well known in the New England area. And his son had decided for the first time to put an earring in his ear.

When I noticed it, I called him over as all of the players were leaving the locker room. I said, "What are you doing?"

He said, "This is the fashion now."

I remembered that when I was growing up, the fashion was to have crew cuts, so I said to him, "I saw your dad after the game with all of his friends. Do you think that earring is going to upset him?"

And he said, "Probably."

So I said, 'Well, just think. First, he's got to drive back about 425 miles and he's going to be thinking about this. He'll be kind of embarrassed because he's never seen you with an earring before. And second, he's probably talked about you for the past 6 hours to all of his friends. I don't think he's going to lose any respect or love for you, but I think you're losing respect for him."

I said, "I just want to ask you, if he gets killed on the way back home in a car accident, how are you going to feel? You can put that earring back in on Monday. You're never going to wear it in the locker room, and you're never going to wear it in my office, but you can put it on Monday and wear it wherever the hell you want to wear it. But you're not going up there with that earring in your ear. And if I've got to cut the lower part of your ear off, I am going to do so. I want you to think about what I just said about your dad going back home. If you're the man that I think you are, you will take that earring out of your ear ASAP."

I turned around; he took the earring off and put it in his pocket. Five years later, I heard about the earring story from his father, and 15 years later I was at a game at Harvard and that young man brought his two sons over, and the young boys said, "Coach Moran, will you tell us the story about the earring?"

I don't want to sound like a dictator. I just wanted to play the role of a parent, which I definitely was, because over the course of those 4 years, I was spending more time with their sons than they were. I just wanted to give proper guidance, which was very important.

Speaking of his two sons, I was overwhelmed because it's obvious it's a story he's kept in his mind for years and years. So Steve, don't wear an earring tomorrow...

I was planning to wear a nose ring...

Oh, baby!

Our Wild Irish Rose

The 1971 season proved that the Cornell lacrosse program had reached the pinnacle of success by winning – in a convincing manner – the first NCAA lacrosse championship tournament.

How did that change the landscape of collegiate lacrosse?

Now that college programs realized they could pursue a national title on the field rather than by committee, this made recruiting a lot more challenging. My office received more information on players than ever before. It was evident that high school coaches wanted their players to continue playing in college, and a majority leaned toward the Ivy League.

After 1971 our schedule became extremely competitive. I had approached Bob Kane conveying my belief that the ideal way to build the best program was to play against the best opponents. In 1972, we won the Ivy League title with an undefeated record. One of the outstanding games during that run was a dramatic 11-10 overtime win at Penn. Our returning players from 1971 did a remarkable job, especially since we lost our outstanding goalie, Brent "Bucky" Gunts, in our season-opening scrimmage. Bill Ellis, Bob Shaw, Bruce Arena and Frank Davis were named to the All-Ivy team.

In '73, Navy and Hopkins – both elite programs – were added to our schedule, and we continued our dominance over Syracuse. A home game against Penn was very similar to the '72 game, but it lasted a record five overtimes before we won on a goal by Bruce Arena. A side note, my friend Bill Murray of Ithaca owned the Cornell Barbershop downtown. He normally closed at 3 pm on Saturdays. The game was being broadcast on WHCU, and Bill and his customers were so absorbed in the game that he kept the barber shop open. That year, Bruce Arena, Jim "Brooks" Bradley, and Mike Emmerich were named first team All-Ivy. We finished 5-1 in the Ivy League, and we won our last eight games.

That winning streak continued into the '74 season, and the players who were ineligible as freshmen were now stepping up to help the varsity team. We won our first three games before losing to Johns Hopkins. After the Hopkins game in Baltimore, we went on a nine game winning streak, enabling us to qualify for the NCAA tournament. In the first round, we beat Virginia to get to the semifinals at Maryland, where we lost. The All-Ivy selections that year were Jim Trenz, Mike French, Bill Marino, Dave Devine, and Mike Emmerich.

In 1975, we were undefeated in the Ivy League, and were 14-1 overall. In the NCAA tournament, we beat Rutgers in the first round but lost to Navy in the second round. It was strange we had three players make the All-Ivy team that year – Eamon McEneaney, Bill Marino, and Dave Devine.

As I recall, it was after that 1975 loss to Navy that Eamon McEneaney approached you after the game and said, "Coach, that's the last time we will lose a game while I am at Cornell."

That is correct.

The Ivy League was gaining legitimacy and credibility, but until 1976, no other Ivy team was able to win the tournament. Obviously that changed in 1976, when your team reached the top of the mountain again. I know there were many building blocks to those legendary teams of '76, '77 and '78, and a bit later we will talk about several of those players. To start, I'd like to learn more about the player who is synonymous with that magical era. Of course, I am talking about Eamon McEneaney, who was an accomplished author as well as one of the best players ever to

pick up a lacrosse stick. Am I correct that writing was important to Eamon from an early age?

Yes. Eamon wrote his book of poems called "Bend in the Road." Eamon wrote those poems during some leisure time, and I remember that they took shape on pieces of scrap paper or napkins. He worked on them while on bus trips and when he had time in the locker room.

I first met Eamon when I was playing softball at Sewanhaka High School. Eamon had older brothers and they used to come around and, of course, he stood out.

How old was he at that point?

Eamon was about 9 or 10. He and his brothers came around, and of course, they looked like little leprechauns. They definitely were Irish looking. They were on the move all the time. Eamon's brothers were outstanding athletes. He was a tag-along. He would just smile, and his eyes—he had the combination of an angel, a devil, and....

And everything in between?

And everything in between... That's good. And I remember when the teams in the neighborhood played against us, he came over with his brothers and harassed us, which was pretty interesting. I had never been harassed by a 9-year old kid. You know, it was really comical because they definitely cheered for the home team. In those days, we still had the Brooklyn Dodgers, and the Giants were still at the Polo Grounds in New York. I was a Giants fan and I remember going to Brooklyn Dodgers games, and the way the fans harassed the players was very brutal. I never thought I'd be playing softball on an amateur level and take so much harassment from one family.

As the season went on, we really got to know who the McEneaney's were, although I had never met their parents up to that point.

How many boys were there?

The family had four sons and a daughter, I think. I'll have to double check that.

Little did I know we were going to get together in a future life. As the years went on, I coached against his brothers who played at Sewanhaka High School. I was coaching at Elmont and Manhasset. Eamon's brother, Blayney, who played against me, was an outstanding quarterback. I remember that summer, I knew he was going to be playing against us. It was an opening game, and it was right before the Jewish holy days.

I knew we played on Friday and I told him the date. I said, "I'm looking forward to seeing you. I'm not going to retaliate with harassment, but we are going to be all over you come game day." Sure enough, we were. We won 27-0. And he got flattened about six or eight times. I remember one particular situation... They had a huge tackle who was supposed to protect his blind side, but the tackle unfortunately was not quick enough for our defensive people. Blayney had a lot of conversations with the tackle, so I think we distracted him. I don't believe in revenge, but I was thinking about the days I used to take a lot of harassment from Blayney and his clan. That's how my relationship with the McEneaneys started.

When I came to Elmont full-time, and became the Director of Athletics, I was fortunate to be able to reinstate lacrosse. So here again, we're going to be butting heads with the McEneaney family.

Our relationship started in the early 1960's, and we remain very close to this day. I arrived at Cornell in October of 1968, and by that time the smallest of the leprechauns had become the king of Long Island athletics, both in football and lacrosse. In fact, if they had early recruiting, he probably would have had ten schools wanting him to commit when he was a freshman in high school. He was a continuous highlight film on the athletic fields. He had an outstanding vertical jump, quick feet—probably the quickest feet that ever stepped on an athletic field on Long Island. We're talking about great players, like Jim Brown and a whole slew of top players that came out of Long Island, like Matt Snell of New York Jets fame.

Eamon became a complete athlete. He was wiry; he was quick. His dad actually came from Ireland and was a scholarship runner at the University of Texas —and he told me something that we might want to start doing with babies. When Eamon was a baby, he would sit him on the floor and he would play footsie. Eamon would put his feet up against his father's feet and he would play footsie, which developed his reflexes and coordination in his feet. Maybe that's something we should train our Olympians to do, because Eamon could have been a great track star himself, but he decided to stay with football, basketball, and lacrosse. My firm belief is, he would have excelled at whatever sport he had taken up.

When I got to Cornell in 1968, I kept thinking of players on Long Island. Eamon was in junior high school at that time. He was definitely on the blackboard when I looked at my future recruiting. I knew he would have to excel as a student, and when I thought about players on Long Island for the future, of course his name always popped up. Having gone to Sewanhaka High school, and played for the same coaches that he played for, I stayed in contact with them and, of course, they gave me updates on their players.

That was obviously before coaches had video clips available to send...

Yes, it was. It appeared that Eamon was spending a lot of time on the athletic field. Of course, he was spending time in the classroom too, but I think his concentration might have been on creating plays, getting a good run in football, developing sequences that he could use in lacrosse, and thinking about picks and movements that he could use in basketball, He seemed to focus more on those things than he did on geometry, chemistry or biology.

During his first two years of high school, his "weight" was very heavy on the athletic field, but he was a lightweight in the classroom. During one of my visits, I had a meeting with Eamon and his guidance counselor. He was a sophomore, and I tried to convince him how important it was to really do well in school. At that time, he had a full set of teeth, and the teeth would be pretty important in his future career as a business executive. He smiled and nodded and we shook hands. I patted him on the back and told him how proud I was of him representing Sewanhaka High School. I made sure he knew the fight song because, unfortunately, it was no longer very important to a lot of athletes at the high school. However, it was very important to all of us who played there and graduated from there.

During his junior year, his high school coach asked me if he could bring a team to Ithaca to play some central New York teams - like Corning, Ithaca High school, and some scrimmage games against other upstate teams. It was a spring trip for Sewanhaka, and I tried to get the cost down as much as possible. They dined on campus, and we all know that Cornell Dining is one of the best in the country. They slept in the old Schoellkopf Hall, and I think the height of the average guy in the first world war, when that was built, was probably about 5'6," so these beds were pretty small and rickety. And they were bunkbeds. It was March so it was a little chilly. And the blankets were, of course, part of the beds. The blanket came from Army surplus. It was comfortable enough to stay there for a few hours. A good night's sleep was often a different matter. The wind would blow through the building, and I think the Sewankaha team thought we put them in a haunted house because I went up early on the first morning to make sure everything was okay, and the young men walked to the showers and the lavatory and their eyes were popping. So it was very obvious they didn't get a lot of sleep.

They scrimmaged against one of the high schools, and we had an opportunity to watch Eamon play. It was a trip that brought them all together, and brought them to a college campus for the first time. It gave them an opportunity to meet our players, and an opportunity to play against good competition in upstate New York, which had never been done before. Several of the players on our team knew Eamon. Bruce Arena was from Franklin Square, and Jay Gallagher was from Garden City, both on Long Island. They, of course, took Eamon under their wing while he was visiting and encouraged him to do well academically in his junior and senior years. They stayed in touch with him, which was really nice throughout those two years because both of them lived within about 4 miles from where Eamon lived.

Those guys knew something special when they saw it?

Oh yeah, definitely. They were both very good athletes. They realized that Eamon was a special player who could really help us at Cornell in the future. So, our recruiting of Eamon was ongoing. Encouragement came from a lot of people. We had Cornell alumni on Long Island that heard we were interested in Eamon McEneaney. Bruce Cohen - who was an all-American lacrosse player at Cornell in the late '60s - was instrumental in my getting the job here at Cornell. Those players were all looking for talent for us, all over Long Island. That was really a key because I did not have a full-time assistant. To have someone be able to jump-start my recruiting by looking at players for me, and finding out if they were qualified to be accepted at Cornell, and tell them a little bit about Cornell, that was all very helpful. That was a little bit different method than is used today because alumni can't play a major role, based on the NCAA rules. At that time, we weren't going against any rules. We were trying to indoctrinate young men on the value they could get from a great education, combined with an opportunity to chase their athletic dreams.

In 1973 it came time for us to really pursue Eamon. We were playing at Yale, and Blayney brought Eamon to the game. It was a very physical game, and both teams played very hard. Yale had a tough player by the name of Gary Fencik, who went on to play in the NFL for the Chicago Bears. Bruce Arena and Jay Gallagher were on the field for the game, and they both had outstanding performances. Eamon had strong connections with them, and I was pleased to see them step up with him watching. At that time, Eamon was being heavily recruited by teams in the Big 10 and in the ACC. I knew that our strong performance would be a selling point for our program.

He was being recruited in multiple sports?

Yes, for football and lacrosse. And there's no doubt about it. I personally believe he could have played Division I basketball or, at least Division II because of his jumping ability. His vertical jump had to be the best, at that time, for a young athlete.

Did I hear you say that at 5'10," he could dunk a basketball behind his head?

That's correct.

After the Yale game, he and his brother spoke extensively to Bruce and Jay, and of course, I spoke with them as well. We had an alumnus by the name of Clarence Fauntleroy, who was a Hall of Fame lacrosse player at Cornell. He also played football. And believe it or not, he went to Sewanhaka High School. When I was growing up, I was a ball boy at Sewanhaka and Clarence was my idol. He was the youngest guy in New York State to be able to play varsity football. I think he graduated from high school at age 16. So there he was, playing varsity football probably at age 14, and he had to get special permission. But he, without a doubt, was my idol when I was growing up. Clarence was kind enough to put on a reception for us. I asked Bruce if Eamon and his brother would like to join us, but he said they had to get back to Long Island.

As I got on the bus, Bruce came up to me and said, "Coach, you gotta tell Eamon that he's going to start at Cornell." I said, "What do you mean?" He said, "All the schools that are recruiting him are telling him that. Maryland said he would be an instant starter." I said, "Bruce, number one, freshmen are not eligible to play at Cornell." He said, "He doesn't know that." But I said, "Bruce, I can't lie to him. Second of all, I've never told anybody they're going to start. I'm telling him he can make the team." Bruce pleaded, "Coach, if you tell him he can only make the team, he's going to go to Indiana for football or Maryland for lacrosse, or someplace else for lacrosse, maybe Johns Hopkins." I said, "Well, tell him we're very interested."

So, of course, I got off the bus, went over to Eamon and I said, "In order to keep the Sewanhaka tradition of going to Cornell, it's very important that you give us a lot of consideration and a lot of thought." He had that great quick look and smile. As I mentioned, he had all of his teeth at that time, so he had a big smile. We shook hands.

That summer, I worked a couple of lacrosse camps on Long Island. One camp was at St. Paul's School, in Garden City. Eamon was actually working. He wasn't a camper. I'm sure his dad had him tied into some manual work, because one day he came over and he looked like he was probably digging ditches because about 80 percent of his clothes were covered with mud and dirt. It was very obvious he didn't have a summer job as a life guard, and he definitely was not on the golf course.

He came over on a couple of days and watched me coach at the camp. After one of the evening sessions, we had an opportunity to have some Cokes together and talk about his future. Camp had ended, the fall season had started, and we were starting to get Eamon to think about coming up for a visit to Cornell. In those days, the recruiting was different—you went to the high schools. You contacted the parents. You made very few home visits unless you thought it was imperative. And when I say "imperative," that meant that the family had several children and finances were an issue—of course, we had no athletic scholarships at Cornell. It was all based on need. And it wasn't based on how much I needed him, it was based on his financial need! We made phone calls to the parents, and guidance counselors were a tremendous help to me, as were the teachers and coaches.

I went down to Long Island for a recruiting visit. In those days, if I played my cards right and I scheduled right, I could visit ten schools in a day, starting at 7:30 in the morning and ending at 4 o'clock in the afternoon. All of the high schools were within five to eight miles of each other in Nassau County, a little bit farther apart in Suffolk County and, of course, I would go up into Westchester for a day, and go to New Jersey for a day. All those trips were set up weeks in advance to align schedules.

Well, Eamon's guidance counselor was really leery of his academic accomplishments up to that point. One of the areas that really stood out when I looked at his academic information was his ability to write. He sketched as well. I thought about potential matches, and I knew we had a program in the College of Agricultural and Life Sciences under the title of Communication Arts, and I said to myself, you know, he may qualify for that type of program. I called him that night to tell him about that program and he was very enthused.

At the same time, many other schools were setting up visits. In those days, the NCAA was cutting back on visits, or attempting to. They were starting to pass legislation regarding the number of visits you could take, because they were finding out that young men from Buffalo, for example, when there was snow on the ground, would be going to Arizona or Miami for recruiting visits, when really what they were doing was taking a vacation from their tough weather.

At that time it was around five visits, and it wasn't really monitored by the NCAA fully, so Eamon was really starting to get calls, and his visit total was starting to go up.

He was having several full scholarships offered to him?

Correct. One of the things I thought was very important was to get his visit solidified, get it organized, and get him up to Cornell as soon as we could. His visit was going to be scheduled after the football season, because his team was a top team on Long Island at the time. In fact, I think they were in the running for the Rutgers Cup, which is symbolic of the best team in Nassau County. Eamon was a quarterback; his ability on the football field was exceptional. He couldn't throw a 60-yard pass but he could certainly put the ball 40 yards out there and hit receivers without any problem. His quickness was an asset.

During that season, when they were vying for the championship, they played an important game against Lawrence High School. Eamon also played as a defensive player, which was unusual. As a rule you want to protect your quarterback, but he was such a great free safety that they thought it was important to keep him on the field. The coach sent in plays via a "shuttle system," and one of Eamon's teammates was a young man that had a slight speech impediment. This young man came over with the play, and I guess the young man was a little nervous, and he might have stuttered. The play was supposed to be a quick pass, whatever the number was, and it sounded like quick kick. Eamon was a little baffled, as they hadn't really quick-kicked with him that year. Eamon decided to get into a shotgun formation, and the coaches were a little concerned because they anticipated a quick pass to the tight end. Eamon got back, faked a pass, and kicked the ball. That probably made two coaches faint on the sideline, because Sewanhaka was losing, and the quick kick gave up the ball on third down. It turned out that his kick rolled all the way down to the 2-yard line. Lawrence High School could not move the ball; so they attempted to punt. The punt was blocked and went into the end zone, and Sewanhaka recovered and won the game! Eamon – once the pesky and annoying leprechaun – was now the hero of Sewanhaka High School!

Thanks to a miscommunication…

That's right. So this just gives you an indication of the luck of the Irish. There's no doubt he had a shamrock somewhere on his body that day!

When it came time for his visit, I always sent the parents an itinerary in advance. The itinerary included me picking up every prospect upon his arrival. At that time, we were fortunate to have some recruiting funds to be able to fly three or four players to campus, and of course, he was going to be one of them. I sent the itinerary to Eamon's home with information that his airline tickets would be coming a week or two before his visit.

Regarding the actual visit; we would get some nourishment before we started the day, and we would then visit with professors who taught in the area of the prospect's academic interests. We would go to some classes, spend time with some of our players in class, and then we would take a complete tour of the campus. One of the locations we would go to first would be the library. That was important because it was like an athlete walking into Madison Square Garden for the first time. If you go into an empty library, it doesn't mean anything, so we made sure we went when the library had wall-to-wall people, and that gave our recruits an idea of how important it was to be prepared to study when you came to Cornell. And then they had a little tour of downtown Ithaca and Collegetown. A visit would last for 48 hours. That was the rule that the NCAA had implemented.

So, the visit was all set up. I picked the date, told the McEaneaneys what the date was. We made it for two weeks after his football season. I knew he was going to visit Penn State. He was also going to visit Maryland, and I believe he had scheduled a visit to a Big Ten school. I wanted his visit with us to be the last on his schedule, and I planned it that way.

I did not have a full-time assistant in the office every day, but I did have Mike Waldvogel (who would later win several Ivy League titles as the head coach at Yale, and earn induction in the National Lacrosse Hall of Fame). He was serving as a part-time assistant coach while teaching at nearby DeRuyter High School. Recruiting was difficult during the day, so the majority of recruiting efforts took place later in the day. I would take the recruits around, and some of the players would help out. It really worked out very well, it was very efficient.

Each prospect was asked to come on his visit with ten questions, some of which could be asked by their parents. They had to be typed out, and we instructed them to put them on 3x5 cards and carry them in their pocket. When they arrived, they were to ask those questions. What that did was, if we had seven young people on campus, when we were having lunch together, there was an opportunity for seventy questions to be answered. We wouldn't answer all of them at lunch, but we would answer them throughout the day. And they could consist of "Who wakes me up in the morning?" to "What are the details of financial aid?" to "Do you really think I can play here?" They asked a lot of questions about academics, about the culture at Cornell University, and the lifestyle in Ithaca, New York.

I was very confident that I got all that across to Eamon. It was going to go well. The week before his visit, I had seven young men on campus. In fact, five of those seven ultimately came to Cornell.

It was about 6 o'clock at night and all seven were going off to dinner with some of our players. I was going to meet them at a hockey game, and it was going to be a great night. It was going to be an exciting hockey game, and the electricity of a packed Lynah Rink was always an asset in giving prospects a sense of what the spirit on campus was like.

I got a phone call at home. It was Eamon McEneaney. I said, "Eamon, it's nice that you called. I was going to call you on Sunday and get everything all set for your visit next week." He said, "Coach, next week? I'm here now." I said, "You're where?" He said, "I'm at the pay phone outside your office in Teagle Hall!" I said, "Eamon, I do play my share of pranks. This is not a prank, is it?" He said, "Oh, no, Coach. I'm here." So I asked, "How did you get here?" He said, "I took a bus." I said, "Eamon, I had a plane ticket for you." He said, "I don't like to fly. I took the bus, and I walked from the bus terminal up to campus." I asked, "Eamon, you walked from the bus terminal up to campus?" He said, "Yes Coach. I didn't think it was too far because when we came here to play, everything seemed pretty close." I said, "Yeah, Eamon. When you were here, you went from the dining hall to Schoellkopf dormitory, to the field. But from the bus up to campus is pretty far." He laughed and said, "Yeah, I found that out!"

So, your number one prospect walked over 2 miles, half of it straight uphill, lugging a suitcase?

You got it...He said, "I started walking and when I got to the first hill I asked some man "Where's Cornell?" and he said, "Up the hill." I got up the first hill, got to the second hill, and it was a lot of stores, a lot of activities, and I saw some students and I asked one of them, "Where's Cornell?" He said, "Up the hill," so I went up another hill, and I got to your office!"

I said, "Eamon, stay right there. Don't move. Jay Gallagher and Bruce Arena will pick you up in 5 minutes." I knew it was going to take me at least a half hour to get back to campus, so I called Bruce and Jay, and I said, 'Bruce, take him to the restaurant in the Statler Hotel. Get him the best meal on the menu, whatever he wants. Okay?' The ever-resourceful Bruce Arena said, "Coach, can we eat also?" What was I going to say? "Yeah. No problem." So Bruce and Jay took Eamon to the Statler.

I came up, and as always, valet parking was very helpful to me. I knew a lot of the valets at the hotel because of all the recruiting we did, and parents would often stay there. Pat and I went in for entertainment, so they parked my car very nicely. I said, "I'm planning to go from dinner over to the hockey game." The valet said, "Coach, don't worry about it," so that was a help.

I sprinted up to the dining room, and there were these three smiling faces. I did not let on about him coming a week early, because I didn't want him to be embarrassed in front of Bruce and Jay, but they already knew. They didn't say anything either. After dinner, we went over and caught the second and third periods of the hockey game, which was very exciting. And then, of course, we had to arrange housing for Eamon. Usually a player stayed with a host, which was a lacrosse player, and in those days we were fortunate to have lacrosse players room together. For example, two engineers would room together, two players in pre-med, pre-vet — so the hosting arrangements were excellent when we hosted recruits. When we had them visit, we would learn if they were interested in pre-med or pre-law, and we would match them up with players that were in those courses.

We definitely wanted to do a lot in those 48 hours. Now, of course, Eamon's itinerary was for the following week. At the hockey game, I was sitting near Dr. Len Feddema, the Director of Admissions for the College of Agricultural and Life Sciences. He was always very helpful in meeting with prospects when we hosted them on campus. I told him my story, and I knew he was close friends with our team faculty adviser, Scotty Johndrew. Scotty was amazing. He was in poultry research in the College of Agriculture and Life Sciences. When I mentioned Eamon's name, Dr. Feddema said, "Oh, yeah. We know a lot about that young man. He could be one of the best athletes we've ever had here at Cornell." I was sort of astonished that he knew about Eamon, so I said, "Eamon actually came up a week early." So Dr. Feddema said, "Let me go and speak to him." After the hockey game, he went over and spoke to Eamon, and he arranged for Eamon to meet with him at 10 a.m. the next morning for breakfast.

We picked up Eamon at about noon from Dr. Feddema's office, and I didn't realize this, but Eamon had brought a lot of his writing and poetry that he had written at school. He brought some artwork and sketches, and Dr. Fedemna was very impressed, evidently.

We had planned to meet with all of the recruits at 1 o'clock at Teagle Hall, and we went over any questions they had. Eamon didn't have his ten questions written out on a card, but he probably asked twenty questions. It was like facing a dodgeball, and the ball kept coming! The questions kept coming, and we couldn't dodge them, because they were all legitimate. "Are we going to buy new uniforms?" "What kind of sticks are we going to use?" "Can I play football?" Can I play basketball?" So, of course, all of those questions had to be answered. Then we had players chime in about school, about financial aid, and we went through all of the important things they would need to know to prepare for life at Cornell.

There was a basketball game that night. I always tried to choose a weekend where there was athletic activity, be it wrestling, basketball or hockey. During the fall it would be football, of course. I actually took a couple of recruits to see the cross-country race one fall because one of them had been a cross country runner. It was a beautiful fall day and the meet was Army against Cornell. It was important for these young men to see every possible activity and venue that we had at Cornell. The famous Cornell Dairy Bar was a hit because of the ice cream.

In the afternoons, our players would play basketball at Barton Hall. It was a chance to let loose, and they invited the recruits to play. Now, some had sneakers with them; some didn't. We did mention in the itinerary that they might be playing basketball in the afternoon, and that was pretty exciting for some of them. Our players got sneakers for the prospects that didn't have them, arranged for them to get shorts and towels, and they dressed out at Teagle Hall locker room.

That took care of the afternoon. Then we had an early dinner and went to the basketball game. There was some social involvement on campus, and the hosts took the players to some parties or other events. Eamon was going to be staying at SAE with Bruce and Jay, mainly because the housing had already been set up for the other recruits and we didn't get a chance to set up Eamon's. That worked out nicely, as it gave him a chance to see what fraternity life was like. We also had our other hosts take the young men to their own fraternities, to give them a broader look at what Cornell University was all about.

They planned to take Eamon and the other prospects to a Cornell varsity basketball game that night. I needed a break so I didn't go to the first part of the game. I caught the second half, and when I looked around I saw a couple of recruits had been there and left. One of the recruits said that Eamon had been there and he left with Jay Gallagher and Bruce Arena. I thought, "Oh, that's fine."

Now, I was going to pick up Eamon because he was going to return to Long Island by bus. I was going to pick him up at 7 a.m., go to church at 8 a.m., have breakfast, and get him to his bus which was scheduled to leave at 11:00.

The rest of the recruits had varying travel plans and schedules. Some were flying back at 1 o'clock, some at 2, others were being picked up by their parents. The final event of their visit was a big group lunch at Willard Straight Hall, which had a fantastic brunch on Sundays.

Late Saturday night – actually, it was probably closer to 12:30 or 1 o'clock in the morning – I received a phone call. It was Jay, and he said, "Coach, I'm sorry for calling you this late, but we've been watching you all weekend and you've been working really hard with all of these recruits. You must be exhausted." He said, "Why don't you sleep in? We'll take Eamon to breakfast, then to church, and get him on the bus." I said, "Jay, I'm embarrassed by the fact we've got this whole weekend screwed up." He said, "Coach, it's not screwed up.That meeting with Dr. Feddema gave Eamon a chance to go through everything that he needed to." He said, "You had seven people in there all weekend, and then Eamon showed up, now there are eight people. We'll take care of Eamon." I said, "Jay, I really want to speak to him." He said, "No, he's sleeping right now." I said, "Okay. Well, tell him I'll call him Sunday night."

I went back to bed. When I got up on Sunday I assumed Eamon was on his way through Binghamton by that time. I went to church, and after church I met with all the recruits and their parents. In fact, some of the parents joined us as they were picking up their sons, so it was a great dialogue at breakfast.

I couldn't wait for Sunday night, because I definitely wanted to speak to Eamon, and to his mom and dad on the phone, being sure not to tell them that he was there a week ahead of time. I told him not to say anything either, because I didn't want them to be embarrassed. He got on the phone and said, "Coach, that was one of the greatest weekends I ever had on a college campus. If I can get into Cornell, I'm coming." Well, with that, I don't think I was shaking, but I know my friggin' knees were knocking. I said to myself—that's fantastic. I said, "I'm actually coming down to Long Island on Wednesday. I'm going to be meeting with some other young men that are interested in Cornell. I may stop by your high school just to say hello." He said, "That'd be nice." Well, we hung up and I was sort of jumping around, like I just won—I don't like to say Super Bowl because it's overused—but it's like.... It was like I just added another person to my family, and the family was quite extensive. We had thirty-two players, plus my three lovely and wonderful children. But I knew getting him through the admissions process was not going to be easy. So I drove down to Long Island and at about 11 o'clock in the morning, between appointments, I got a break for about an hour and a half. I could either go and have a nice lunch, or pick up a sandwich, eat it in the car, and go visit my high school.

To this day, I still visit my high school every time I'm on Long Island. I walk on the football field, which is also a lacrosse field. The football field is like a golf course green. The tradition... you can feel it. You can look around and start thinking about the games you played there, both in lacrosse and football. You think about the coaches. So I took a little walk on the field before I went into the guidance office.

Of course, I wanted to speak to the guidance counselor about Eamon. As I walked in, the guidance counselor said, "Richie! What a visit Eamon had! I hope he can get into Cornell! He came into my office Monday and Tuesday, and I've never seen a young man so excited in my life! You guys really plan some outstanding weekends for your recruits." I said, "Well, we try to do the best we can." She said, "I never heard of an itinerary like that. The basketball game—you try these guys out by playing basketball?" I said, "Not really. It's sort of recreation." She said, "Well, Eamon told me it was a try-out to see how quick he was and see what their agility was like." I said, "Not really. We really don't do that." I thought about it, and I remembered that Notre Dame had done that with their football recruits. They had them come in and play basketball, which is great. So she gave me a new idea. I said, "Is he available?" She said, "Yeah, but let me tell you about the basketball game. He came down on Monday after he returned, and I said. 'Eamon, where did you get that cut over your left eye?' He said, 'Playing basketball.'" I said, "I didn't know that." And I was thinking about Jay Gallagher and Bruce Arena… they took him to the bus station because they didn't want me to see him.

So he came down, and he had a huge bandage over his right eye. It was very obvious he had stitches. I said to him, "You got hit in the basketball game?" He said, "Yeah. I was going up for a rebound and this guy came up and clocked me as I was coming down." I said, "Really? Did you have to go to the doctor?" He said, "I went to the hospital." I said, "Well, I gotta figure all this out as far as the bills and stuff." He said, "Coach, don't worry about it. Everything's going to be taken care of."

I said, "Okay. Let's go out in the hallway."

So we got in the hallway and I said, "Now, tell me how that happened." He said, "Coach, I can't lie to you. I was at the SAE party and I love to dance. I was dancing with this guy's girlfriend, who happened to be a very good dancer. The guy got upset and he happened to be a 275-pound tackle on the football team. If I knew it was coming, he would have missed me, but he blindsided me and hit me in the head." He said, "Coach, number one, I didn't go down. And number two, I kicked him in the groin and I knocked him down. And with that, all the SAE guys separated us. It was obvious I had to go to the hospital." He said, "You know when you got that phone call at 1 o'clock in the morning? I was in the hospital. Please, don't tell the guidance counselor because I don't want my parents to know what happened." That secret was kept for a long time.

So then it came time to get Eamon's application in, and in those days, schools would pay the application fee for scholarship athletes. We had no scholarships, so he had to submit $25 with his application. The application came in, and it was very well done. You had to write an essay in those days, and his essay was excellent. He got a tremendous amount of "plus factors" in the application, including great recommendations from his biology and chemistry teacher.

It came down to decision time. Well, we were in the thick of our season. We were in play-off contention, and it was hard to worry about who was getting accepted and who was not getting accepted. When we got to the end of April, all the acceptance letters were going out. Sure enough, Eamon was accepted. It was kind of like New Year's Eve. I was always delighted when young men got accepted, but this was exceptional. He came from my high school. He had to work extremely hard to get into Cornell. He turned down opportunities at other schools where he would have had a full scholarship. And his dad, with other children in the family, was going to have to get involved with financial aid. That was tough, to have a parent give up four years of a free scholarship opportunity for his child to go to Cornell. He and his dad debated often about his choice. Finally, I feel his brothers did a lot to convince their father that Eamon should go to Cornell. One brother, Blayney, was the quarterback at Yankton College in Kansas, the same school attended by Lyle Alzado. Alzado was an outstanding lineman at Lawrence High School on Long Island, and also with the Oakland Raiders. I think Blayney understood how important Cornell was to Eamon.

When Eamon came to Cornell, the toughest thing for him was that freshmen were not eligible to play on the varsity; otherwise, he would have set records that never would have been broken. That freshman team was like a Who's Who in college lacrosse. It was just a great group of players, one of the best freshman classes I ever recruited. I was actually worried about the competition because, outside of some junior colleges—and we did play Hobart and Syracuse—our schedule was not as strong as the varsity schedule. But Eamon was very enthused, and he did a lot of great things. I think one game he had eleven assists. Another game he had eight goals. He was a great team player. He was a component that every coach in the country would love to have. He was the quarterback. He was the point guard. He was the feeder in lacrosse. He was dynamic. Our freshman games sometimes attracted a thousand people. It definitely was a fabulous group of recruits. The word started getting around about how athletic, how good this group of players was and would be, and in '75, they all came up to the varsity.

Getting back to the financial aid issue -- Eamon got a job in the fraternity house. We had about two dozen jobs where our players could get meals. Sometimes it was breakfast, lunch, and dinner. It depended on the chef. Most of them got the full complement, because they were all great people and the chefs loved them, and because they left the place spotless. They took a lot of burden off the chefs. Eamon's job was cleaning pots and pans. I remember meeting the chef at one of the games, and he said to me, "I've never seen pots and pans shine so well." I thought, what the heck has Eamon been using to shine these pots and pans? Hopefully it was not Brasso.

What is Brasso?

Brasso was a cleaning compound that you used in the Marine Corps for shining your buckles.

We tried to get them summer jobs in construction. A gentleman named Mr. Harter had an extermination company, and a number of our players worked for him. We tried as much as possible to take away the burden of the cost of Cornell from the parents. Those players were committed to doing that, and that's why they are so successful today - because of all the commitments they had to make in order to get a Cornell education.

So… I must ask… when Eamon showed up for his recruiting visit, and it was not even his time to be there, I know that the coach in you, the Marine in you, really likes people who can follow instructions. But I am guessing that you thought it would be easier to teach somebody to follow instructions than it would be to teach him to be the best high school lacrosse player in the United States.

Oh, baby! Very much so! And I think he was so anxious to compare Cornell to the other schools, because without a doubt, the other schools were giving him mandates that he had to give them a commitment ASAP. I didn't think that was a very proper way to do things, but then again, I was not in that kind of high-powered, high-pressure lacrosse program, in the sense that we didn't have scholarships to offer. If someone didn't take a scholarship, the coaches at that school would have the opportunity to offer it to someone else. So there were intangibles that we couldn't control, but I think all those things from his visit came into play: the culture, the environment… I don't know how much the fight took part in his final selection. I was kidding him. I said, "Did you come back here to get even with that guy?" He said, "Coach, when I was playing football, we played against each other. We played alongside each other," Eamon was a wide receiver at Cornell, and a fine one at that.

After your team's loss to Navy in the 1975 NCAA semifinals – Eamon's sophomore year – he said that would be the last loss he

would experience in a Cornell uniform. How did that statement resonate with you?

I felt, with his leadership and work ethic, he would do everything possible to make sure his teammates shared that goal.

Did you have any indication that the 1976 team would embark upon the longest winning streak in NCAA history?

I did get a slight indication, because in every intramural activity, the lacrosse players excelled during the offseason. Their athletic skills in other sports were outstanding. It was an era when many athletes played more than one sport. Some played football, some played soccer or hockey, so their focus and conditioning stayed sharp year 'round. I am still a firm believer that if a young athlete wants to compete in more than one collegiate sport, and can handle it academically, I would approve of that without any hesitation.

Those teams played before the term "Dream Team" was coined, and I would like to know - given their focus, determination, collective work ethic and chemistry - if they were your version of a dream team?

My definition of a dream team is one that has leadership, teamwork, integrity, perseverance, tenacity, and love for one another. The results from those years certainly prove what those teams were all about.

You told me a lot about Eamon as a player, and that he was a person who was willing to adjust his game for the betterment of the team. I get the impression that trait held true across many areas of his life.

Yes, it certainly did.

I understand that he was a natural leader, and that people gravitated to him because he had that personality and he had that work ethic. I know this chapter will not be the easiest one for you, but I have heard you say how proud you were of your players, to see them go out after graduation and use those life skills that they brought into Cornell, and refined on the field, and in the classroom. And I know you are proud of your former players for their professional accomplishments, and for their contributions to their families and communities. You are proud

of them for being professionals, coaches and leaders. Speaking of leadership, and the ability to think on your feet, I'd like to ask you about that 1993 incident when the World Trade Center was attacked with a truck bomb and Eamon was instrumental in helping people get out of there. I'm going to guess that didn't surprise you that he stepped up so courageously in such a critical time.

That's correct, Steve. Leading up to that day, we had established a network of players out in the corporate world, giving assistance to graduates. Eamon, along with Jay Gallagher, Chris Kane, Tom Marino, and other alumni started to reach out and offer opportunities to many of our graduates, to start their career with Cantor Fitzgerald. They also helped place them in jobs in other investment groups. Eamon was a catalyst in getting people out into the eye of the finance world. That, to me, was really a great thing because it enabled some of our players to have a super contact. And those contacts kept opening up, building up, because after he hired one former player, that individual became a person that we could rely on to try to help the next Cornell graduate.

Eamon was very settled in his position with Cantor Fitzgerald. In the first bombing incident, in 1993, a bomb-laden truck was placed underneath the World Trade Center. You know, it's unbelievable how things happen in my life. I happened to be at a convention in Baltimore in 1996, and I met a gentleman who had actually been in the Secret Service and the CIA. He explained to me that if that truck had been parked a number of yards nearer a support column, the building might have come down at that time. It was ironic how they tracked this down. The truck, of course, was a rental, and unbelievably, they found the ID number of the truck and tracked it down.

During that period of time, Eamon guided sixty-five people down 105 flights of stairs.

As I understand, that stairwell was filling up with smoke and the lights were not functional.

That's correct. The stairwell was filling up with smoke, and the lighting was definitely not adequate. Eamon led them down, and about every ten levels they would count off and then proceed to keep going down.

He had the men in the group take their shirts off and had people use them as a filter for the smoke. They put them over their noses and mouths so they could breathe better as they proceeded down the stairwells.

So, when I heard this, I really felt terrible about what had happened. I also felt that if someone was there to help other people, I would assume it would be Eamon. He had a strong bond with people. He was very likeable. He had that little bit of an Irish swagger. He had great feeling and great compassion for people, so he did the right thing and helped those people survive.

Did you ever talk to him about this, Richie? Was that a drill that people had worked on ahead of time or did he think of that spontaneously?

I never talked to him about it. He had a lot of accomplishments on and off the field. He never once mentioned what he had done. He said he was just there and available to help people. And that's the way he would go about things. During one of my times in the city, he and I went to lunch. As we were walking down the street, there was a gentleman that was looking like he was having some hard times. Eamon said hello to him, and said, "I'll see you on Thursday." I walked another block or so and I was a little inquisitive. I said, "Eamon, do you mind if I ask you who that gentleman was?" He said, "Yeah. He's a fellow that was in the finance business, and unfortunately, he lost his job. I get an opportunity to meet with him every Thursday to see if I can help him out, and help his family out." So that was the type of individual that Eamon was. It's a credit to his family and it's a credit to him that he was so caring and so willing to share.

You spent a fair amount of time with Eamon and Bonnie and their four children over the years, and you speak of them like you perceive them as your extended family.

That's correct. When Brendan was born, it was an extremely unbelievable day for Eamon and Bonnie, and of course for all of us because Brendan became part of our family. When I say "family," sometimes that word is overused, unless it's your immediate family, but he became part of the Cornell family.

So we were delighted about that. Jennifer was born after Brendan, and then Kyle and Kevin came along. It was the making of a beautiful family. They moved to New Canaan, where there were a number of opportunities for Eamon and Bonnie, and their children.

I know this part is not easy for you, and it is obvious that you are very grateful for the relationship that you have with the McEneaney family. If I may ask - and please understand that we can back out of here any time with any of this - but when the actual attack happened in 2001, when Eamon and 3,000 other people lost their lives, did you find out about it afterwards or were you aware of it as it was unfolding? I'm sure you remember that day.

Well, remembering that day is quite difficult. My wife and I were going to look at a boat and wanted to take our daughter, Jennifer, with us. We had a home on the lake and we thought it would be nice to have a boat for the grandchildren and friends that visited. During the drive to Jennifer's house we didn't have the radio on but when we arrived at Jennifer's house, she met us before we even got out of the car. She said, "You've got to come inside quickly. A plane has just crashed into the World Trade Center."

Was Jennifer aware that Eamon was in the building at that time?

No. And then another plane crashed, and we started hearing reports about planes that had been hijacked, going off radar screens, and going in directions that they were not scheduled to go in. And then we started hearing reports of people that were dying, people that were trapped. And they did mention Cantor Fitzgerald. And if I'm not mistaken, I think the firm occupied Floors 101-105. That was just a few floors up from where the plane hit, and from there up, there was heavy damage. Some people had gotten to the roof, and some of their phone calls indicated they were hoping helicopters would come and get them. But it happened so quickly... It didn't turn out that way.

And I just sat there in shock. Everything sort of stopped for me. It became very confusing. I was horrified. I couldn't look at the TV any longer, but I could hear the accounts. Knowing where the Trade Center was, having had a chance to view it when I visited Long Island. I will never forget looking across the water at the Trade Center. It was the pinnacle of American success. And there it was, being destroyed.

I knew a number of people that were in that building, that I either had at lacrosse camp at Cornell or worked with at camps in different parts of the country. Also, I recruited some of the men that were in that building. It's strange but we had three players that had left Cantor Fitzgerald within the previous three months to step out into another branch of the financial world. Mike Tanner was a former Cornell football player, and he also worked with Cantor Fitzgerald.

Like everybody in the country, in the world, I was numb. I remember going home, sitting on the back deck, and my mind could not function. The phone started to ring. Our players were calling. Many of them had visited Eamon at Cantor Fitzgerald. They knew exactly where his office was. After a period of time, I don't even remember what the conversations were. I prayed a lot. I went to church. I'm sure people all over the country, all over the world, did something very similar. Everyone hoped that those people would have found some way to be rescued, some way to escape the inferno.

I waited and waited. Someone called and mentioned that the McEneaney boys had gone to the area where they were trying to identify people. They brought pictures. If you remember, the newspapers and television had pictures of all the people, with the hope that they might have gotten out of the building.

I recall there was hope they might be in an emergency room somewhere.

Right… Or had been injured or incapacitated to some degree. That was very difficult.

Over the years, I couldn't bring myself to go to the memorial. Last year, my daughter Kathy and her husband Bill rented a home in New Jersey, on the shore. She said, "Dad, we're going to take the ferry, and we're going to the World Trade Center." I was really reluctant to go. My granddaughters, Lindsay and Adrienne, said, "Grandpa, we'd really like you to go." And I'm glad I did.

The memorial is so inspiring because we lost many heroes that day. Everybody that lost his or her life in that disaster, they are all heroes. The memorial was definitely a wonderful tribute, and I'm so glad that I went. The construction, the beauty, the features are everlasting. I will always remember every feature of the memorial. One section had the steel from the original building. And there are, of course, names of the individuals that are etched into the memorial. Just to get the chance to rub the etchings of the names of the men that I knew that were in that building brought me, in a way, some relief.

There was still a tremendous amount of heartbreak. My thoughts were with them and with their families.

It's a period in my life that is extremely difficult to describe. That day at the memorial gave me a lift, and it gave me a lot more courage than I had previously. My daughter and her husband and my two granddaughters were very convincing, and I thank God that they convinced me to go. We'll never have closure. It's very difficult for me to believe in that because I will always remember looking at those etchings of names, looking at a media tribute that they had regarding the people that lost their lives, thinking of the children that they left behind. There's no greater tragedy for young people than to lose a parent, and many children lost a parent.

We often ask "Why?" But we really don't have that type of power, to really get a feeling of why it happened, and what could have been done so that it didn't happen. It will forever be one of those days that we'll remember... December 7th, 1941 and September 11th, 2001. Those days will always be in my mind because even though I was four years old in 1941, I remember the expression on my parents' faces when Franklin Delano Roosevelt spoke. I remember what my brothers and my sisters' faces looked like that day. And on 9/11, my mind reflected on all of the people that I knew who died in that building, and all of the wonderful things they had done with their lives. And in a way, they continue to do that. They'll never be forgotten.

Three years after 9/11, I was asked to speak at the dedication of a memorial wall at Farmingdale University on Long Island. There were children there, and it was one of the most difficult addresses and testimonials I ever had to give. As I looked out, there were hundreds of people there, honoring the young men and women who had died. To look out and see the faces, and think about some of the fathers that I knew, and how those young people looked a lot like their dad. To realize that their dad was not going to be there any longer... I was very honored to be able to speak at that dedication, and I'll always hold that as a cherished moment in my life.

Richie, I'd like to ask you about the eulogy you did for Eamon, the one that was televised. I wonder how that came to be. Virtually everyone knew how tragic 9/11 was, and felt some degree of pain and loss, but to actually lose someone that you were so personally connected to for a long time, someone you watched grow up, someone you helped grow up, that adds a personal dimension to the September 11th attack that many people never experienced. For you to step up and do that eulogy right after experiencing such a deep loss was very compelling. Who asked you if you would do a eulogy, and would you be kind enough to tell me a little bit about that experience?

Eamon's memorial service was held in New Canaan. Bonnie had asked me if I would do the eulogy in memory of – in honor of - Eamon. That night I stayed at Joe Lizzio's home in New Canaan. The night before, Jeremy Schaap – whose father, Dick was a close friend of mine - was kind enough to come over to Joe's house. He interviewed Jake O'Neill who was very close to Eamon, and Mike French, who was like a brother to Eamon.

In fact, in all honesty, we might have overused the term "Band of Brothers," but these players were all brothers. They still are to this day. They name children after each other. They've been to one another's weddings, bar mitzvahs and baptisms. They had formed a chain that has links that will never be broken.

Jeremy spoke to each one of us individually, and it was extremely difficult for all of us. After that conversation, I stayed up the whole night. I usually do things without written testament, without notes, but I decided that night that I had better write something down.

I sat at the table at Joe's house and started to compose what I was going to say. And something kept telling me "You're not going to be able to put this on paper. It's going to have to come from your heart." Now, I'm very spiritual, and I actually believe that someone was whispering to me to do that. It was unbelievable.

Joe woke up fairly early and I was still at the kitchen table. I went in and took a shower. I got dressed, relaxed on the couch for a while, and at 9 o'clock we left for the church.

It was unbelievable. I felt so refreshed. I felt so under control. I felt that I was taking steps to do something that would hopefully assist the people that would be in attendance, help in understanding about Eamon, Bonnie, his family, his brothers, sister, his mom and dad.

We got to the church early. I sat in the first pew and never really looked around. But I did look forward. I had asked a good friend of mine that sang in the alumni choir at Cornell if he could get a group of people – including my good friend Jay Spiegel - to come down and sing at the memorial service. They were really gracious. They came down on a bus. Once they started singing some Cornell songs, my heart was just reaching out because then it started to become very painful. I was feeling the depth of what I was asked to do.

When it came time for me to go up to the pulpit, I looked around, and it was as if I could see every eye. I could see in the eyes of the people that they were feeling the same way I was feeling. I started off by telling some stories about Eamon, talked about when I first met him - how he used to heckle me when we played in the softball league, when he was 10 years old. I talked about his recruiting trip. I talked about Eamon the son, the husband, the father, the player, and the friend.

Some people say that when you cry it could be tears of joy. I cried during my talk. And the good Lord helped me convey what was necessary to convey. It was my opportunity to give a verbal send-off to a person that we all loved.

It sounds like you presented it both as a going-away gift to Eamon, and a heartfelt gift to his family.

Every day leading up to that day, my thoughts were "Please let me do the right thing. Please let me say the right thing." It wasn't a good-bye because I know we're going to have an opportunity to get together again, but it was an opportunity to convey my feelings on behalf of my players, Cornell University, and all the people that knew and loved Eamon.

It's an honor to be asked to do something like that.

Yes, it definitely was. I feel for the president of the United States, with the recent tragedies we've had. He has to speak at these memorial services and really doesn't know a lot about the men and women he is honoring. Yet, he helps console the grief that everybody has. And the grief is a national grief. At Eamon's memorial service, it was a national grief because it affected the nation. It affected the world.

It's astonishing. Eamon would travel to Ireland periodically, and he would take some new employees of Cantor Fitzgerald to travel with him. The objective was to get to know them better, to play golf with them, and visit the pubs. There were some great stories about him in Ireland. One that I remember involved the fact that the Vikings had a lot to do with settling Ireland. Eamon was in a pub one evening where he met some locals who had lived in Ireland all their lives. Great pride, great tradition and wonderful hospitality.

They got into a discussion about the Vikings and one guy said to him, "Eamon, you don't know what you're talking about." And Eamon said, "Well, why don't we do this? We'll meet here tomorrow night. If I'm correct about the Vikings in what I stated, you buy all the drinks. If I'm incorrect, I will buy all the drinks."

He went back that next night with the group of gentlemen that he brought to Ireland, and there was complete silence in the pub. One guy was playing the banjo, another guy was playing the violin, and there wasn't a peep. Normally, you hear vibrations all over the bar. Eamon walked in, walked down to the end of the bar, pounded on the bar and said, "My story about the Vikings was true." And with that, everybody started to clap, laugh, and started to sing. Music started. And everybody was so overwhelmed that this American, this Irish-American knew so much about Ireland.

I didn't ask him if the guy ever bought the bar a round that night, but I guarantee he didn't, because Eamon would have stepped up and not accepted it.

You had to ask me a question and I went over.

No, this is all good, Richie. You know...what people value about you is how deeply you care about people and connect with them. This is a nice glimpse into that.

As we all grow older, we go to a lot of ceremonies, a lot of memorials and celebrations of life. And it sounds like you and I are on the same page here – we agree that it's very sad when you lose somebody but it's even sadder when nobody steps up and captures the depth and the color of their life, and that is not an easy thing to do. To use a cliché - I don't think wild horses could have kept you away from there when Eamon's family needed you.

Definitely not. You know, that night I stayed up, you would think that after a day of travel, and staying up all night at a person's home, that I'd be worn out. There was something that gave me an ability to not worry about sleep, not worry about being tired. And yet, I had been up for over 24 hours. And there's no doubt in my mind that someone was behind that. When I need assistance, I always think about my wife and family, my mother and father, my sisters and my brothers. I know they reach out to help me. I'm sure that night there were a number of people that reached out to help me both prepare, and be alert, to do what I had to do.

Maybe a little nudge from Eamon?

Could have been... There are times I feel that there are people that are giving me nudges over the years. Bonnie wrote a wonderful book, entitled "Messages: Signs, Visits, and Premonitions from Loved Ones Lost on 9/11" ... Her book details many accounts from people who believe, as I do, that we are assisted by departed loved ones.

February 11, 1961

The Moran Clan
Front: Quinlan, Eamon, Lindsay, Adrienne, Ryan, Chase and Kylie. Back: Kevin, Melissa, Finn, Pat, Richie, Kathy, Bill, Louie and Jennifer

The day John Moran became a U.S. citizen.

Catherine and John Moran, with 2 year-old John and 4 year-old Mary.

Pat as a University of Maryland cheerleader! (The brightest one in the bunch!)

First trip to Ireland together.

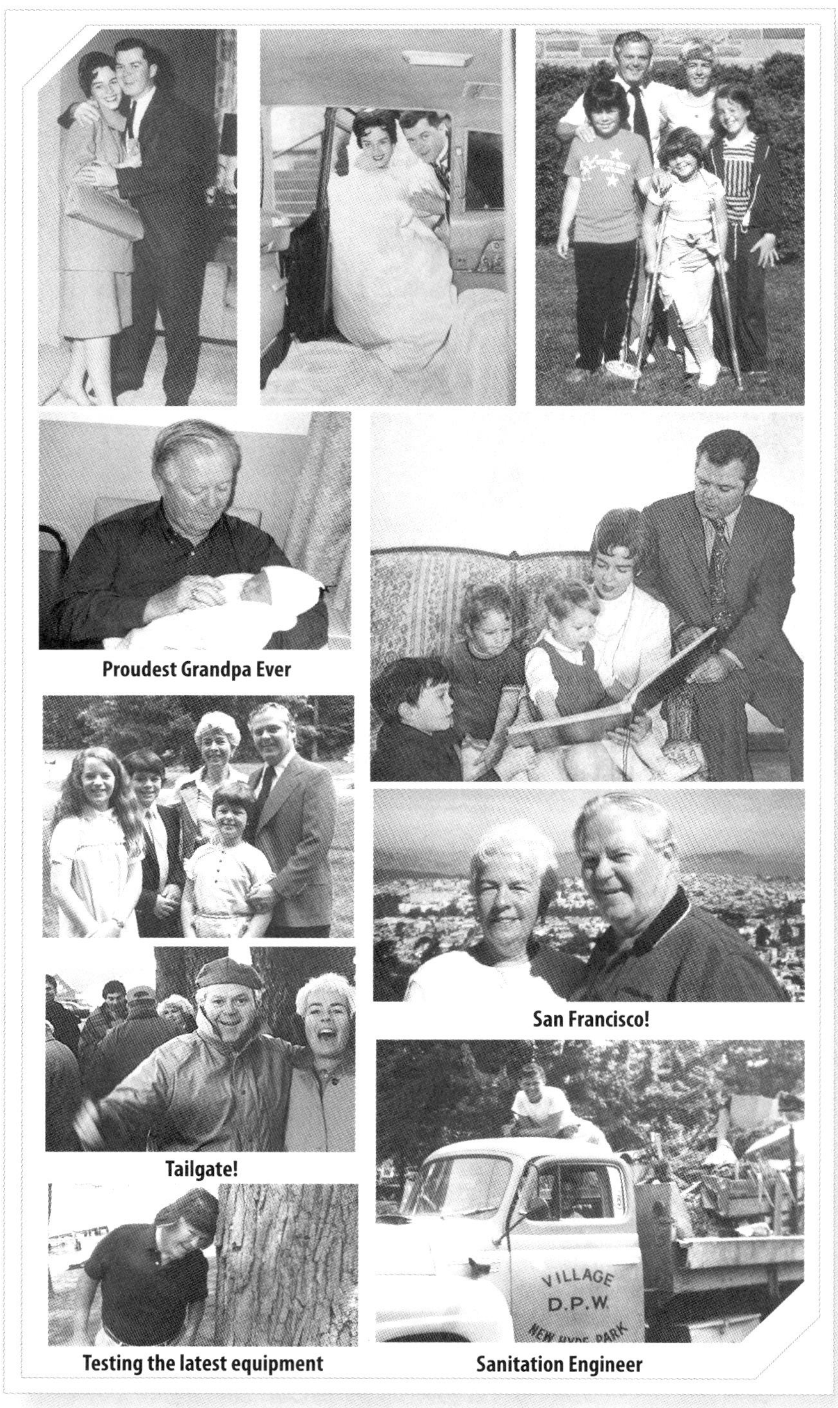

Proudest Grandpa Ever

San Francisco!

Tailgate!

Testing the latest equipment

Sanitation Engineer

Miss Pat Smith
Phi Kappa Sigma
1959 Girl of the Year

Kevin Moran

Mike French, Richie, Glen Mueller and Walter "Pop" Scholl

Richie with United States Senator Hillary Clinton

I Love Cornell

Ashford Castle - Cong, County Mayo, Ireland (With Chuck Feeney)

Post-game interview, 1971 National Championship win.

Eamon McEneaney's Hall of Fame Induction

1971 team member and Four-star General Jay Paxton

1988 Seniors: Joe Lizzio, John Wurzburger, Coach, Kevin Moran, Tim Goldstein, Matt Gleason, Karl Lehman, Mike DeStefano, Brian McCormick and Charlie Caliendo

First day as a coach, Manhasset High School

Aggressive on the ground ball

Sewanhaka Midfielder – 58 Straight wins

1959 NCAA National Champs, UMD

Ireland Lacrosse

With Bill Marino

Hall of Fame Induction

Tom Marino, NCAA playoffs

Cornell/Notre Dame joint trip to Ireland

Mike French, eye on the prize, 1976 National Championship Game.

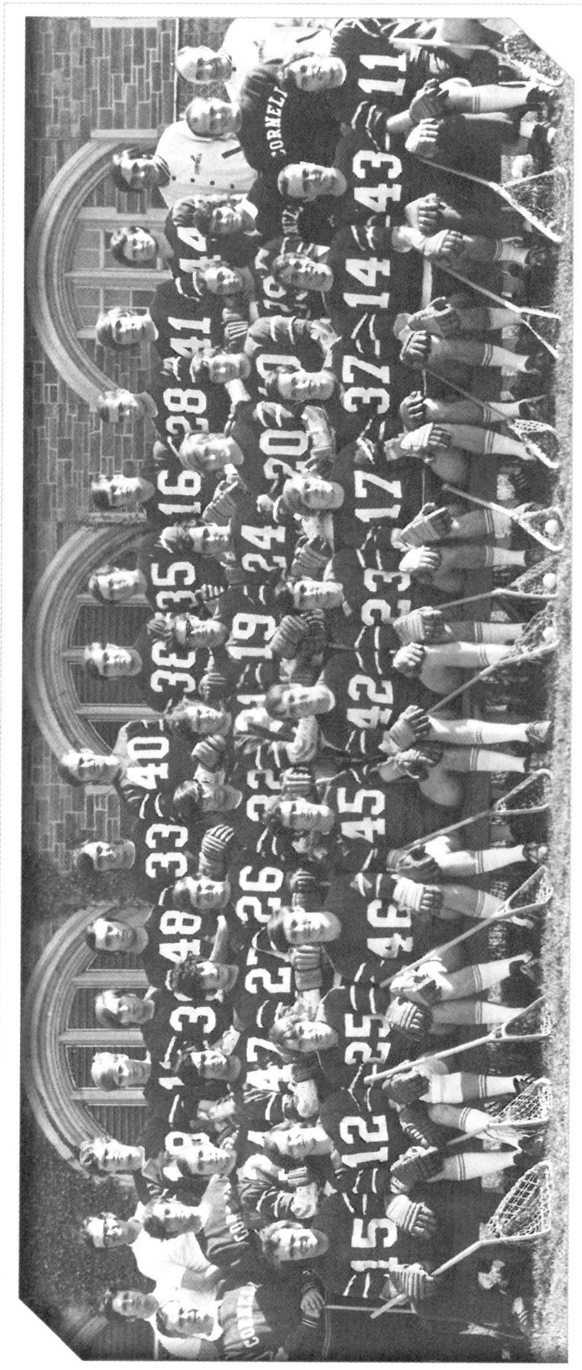

Photo courtesy of Cornell University

1971 Team

First Row: **Bob Rule, Frank Davis, Glen Mueller, Bill Ellis, Mickey Fenzel, Tri-Capt. John Burnap, Tri-Capt. Bob Shaw, Tri-Capt. Al Rimmer, Rob Wagner, Bruce Teague, Hank Olivier, Bob Buhmann**
Second Row: **Coach Richie Moran, Asst. Coach Mike Waldvogel, Matt Sampson, Harry Nicolaides, Bill Reed, Pat Knapp, Craig Bollinger, Gregg Wellott, Craig Pollak, Bill Molloy, Bucky Gunts, Pat Gallagher, Art Fried, Manager Barry Freilicher, Trainer Rick LaFrance, Faculty Advisor O. F. Johndrew Jr.**
Third Row: **Manager Stan Fish, Manager, Kim Eike, Tom McHenry, Tom Mygatt, Jim Skeen, Russ Greene, Chuck Keibler, Matt Olenski, Larry Croucher, Jim Bradley, Larry Young, Jay Paxton, Steve Alms, Jim Nowak, Bob Cali.**

Photo courtesy of Cornell University

1976 Team

First Row: **John Griffin, Jon Levine, Steve Dybus, John O'Neill, Tri-Capt. Ted Marchell, Tri-Capt. Bill Marino, Tri-Capt. Mike French, Albin Haglund, Robert Mitchell, Dan Mackesey, Advisor Scotty Johndrew**

Second Row: **Coach Richie Moran, Dave Bray, Bob Katz, Vince Shanley, Bob Jackson, Eamon McEneaney, Frank Muehleman, Reiley McDonald, Gary Malm, Paul Sadowski, Joe Szombathy, Brian Lasda, Announcer-Statistician Kim Eike, Junior Varsity Coach Scott Anderson, Asst. Coach Mike Waldvogel**

Third Row: **Asst. Manager Dave Hohreiter, Chuck Weibe, Jim DeNicola, Bob Henrickson, John Sierra, George Lau, Ned Gerber, Bob Mathisen, Tom Marino, Britt Britton, Keith Reitenbach, Chris Kane, Trainer Rick LaFrance, Manager Bill Messina.** *Not Pictured:* **Greg Raschdorf**

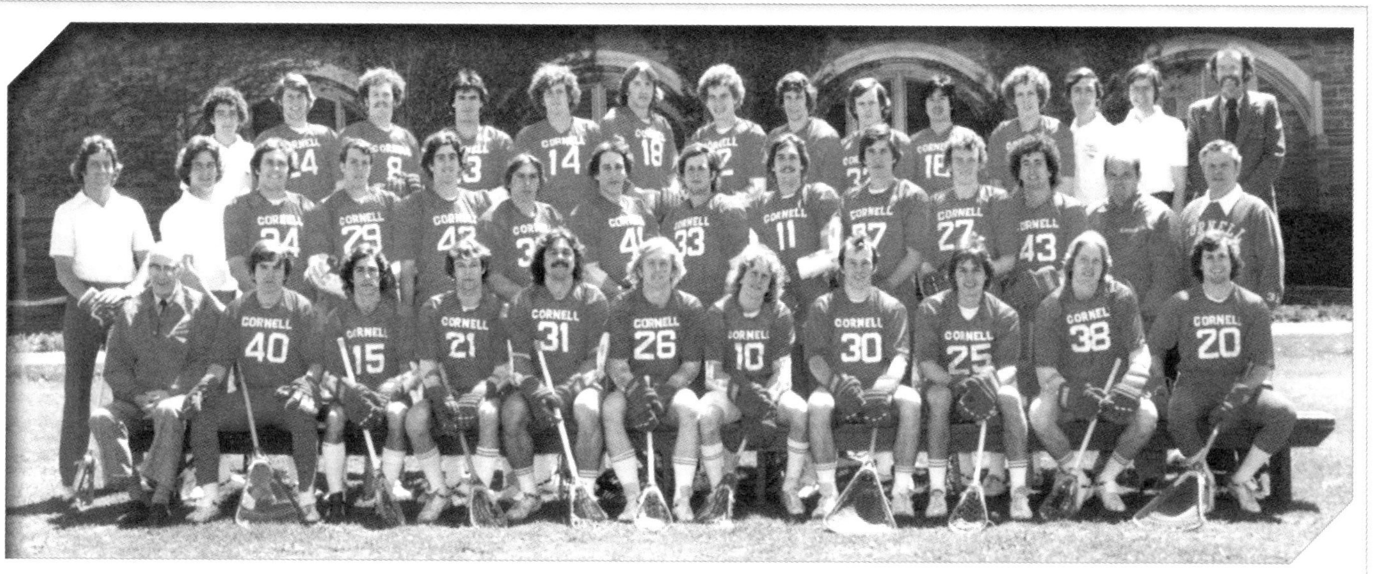

1977 Team

First Row: Faculty Advisor Scotty Johndrew, John Griffen, Thomas Marino, Robert Annear, Brian Lasda, Tri-Capt. Gary Malm, Tri-Capt. Eamon McEneaney, Tri-Capt. Daniel Mackesey, David Bray, Vincent Shanley, Robert Jackson
Second Row: Asst. Coach Michael Waldvogel, Varsity "B" Coach Scot Anderson, Paul Sadowski, Peter Kohm, Chris Kane, Robert Mathisen, Robert Katz, James McDonald, Joseph Szombathy, Frank Muehlman, Keith Reitenbach, Joseph Marletta, Trainer Rick LaFrance, Varsity Head Coach Richie Moran
Third Row: Manager David Hohreiter, Robert Henrickson, Craig Jaeger, John Sierra, Brian Conroy, John Gerber, Joseph Taylor, Greg Raschdorf, Charles Weibe, George Lau, Stephen Page, Asst. Manager Barry Pineles, Asst. Manager Rod Iwanczuk, Statistician Kim Eike.

Photo courtesy of Cornell University

Photo courtesy of Cornell University

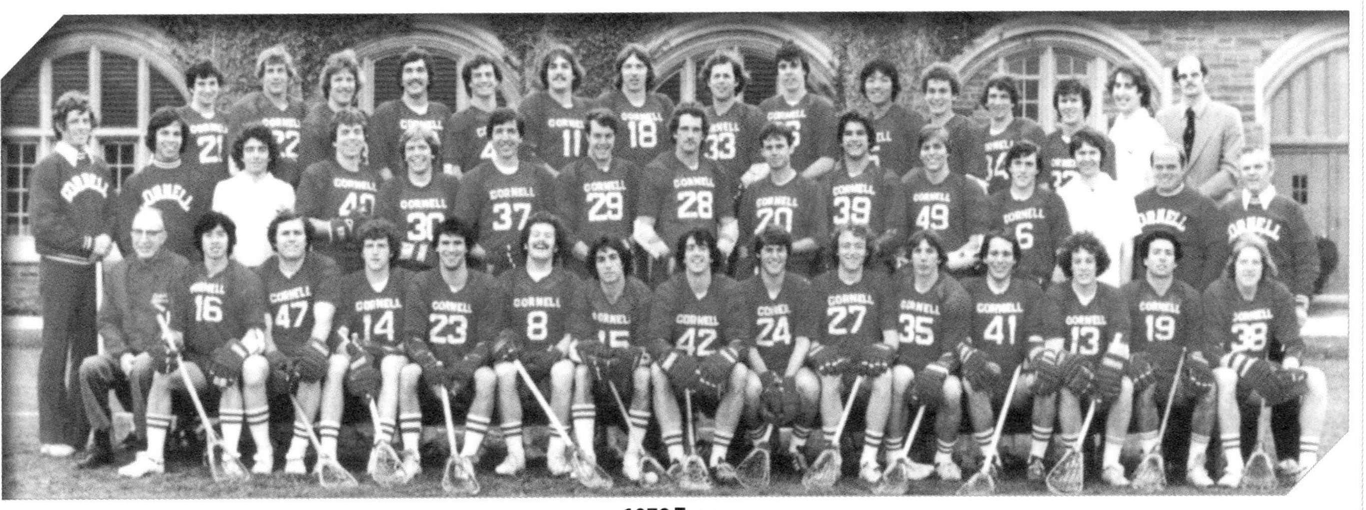

1978 Team:

First Row: Scotty Johndrew (Faculty Advisor), George Lau, Paul Sadowski, Brian Conroy, John Sierra, Craig Jaeger, Tom Marino (Tri-Captain), Chris Kane (Tri-Captain), Robert Henrickson (Tri-Captain), Keith Reitenbach, Bob Mathisen, Bob Katz, Steve Page, Joe Marletta, Vince Shanley.

Second Row: Mike Waldvogel (Assistant Coach), Bruce Arena (JV Coach), Dave Hohreiter, John Griffin, Bob Capener, Frank Muehleman, Peter Kohm, Cutty Cleveland, Bob Jackson, Jeff Dingle, Laurey Millspaugh, Jim Power, Rob Iwanczuk (Manager), Rick LaFrance (Trainer), Richie Moran (Head Coach).

Third Row: Jim DeNicola, Charlie Wood, Tom Breen, Jim Buckley, Wayne Meichner, Joe Szombathy, Ned Gerber, Reiley McDonald, Tim Guba, Randy Wong, Joe Taylor, Greg Raschdorf, Chuck Wiebe, Al Levine (Manager), Bob Luria (Statistician).

1978 Team (JV):

First Row: Bob Barron, Dave Walter, Kenny Katz, Sam Edwards, Jim Sheehan, Matt Wigsten, Tom Wagner (Co-Captain), Henry Reed (Co-Captain), Greg Hansen, Jon Graham, Woody Jay, Jim Hauslein, Scott Harrison.

Second Row: Bruce Arena (Head Coach), Eamon McEneaney (Assistant Coach), Bob Boehringer, Joe Ripa, Joey Holihan, Dan Titus, Scott Koenig, John Roche, Sam Greason, Art Palmer, Brian Meyers, Jay Bloom, Jim Howe, Don Devine (Manager), Dave Hill (Manager).

Third Row: Tim Guba, Marty Cooper, Kevin Rogers, Chris Berry, Dave Furiness, Laurey Millspaugh, John Mutch, Mike Lynch, Tom Enright, Tony Scialabba, Rob McChesney, Carl DelBazio, Jay Ernst.

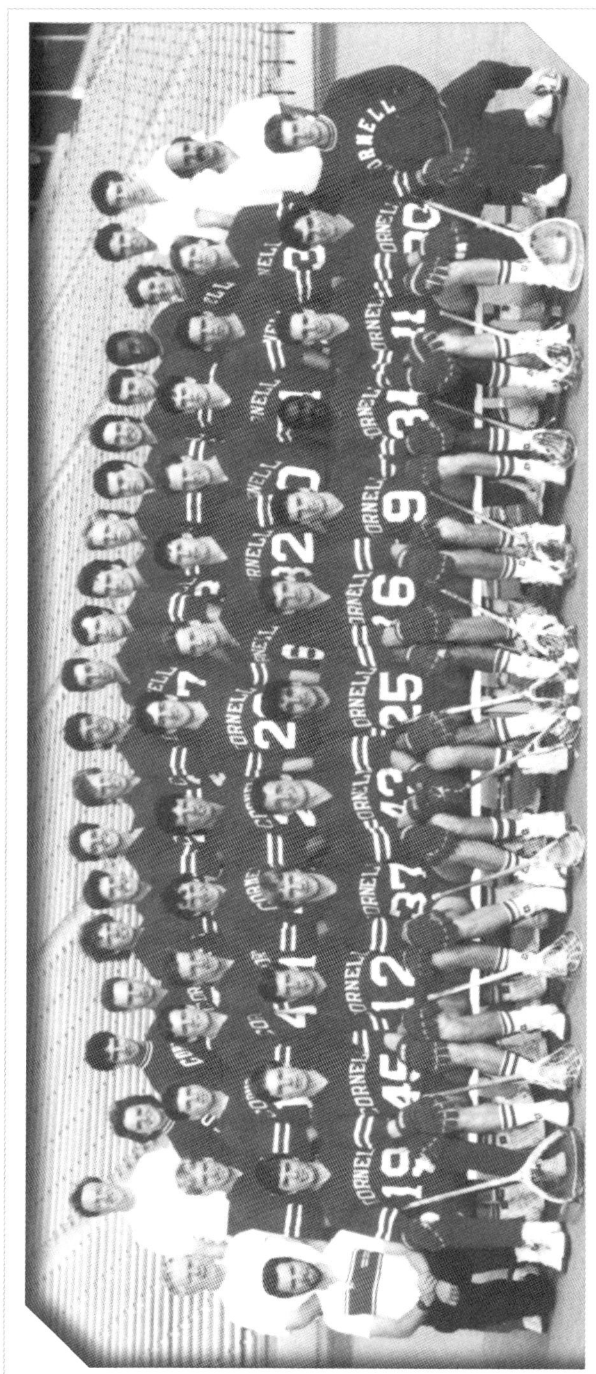

Photo courtesy of Cornell University

1987 Team

First Row: **Trainer Tom LiVigne, John Colucci, Evan Conway, Steve Long, Todd Francis, Tri-captain Steve Paletta, Tri-captain Paul Kuehner, Tri-captain Tim Vivian, Bob Cummings, Aaron Jones, Tim Mulligan, Chris Modesti, Manager Frank Guarnieri**

Second Row: **Head Coach Richie Moran, John Wurzburger, Tim Goldstein, John Rossettie, Matt Gleason, Tim McDevitt, Karl Lehmann, Mike DeStefano, Mike Cummings, Jim Ciquera, Paul Schimoler, Geoff Hall, Charlie Caliendo, Tony Morgan, Asst. Coach Jerry DeMeo**

Third Row: **Asst. Coach Keith Reitenbach, Manager Melanie Cavo, Manager Larry Carbone, Matt Schultz, John Miller, Dave Dunlap, Mike Hays, Bill O'Hanlon, Vince Angotti, Steve Meyer, Chris Tierney, Brian McCormack, John Heil, Kevin Moran, Chris Marzullo, Paul Shea, Manager Mike Strickland, Manager Naomi Hyman, Faculty Advisor Phil Marcus, Graduate Asst. Mickey Fenzel (missing: Joe Lizzio)**

Building Blocks

Richie, you wanted to talk about how championship lacrosse teams are built, and my guess is, like any building project, you start with a foundation. In this context, what are the components that go into building the foundation of a championship lacrosse team?

As you start organizing your program, you think of components that are going to be very important - like conditioning, mental preparation, physical preparation, fundamentals and drills, all of the things that are extremely essential to develop early on.

Let me ask you before you go any farther... when you were looking at a particular athlete and thinking about how you were going to incorporate his skills into your system, those components had to take a backseat to what had to happen to get that athlete to come to Cornell in the first place, right?

Yes. That is true.

So starting there, what pieces of that puzzle did you have to look at, and who helped you do that?

Basically, I'd be in contact with the coaches from many high schools. In May, I'd send a personal letter out to every high school that was in the high school athletic directory throughout the state, and beyond. It was a questionnaire, asking them to recommend an athlete, or athletes to us. I'd put in what's essential to be accepted at Cornell, the range of SAT scores, what's involved as far as financial aid, so that they would get a pretty good overview of what their young man could expect once we got in touch with him.

Once that list came in, I'd start sending out personal letters with a questionnaire card. The questionnaire card was a card the size of an envelope that contained personal information on the front, and academic information on the back. That would give me a chance to initiate our communication, our first method of getting to know one another. I would then contact the guidance counselor at that school to find out about the student academically, to get more information, and also I would contact some of the coaches that he may have played against to find out what type of player he was.

In the late '60s-early '70s, there really wasn't a lot of filming done so the advantage that coaches have today of looking at a player on film were really nonexistent. There was some game film but it was on 8 millimeter.

And these films had to be mailed, so it was cumbersome and expensive?

Yes, and it really didn't give me what I was looking for. I was looking for the skill level. You could see it somewhat but it wasn't defined as well as it could be defined verbally by his head coach and/or opposing coaches.

This method was very successful for our program. I had one assistant coach, Mike Waldvogel, and we pursued the candidates. If we felt that the candidates had a strong interest in attending Cornell, we would visit their school. That took a lot of time. I would go on the road for a week, come back late Friday night, spend some family time, and go on the road again Sunday. Areas like Long Island were pretty easy to recruit from because the schools are within 15 minutes or a half hour from one another.

Since our seasons overlapped, I saw very few actual games. It was really a personal visit to the school. I'd arrange for the young man to meet me in the guidance office. If his coach could make it, and he had a free period, I'd try to work around that. I would personally speak to the young man alone. Then, if possible, I'd speak with him with his guidance counselor and coach. And then I'd be off to another school.

So, it involved developing a portfolio on each individual that I could look at and keep track of. Did the young man play other sports? I would have friends of mine that might be in that area go to games and take a look at him playing football, basketball or soccer, and that was extremely helpful.

We had a network of alumni and personal friends that would also look at the candidates we were interested in, in their area or their neighborhood. That was very productive.

A lot of these people had an intimate knowledge of Cornell and what would make a good match, right?

Very much so.

It seems almost like a sales scenario where several other coaches are showcasing their product. I'm going to guess it was helpful for you to have seven different colleges within the university, increasing the likelihood there would be a match with that particular young man's skills and interests.

That's right. During that time, there was a gentleman, Sol Goldberg, who worked in Media Services at Cornell. He put together a group of slides that I'm sure are archaic now, but were not in those days. We had that slide production and while I was talking to the young man I would put the carousel on. It would be up on a wall and we'd be facing that while I was talking to him about Cornell.

Showing them the fall colors, ivy-covered buildings, gorges, spectacular views and the beauty of the Ithaca area?

Yes. The slides contained information on the various colleges, so the guidance counselor frequently sat in on it because it was helpful to him or her. And it was extremely helpful for the athlete. Then it came down to when we were finally able to get all the athletes together on one occasion. We would invite them to an event that was sponsored by lacrosse alumni and Cornell alumni, in various areas, like Long Island, Connecticut, New Jersey, Baltimore and Washington, D.C. The Cornell Clubs in those areas were extremely helpful. Cornell University had produced a truly amazing film that we would show, and then we'd have a presentation. Some former players would speak about the values at Cornell, what they obtained by going to Cornell, the degrees that they received.

The opportunities that might lie ahead?

Yes, and how lacrosse played a part in their careers. And then we'd have some gentlemen that graduated in the '40s or '50s talk about their lives. These testimonials were a part of a night of information that would be useful to the athlete and his parents. Typically, we would try to time it when Cornell had a representative – for example, in financial aid or admissions - in that area, and we'd invite them to the event. That was very helpful because it gave parents a chance to meet us personally and ask questions.

House visits were not really big in those days. If I felt the parents wanted further information, and they wanted it to be private, I would definitely visit their homes. But mainly it was going to the schools, meeting with the guidance counselors, meeting with the coaches, meeting with the player. Then we would have an event in that area before applications were due. We would put together a format that the prospective student and his family could follow.

We were there as a resource. Working with the guidance counselors was very helpful because young men were being recruited by a lot of schools, and not just for lacrosse. Financial aid was a big factor in a lot of the homes. We could provide some summer jobs for the players. We could provide jobs on campus. Notice we're using the word "jobs." To speak to a scholarship athlete today, and tell him that he's going to work in a fraternity or sorority house washing pots and pans and waiting on tables, I don't think they'd be very receptive. However, those players were very determined to come to Cornell. They were very interested in Cornell academically and athletically.

I personally believe that the methods that we used gave them a pretty good insight into the sequence of opportunities that could happen for them. It's very difficult at age 16 and 17 to start making lifelong decisions or commitments. I would never force a young man into making a commitment. The value of the guidance counselor was very important because I would drop them notes periodically, send them a Thanksgiving card, send cards to the coaches at Thanksgiving or Christmas. And I'd call the guidance counselor every once in a while if I felt that the individual that we were interested in might have had some other schools way ahead of us. If they did, then of course, my interest level would decline. I was still interested in the young man, but if we were number four or five on his list, in all due honesty, once you get past one or two, you're really not in the battle. Not that I wanted to be combative; I just wanted to be efficient with my time, energy, and available resources.

In 2016, any coach can send out 300 e-mails a day. He can attach game film clips from a game played 5 minutes earlier. That's

pretty easy. It's a pretty level playing field. I'm going to guess that 40 years ago, somebody with your tendency to really want to remember people's names, someone who was always reaching for a pen and paper to send a thank-you card, and a greeting card or a birthday card really stood out from the crowd. I'm sure your genuine concern for people was obvious, and that it set you apart from a lot of the other recruiters.

Well, I thought it was essential to use a personal touch. As for the initial letters, we were fortunate. I had a secretary for 1 hour a day, a student. We had a system where we could put letters put into a system that could be copied. It was personalized, using the recruit's first name, and I always put notes on them.

Sort of an early word processing system?

Correct. Word processing—thank you. You do pretty well for a young guy! I would definitely use that word processing system and then, of course, personal notes. Quite a lot of letters went out. It was good because it started letting coaches know that Cornell was on the map, that we really wanted to strengthen the program. We were going to bring in excellent student athletes. And whenever I went to conventions, I always found time to gather all these coaches together for a coaching session, questions and answers. So I got to know them personally. In fact, a lot of them today are still my friends.

In the recruiting process, I sometimes went to visit a home and to meet the family. A lot of times, the parents were really very gracious and invited me for dinner. I would sit down in the home, and I always brought a host gift. If it was around Christmastime, I brought a couple of poinsettias. I'd sit down and I would see five siblings at the table, and I knew that the parents would be making a gigantic financial sacrifice to have their first child go off to an Ivy League school.

Sometimes, after having dinner, I'd sit down with the parents and the candidate, and I'd always want the brothers and sisters to sit in because I wanted to get to know them. Then we'd have a session. I would meet with the dad and mother. The topic was often, "Coach, we'd really love to have our son come to Cornell, but that would mean maybe our other four children might have difficulty going to a school like Cornell financially." Maybe they would have to consider a junior college. That was always tough. And that's why I went overboard to try to provide jobs and opportunities for the athlete to help with the financial commitment of coming to Cornell.

That enabled a lot of parents to feel like we were really going to work together. If a coach were to tell you he was "only concerned about the athlete," he certainly couldn't be on my staff, because your concern had to be for the parents as well. I always put myself in that position. At that time, I had one child, a son, and I put myself in that position and tried to ease some of the difficulty that they were going to be facing.

Now, this is a tough one…were there times when a player had a dream to play for you, he wanted to come to Cornell, his parents were onboard, his coaches were onboard, but it just wasn't going to happen. He just was not going to be able to get there academically. That had to be tough.

That was very tough. When a young man got turned down at Cornell, I made a personal phone call to his parents.

Now, believe it or not, some of the young men didn't get into other Ivy League schools but I was really pleased that they had picked Cornell at that stage as number one. If they did not get accepted into another Ivy League school, and they were still in the waiting process at other schools, I would personally call those coaches and tell them how outstanding that individual was not just as a player, but as a person—and if they could, they should do anything possible to get him accepted.

So when the deadline came and a negative decision came, I really didn't end my connection and compassion for that individual and his family. To this day, I'm still friends of parents whose sons went to other schools. I've seen them at various athletic events. Some of their children actually came to Cornell, and they often talk about how their interest in Cornell started. To this day I still feel some stress, to be honest with you, and disappointment. I know they've done well. I see people from time to time and I remember one young man saying "Coach, I wish I had played for you at Cornell." And I tell him, 'You did. It's just that you weren't there in person." And to me, that's pretty important.

I was an usher for a young man who didn't get accepted at Cornell, but we became such great friends. So the bonds and ties that you make and create with people are, in my mind, everlasting.

It sounds like the admissions process was a complex balancing act. Was it a tough path to navigate?

The colleges had set dates when they would notify the students. I would always try to encourage students that had strong academics - and had Cornell number one on their list - to think about applying "early decision." And that worked out well, because some of these students got into Cornell early decision, which would be in December. Now, if they went through the regular admissions process, my greatest concern was they might be coming from a high school from which a number of students were applying, and Cornell was going to look at the top ten students at that school.

So, early decision was a big help. For the other students that went through regular admissions, it was a tough application process. Essays were very, very important. Your academic standards were very important. At that time, class rank was an important issue.

Some schools are larger than others, obviously. For example, the high school I graduated from had 875 graduates. You could be a top student and be number 40 in your class. Someone that came from a school of 100 students could be number 10 at that school. So the range of admissions processing was extremely tough.

We were permitted to send a letter of recommendation. Believe it or not, it was called a "pink slip." I have no idea why they decided to send out pink slips. Today, a pink slip means you're no longer in the mix. We typed that pink slip out, put the information down that we had about the individual athletically, because they had all the academic information. In some cases, we felt it was helpful and in other cases we felt it was detrimental because the student probably would have gotten into Cornell anyway. Sometimes they were turned down, and having a young man turned down was very difficult.

We really didn't find out about the final decision until towards the tail end of April. Our practice season started in February, and in April we were in the thick of our schedule, and we were still heavily into recruiting. There were times when I would leave practice and drive up to Rochester, or Syracuse, to continue to encourage a young man to stick with us, because the other colleges and universities that gave scholarships sometimes wanted a commitment by March. In many cases we would not learn until the middle of April who had been accepted. That could be tough, because the financial details may not have been clarified until May.

The Ivy League had a "compare system," so no one in the Ivy League could present a brighter picture about acceptance. They were all on an even plane. That doesn't exist today. It was a checks and balances system to assure that no one school was offering more financial aid than the other school. One was not over-accepting students because of their athletic prowess, and that was a very good system.

I know that you wouldn't have been able to grind it out as hard as you did in the recruiting process unless you felt that the product you were representing really was going to deliver on what you were telling people. You clearly believed in the bigger, long-term picture.

That is correct. I did, and I still do. You know, it's interesting, Steve. Over the years I coached, there were some disappointments when players couldn't get accepted. But then again, you've got to understand that the interest in Cornell is international. Students from all over the world want to come here. There are only a certain number of spots. It's very difficult for the admissions department to pick everyone, otherwise, we'd have to build a university two times the size of Cornell.

So, it could be disappointing. It was always tough when we had to compete against some of those individuals. But I'm happy for their successes. So in a way, they were part of the program somewhat. I still have their questionnaire cards. In fact, I took one out the other day for Jon Levine. It was really interesting. I can say he was a miracle acceptance, but that was in the '70s.

The Immaculate Exception?

Yes. And he definitely was a wonderful young man. He's now an extremely successful dentist on Park Avenue. His two sons, Cody and Julian, came to Cornell. His wife Stacy is a remarkable person. So I created a Cornell Family. He's a twin. His brother went to Maryland. I met him at a camp on Long Island at St. Paul's school on Long Island, back in 1972. Jon was a left-handed player, which is not easy to find. He was very aggressive, and a very accurate shooter. At camp, I gave him a questionnaire. He filled it out, and 1 hour later he gave it back to me. And from that day on, we've been inseparable. I have been to two bar mitzvahs. I hope to be at Cody and Julian's weddings...

Did you hear that, Jon? Get those invitations in the mail.

I remember them coming up to a Cornell event when they were young boys. And kiddingly, I said that they had won a raffle and they wanted to know what it was. I said they were going to stay with me for a week on the lake. Their excitement level was amazing, that is until I told them we'd get up at 6:00 in the morning and go out jogging, and at 7:00 we would cut wood, and at 7:30 we were going to have breakfast. They never came.

I don't blame them...Back to admissions... the decision has been made. They got in. Did you send them some sort of preseason conditioning plan, or some sort of care package on how to prepare for life as a Cornell student and as a Big Red lacrosse player?

The first thing I would do was send a package of information to the parents. It would contain a lot of useful information about Ithaca, the Chamber of Commerce, hotels, dining facilities, information about the campus, and pamphlets describing the surrounding areas where they could go visit. It would give them a base of knowledge of what the best routes would be to come to Ithaca, and let them know that we had an airport. It would tell them a little bit about student health services, tell them about our medical system here. So I wanted them to get a really definitive idea of everything that was available. This could be at their fingertips. With that, I would invite them to our lacrosse banquet that we had every fall, during homecoming.

In those days, Parents' Weekend was on the calendar but many parents returned on Homecoming Weekend to attend our team banquet. We had hotel rooms reserved. At that time, it was the Sheraton, and the banquet was also held there. We got football tickets for them, and we had a huge tailgate. Johnny Russo's band played and it was very festive. It was an opportunity for all the parents to meet each other. That whole weekend was great. We let everybody know about Cornell lacrosse tradition and Cornell University. I was never one for buttons with the player's picture on it, but I was in favor of name tags, so a person could identify a player with his family. At the banquet, I introduced each player individually and offered some comments about them. We honored our players from the year before, and we had some great speakers. In fact, one year we welcomed Joe Holland - a former Cornell football player and the son of the famous Jerome "Brud" Holland, the first African-American to play football at Cornell and the U.S. Ambassador to Sweden under President Nixon.

Once, I was asked by a dad from Baltimore who our upcoming speaker would be, and I jokingly said "George Bush." Apparently, he passed this information on to the authorities, and the local sheriff and state troopers called me. I learned you had to be very careful about who you pulled pranks on!

Homecoming Weekend is in September, and that's a nice time of year to invite people to visit Cornell.

Yes, it is. We had not even started fall lacrosse then. I always waited until the players were here at least a month and a half so they could get acclimated to schoolwork, college life, and to adjust to being independent. For example, they had to wake themselves up, do laundry, and learn to manage their time.

So, their initial job was to get acclimated to school, to the area, to being away from home?

That's correct. We did have 12 days of fall practice. It was intense. One of the advantages about fall practice was that I always allowed walk-ons to try out, and they stayed with us for 12 days. An athlete develops at certain stages of his life, and if a young man had some lacrosse background, athletic background, I would open the door for him. We'd practice up at Helen Newman Fields. There were three fields side-by-side so we weren't hurting for field space. We paid a lot of attention to every athlete that was on that field. Some of the players knew who the walk-ons were, and believe it or not, they were very willing to work with these young men for the betterment of the team. It was a great atmosphere.

When we finished practice, as the sun was setting, we would do the Cornell cheer, and it would echo through North Campus. To this day, a lot of players remember that, how it echoed. And when the sun was setting, and the beauty of the fall, and the fact that you just finished wind sprints, you would get up together as a team. And the first cheer was "I love Cornell." And I'm sure it startled some of the students that were in the dormitories, because they had their windows open and they heard that echo.

How many players were yelling this at the same time?

With walk-ons, we probably would carry close to fifty players. Our normal squad would be about 28-32, but we also had a B team. The walk-ons could play with the B team starting in February. We developed some pretty good All-Americans from those walk-ons.

Did it make you wonder how you missed them coming in?

It's interesting. They came to Cornell and applied for a certain academic program. They realized that they could try out for lacrosse, and they would be given a legitimate opportunity. They were going to be included in the program, and hopefully enjoy it. Their efforts gave the program some nourishment, because if you show me a young man that tries, I'll show you an extraordinary person. And all these men became extraordinary people, in my mind.

And then some of them would be told "Hey, thanks for coming out this fall." How did they know they weren't really coming back in the spring?

We would put a list up and invite everybody back because we had a B team. Once fall practice was over, I wanted players to do other things. The reason we started fall practice late is because I wanted players that also wanted to play football, or soccer, or to run cross country. I would say 100 percent of our athletes that were on the lacrosse team were also involved in intramural programs, either by way of the fraternities they were in, or the dormitories they represented.

So when lacrosse season had ended in the fall, I wasn't preventing them from going skiing. I wasn't worried they were going to get hurt. I wasn't concerned that they were playing other sports. After the fall, we had a couple of players that played hockey. Somebody might think, well, he's going to get hurt. Listen, you can get hurt in the dining hall. You can get hurt in the dormitory, so it's not necessary to restrict individuals. We had an old weight room at Cornell. All weights were made from a metal bar, utilizing cans that Italian sauce came in. I'd go down to the Italian restaurants, get those cans, and we'd fill them up with cement and put the bar through them. To this day I have no idea what they weighed, but our players would use those weights. We advocated jumping rope; everybody had a jump rope. We had some small weights that were given to me by a local gentleman, and we used those weights. However, it wasn't a weight lifting program at 6 o'clock in the morning like some programs have today. We were more concerned about them getting organized academically, contributing to the university. I definitely wanted our players involved in clubs and organizations on campus, and I wanted them involved in the community. We had them involved with bell ringing for the Salvation Army.

We also had them involved in a "Turkey Run". We broke the squad in halves. The week before Thanksgiving, they would run up Buffalo Street and wind up in the stadium. One team had red jerseys; the other one wore white. It was like a cross country run, and the team that won didn't have to buy turkeys. The team that lost had to go out and buy turkeys, which we gave to the Salvation Army. To this day, there's no doubt in my mind that some of those players still like turkeys.

They'd buy turkeys to donate to various groups, and ringing the Salvation Army bells was a great experience. We would do it for two weekends. We had sheet music, and two players to a bell. In those days, there were several different locations downtown. Well, the first weekend was tremendous. The players sang songs, the Christmas spirit was in the air and they loved it. The following weekend, we got down there on Friday, everybody at their various locations. My assistant coach and I were walking around when we saw two players that came from New Canaan, Connecticut, outstanding players, tremendous young men. There was a bus stop for what was then called the "sheltered workshop," and those players had never seen people with disabilities in their schools or their community. In the '70s, a lot of people with disabilities were cloistered. The interactions with those people were very beneficial to the players, and they never forgot that because I'll see them periodically, and they still talk about that experience.

Later in the afternoon, we saw sleet, snow and rain, and I was not going to give up ringing the bells, but the sidewalks were devoid of pedestrians. So with the rain and snow, I decided to go into some of the taverns and ask them if they would mind if we had some gentlemen come in with Salvation Army bells, and sing some Christmas songs. They loved it, and we went into five taverns. Players sang songs, and we probably collected more money that Friday than any other time in the history of Salvation Army collection in Ithaca. Even the bartenders contributed.

Two years later, I received an award from the Salvation Army, and I read up on their history. It was very obvious that they really do not accept alcohol as a feature of their program, and here I was, in the bar with the Salvation Army kettles!

Whoops...

Tell me about it...So that night at the award presentation, I said, "You can take this award back if you so desire because I definitely violated a very important feature of the Salvation Army: abstinence from alcohol." And I assured them that our players did not drink while they were there, and that all they did was ring the bells and sing.

I still have a video of you and Johnny Russo doing that! You are ringing the bell and Johnny is playing Silver Bells on his trumpet! You have been putting the shake-down on me for Salvation Army money for the last 35 years!

I love that! Another occasion with the Salvation Army, they asked me if I'd open up their campaign. I said, "I'll be happy to do it." It was held at the Pyramid Mall. They had a 16-piece band, and there were about 200 people in attendance. I invited six female lacrosse players and six male lacrosse players to assist in the ceremony. They all arrived very nicely dressed. I wanted them to sing the song with me, so I passed out the sheet music for Silver Bells.

Silver Bells? That's your stand-by?

Yes... I had them practice a little bit. And with that, Max Seibald came up to me and said, "Coach, I can't sing this. I'm Jewish." I said, "Max, I don't think God would be offended if you sang 'Silver Bells today!' I really don't think it has a religious theme!" To this day, whenever Max sees kettles in New York City, he laughs and contributes.

Nice!

You know, "Silver Bells" was written for the Salvation Army.

Was it?

Yes, it was. "Silver bells, hear them ring, on the corners, everyone sings..." I believe that song was written for the Salvation Army in the '20s.

It's true...we learn something new every day. Regarding the taverns, I think you probably felt in your heart that by getting those tavern patrons who were bent on further self-destruction to donate to the Salvation Army instead, you were really saving souls.

That's exactly what I said in my speech, that I was recreating prohibition!

So that speaks to building a championship lacrosse team, and the role played by community involvement, personal character and accountability, generosity, and all those things. You build better players out of better people, right?

That's right.

I know you took great pleasure in watching these young men grow from "green" freshmen, then develop a little more maturity as sophomores, and then into leaders as upper classmen. I also know you enjoy watching them grow as men, as husbands and fathers and leaders in their businesses and communities.

Yes, for sure. One of the joys is that by creating this opportunity to be involved, we were showing that everybody can do something. Get involved. Like the NIKE slogan —"Just Do It!" Our players did it. They went out and also got involved with the Big Brother program and the Make-A-Wish Foundation. I've always been involved with those organizations. The Big Brother program was a tremendous help to the young people in this community. The Big Brother programs help young men really establish a great life. And that, to me, is a great accomplishment.

Continuing our conversation about the building of a championship lacrosse team, and the different pieces that went into the foundation, and what might be considered the framing. Using those building blocks metaphors, I'd like to talk about the personal touches you brought to that process. In my intro to this book, I mentioned that I bring an insider's perspective to this

project, having known you for 35 years. I would like to point out that I bring another dimension of an insider's perspective in that I worked at Cornell Athletics, and saw you every day for the better part of 10 years. While employed there, I held a variety of positions. Sometimes I was addressed as a Physical Education instructor, or as the second in command at the Summer Sports School, or as a tickets and marketing professional, and I was treated in a certain way. Other times, I was the guy who handed out the towels, and I know what that felt like, too. We'll be honest here and say there are some people who treat those two types of people differently. I noticed when I first met you that you treated the towel guys, the custodial guys and the guys that lined the fields the same way you treated the Professors and the Boosters. You treated us all the same way, and that's a tough act to sell for the 35 years I've known you. I've come to see that it's really not an act at all, that you sincerely value people and the roles they play in the workplace and the community.

So, when we're looking at the building blocks of a successful program, let's go around that complex and talk about some of the people who made contributions behind the scenes, people that you'll always remember.

That's an excellent point, and I appreciate the compliment. . Building a program is never done by just one person. I was very fortunate. My trainer was Rick LaFrance.

Yes, you shared that great story about him smashing his head on the back of that bus when he was startled!

That's right... Rick brought a lot to the program. He was a prankster, which was important. He kept everybody loose. He heard all the confessions. He's the one that gave advice to athletes, to make sure that they didn't do things that were going to adversely affect them or the program. That was a very important role that he played.

Doug Vorhis was our equipment man, and he is remarkable. He did so many things that were above and beyond his job description. When you're an equipment guy, you realize that there are going to be times when athletes are agitated because of their performance, or they're just not ready for practice that day, and sometimes they want to take it out on somebody. Well, Doug was strong enough and he had a "turtle back," things just rolled off. He just let it go in one ear and out the other.

Yes… I have heard his wife, Joann, say the same thing!

Ha! And he would find methods to —not retaliate—but sometimes the player would find two shirts tied together, or socks with big holes in them. So it was a method of calming down the individual, and making him smile. So Doug played an important role, a very important role.

Now, when you mentioned an "equipment guy," a lot of people might see that as a pretty one-dimensional sort of job description. But weren't those guys in charge of a lot of the technical things that kept players safe, fitting pads and helmets, the kind of things that were much more important than that title might convey?

They sure were. We converted from grass to turf, and it was important to have proper shoes. In the beginning, we had a shoe bank for visiting teams that came in because many teams didn't have turf fields. It was important that our players had the proper fit, and Doug would make sure the cleats had the proper length for the type of surface. Other days we'd use sneakers on the turf, so we had a variety of shoes.

I always recommended that they put skin lube on their feet, and powder in their socks. Powder in their shoes can prevent turf toe. And we never got a case of turf toe. So I probably should have put that in the medical magazines and got credit. But I don't need the credit. That's only a joke

We had more shoes than Thom McAn. And, of course, the fitting of the helmets was important. I made it a point that I wanted all the players to wear proper shoulder pads. Some high schools never issued shoulder pads; yet the contact is very similar to hockey. You never see hockey players go on the ice without shoulder pads. And we'd stick check, and a check might come up around the shoulder and could easily fracture your clavicle, or injure a bone in that area. So I felt shoulder pads were very important, although a lot of players were not accustomed to using them. We always wanted shoulder pads that would cover parts of the sternum, because you can get hit with a ball, get hit with a check, and to me that was very important.

So Doug had a lot of responsibilities, and I am sure that when we were working down in the polo barns, the aroma was pretty upsetting. I'm sure he and the other people in the equipment room really appreciated it when we brought that equipment back!

I have been in the polo barns... "Aroma" is a kind word.

I'd also like to talk about publicity. We had Phil Langan, who did a great job for us, and then Dave Wohlheuter took over. And all these men really helped us promote our sports in general, and promote Cornell lacrosse.

That was a lot more difficult in those days, before social media and the internet. It required a lot more effort.

It sure was more difficult. Few games, if any, were on television so having the people in the Sports Information office reach out and help us develop an image that the public could read about and hear about was critical. Those two men were very important.

I also want to acknowledge our managers. I can't say enough about them. They just seemed to come out of the woodwork. In fact, a very interesting applicant that we had for manager was a gentleman by the name of Jeff Lehman. We had advertised the position through the *Cornell Daily Sun*, and Jeff was a young man who applied in the 1970's. Jeff was remarkable, and the name may ring a bell when I make the next comment: Jeffrey Lehman eventually became President of Cornell University.

So we laugh about that. I remember when he arrived on campus as President. We went to lunch, and we laughed about it. I was very fortunate in that I liked all the presidents we had here at Cornell. I tried to make myself available if they needed me at any time. I played squash with Frank Rhodes, and I had lunch with Dale Corson on occasion.

You mentioned that friends made that prank phone call, pretending to be President Corson.

Yes. We talked about that one, right? I felt all these things were very important for the build-up of our program. And the managerial situation was great; a lot of those gentlemen went on to great experiences and great careers. Jeff Dann became a Navy pilot. Getting through Naval ROTC was an unbelievable task. Jeff did not like drills. He frequently overslept and missed his ROTC class, and actually didn't graduate until the summer. He went on to become a pilot and he was a great manager, but sometimes a little absentminded. In fact, I once said to him, "Jeff, let me know what zone you're going to be flying in so I'm not in that zone on that particular day!" He is just a tremendous guy.

Larry Carbone was born with one arm. I first came across Larry when I was reading the *Daily News* one day, and on the back cover was a picture of a coach by the name of O'Connor from St. Francis Prep, and next to him was a young boy by the name of Liberato "Larry" Carbone. The story angle was the fact that Larry was given permission by the state of New York to play football at St. Francis Prep.

Years later, I got to know Larry… we were playing Army in a play-off game at Cornell. It was a fantastic game, a great crowd, very physical. We did some great things in that game. We executed our game plan almost to perfection, and Army played a tremendous game as well.

After the game was over, and we had won, people were coming out on the field. I hadn't seen that since we beat Hopkins when both teams were undefeated. There we were in the play-offs, we knocked off Army, and a gentleman came up to me, put his arm around me and said, "I love this game! This is the first time I've ever seen a lacrosse game!" He had one of those Italian Bocce shirts on and he said, "Can I help out in the program in some way?"

I said, "Sure. You can help out as an administrative assistant."

He said, "What's that?"

I said, "Well, I'll explain it to you tomorrow. Why don't you come to my office tomorrow morning? We'll have a chance to talk."

I got to the office about 8:00. He must have been there at 7:30. He was a very patient individual. I told him what his responsibilities would be, and from that day on, we've been inseparable. Larry played Sprint football - in those days it was called Lightweight Football. He played intramural tennis, played intramural lacrosse. He was extremely active athletically.

Larry was interested in becoming a lawyer and when you're a coach, you do write a few letters of recommendation. Larry said, "Coach, would you write a letter of recommendation for me?" I said,

"Sure. No problem." That was the Monday before Thanksgiving. He came in the office and he had 14 applications. If you're familiar with applications to law school, no one question is the same in each application. I think they try to make sure that people understand it's not all the same. So he gave them to me and I said, "Larry, when do you have to have these back?" He said, "Any chance I could get them by Wednesday?" I laughed. So that night, I went home and we spread the applications out on the living room floor, took them individually into the dining room. I dictated to Pat and we did fourteen applications. When Larry came in Wednesday afternoon, they were ready.

I had a work-study girl at the time. Jay Gallagher and I left the office, which was in Teagle Hall. It was a very small cubicle. We went in and took one of the applications and copied it on University letterhead. We proceeded to write down the reasons that Liberato Carbone would like to go to law school. I said he was from Howard Beach, and he wanted to be a lawyer for the mob. I also stated that he was not very trustworthy, that he was the manager for the volleyball team, and on road trips, meal money disappeared. We went on and on and described all the things that people wouldn't want to read in a letter of recommendation.

Larry always had a tendency to put things underneath the chair in the office, and we laughed about it all the time. Jay and I left the office, knowing he was coming up. We could see him outside the window, and when he came in, we had the applications turned so he could read them on my desk. Of course, the counterfeit application was on top. He read it, and the work-study girl came running out after us. She said, "I think he fainted! He was sitting in the chair and he was white as a ghost!" So we walked in and revived him. It's something that stayed with us for years and years. All our players got a chance to hear about the prank that we pulled on Larry.

Today, he's a very successful lawyer. He has a high position with Con Edison in New York. He has a little boy that's about three years old, and I see him four or five times a year. Everybody looks for a silver lining or a bright star, and every time I see him, he brightens up my day because I think back to all the great things he did for us.

One of the most astonishing things is, he wanted to go to law school at Notre Dame, and he wanted to help out with the football team. Every time I see the movie "Rudy," I think of Larry. He didn't get accepted at a few of the schools that he applied to, but he got accepted at Cornell, and I feel he wanted to come to Cornell to stay with us.

On Larry's graduation day from law school, we were very fortunate. We were playing in a play-off game at North Carolina, and from what I understand, Larry was listening to the game with headphones. It was really exciting. They were ahead 4-3 at halftime, and we came out and went ahead 6-4. We hadn't been shooting very well when we got to Carolina. I understand that when we scored the goal that put us ahead, Larry decided that while the speaker at the graduation was offering his presentation, it was a good time to yell out, "Yay, Cornell!" Larry not only enjoyed law school, but he's known for his very loud shout-out during graduation.

I remember that Carolina had a small container of water for us on the bench when we had a workout. That immediately went over the top of the scoreboard and it scared the trainer from North Carolina. He immediately went in and got us huge buckets of Gatorade and water, realizing that the team could not live on a sip of water on a 90-degree day in Carolina.

After our workout, we planned to attend Mass. We had 22 players on our team that were Catholic. That day was Pentecostal Sunday weekend, so we went to Saturday Mass. Our players still had our winter sport jackets on because we hadn't had a chance to change. I didn't know this but the priest was also the chaplain for the athletic teams at North Carolina. He was happy to see the Cornell team. I looked around and I didn't see any North Carolina players. I saw some of their parents. The priest made a nice comment about how great it was that Cornell was there, and he asked if they realized that North Carolina had never lost a play-off game at home.

After church, we all walked out. I was the last to leave. I said, "Father, the bus over there has all the players in it… I want you to do two things. I want you to wave to them. And, if you could, I'd like you to root for us for at least a half. He said, "Oh, I can't do that." But he said, "I'll wave to them." I said, "Father, when you wave to them, when I get on the bus, I'm going to tell them that you wore those red vestments, and the church was draped out in red, and I said, "When you wave to them and I'm on that bus, I'm going to tell them that you wore those red vestments in honor of Cornell University."

And when I got on the bus, there was a huge cheer.

That's a great story. Now, I'm sure you can imagine that, after telling me what you did with Larry's law school application that made him almost have a heart attack, I can't wait to get his testimonial about you for this book...

That would be beautiful!

Continuing our trip down the Memory Lane of the athletic complex, I know that there were some February or March days when there might have been 10 inches of snow on that field in the morning. I'm going to guess that there were times when Mr. Graham and his grounds crew were unsung heroes.

Pat Graham and his crew were remarkable. Plowing turf is tough, mainly because the equipment we had was not designed for plowing turf, and there was always a worry about lifting and tearing up the turf, which could happen very easily. So scheduling a practice could be challenging. We'd get to the office, and I'd always get the weather report a couple of days in advance. Usually we got weather from Chicago, and usually a day or a day and a half later, we'd get almost the identical type of weather that they had in Chicago.

So, we tried to prepare ourselves. Barton Hall was not available because it was used almost 18 hours a day, and as for the polo barns - we'd had enough of the polo barns for 2 weeks. We would try to work out something where we could get a chance to practice, so what we would do is try to arrange to get into Barton Hall early in the morning, knowing that we were going to have snow.

Our first game was usually somewhere around the second week in March. Pat was kind enough to take charge of as much as he could. Pat's staff also shoveled snow, because once you shovel some of the snow off, and the sun hit it, the turf is a lot hotter. So when it was 30 degrees outside; the turf would be about 40-45, and that would help melting.

One particular Saturday, we had planned a double session and that Friday we got some snow. We made some push shovels. We took some boards and put them on the end of broken lacrosse sticks and we pushed the snow off. And by doing this, it enabled us to get it melted so we could get through the afternoon practice.

I also give a lot of credit to my coaching staff - Mike Waldvogel,

Billy Hall, Bruce Arena, Scott Anderson—all these men were really tremendous, and they all went on and had great careers.

People reading the book might think they recognize Bruce Arena's name. He climbed to the absolute top of his profession as a soccer coach, right?

That's correct. He coached the United States National Team. He presently is the coach of the Los Angeles Galaxy of Major League Soccer. They won the pro championship a couple of times.

He's also the same Bruce Arena that snuck Eamon out to get him sewed up after he got beat up at the frat party…

That's correct.

Let me rephrase that: He didn't get beat up. He got punched at the frat party, but then took care of business.

Right…Bruce and I and his wife Phyllis were just together. We were also with Larry Young, one of my former players that was Bruce's roommate. They lived on Seneca Street and that house was unbelievable. They had one guy that was neat, neat as could be. They had another guy who probably would have been a star in that "Hoarders" series on television. If I had gone into that house, I probably would have been carrying a bazooka because probably the best way to clean that house up was to blow those rooms up. There are so many stories from that house, and that night we all got together at Larry Young's house—he lives on Cayuga Lake. Larry was an attackman. He came from Rochester. His father was a minister. I often wondered what his mother and father said when they went to visit that famous house on Seneca Street! I wouldn't be surprised if they made it a part of the historic district, because all those guys in that house created some kind of history.

The stories are just remarkable. They're actually real, and some people look at me in amazement and say, "Did that really happen?" They definitely did happen.

Those stories might be more appropriate for a book written under a different name, intended for a different audience…

Accolades

Richie, I know over the years it has meant a lot to you that you've been recognized for quite a number of awards, and I'd like to ask you about the United States Intercollegiate Lacrosse Association (USILA) Coach of the Year awards. You had quite a run there in the '70s and '80s, didn't you?

You know, 1971 was a building year for us. We had come off a great season in 1970. There was no national championship tournament at the time. It was voted on by a committee. And then in '71, we actually won the championship on the field. The award I received was the Coach of the Year award and that's an award that you really share with your assistant coaches, and the rest of the people that helped us in the program. The support staff, the fans, the players - it was a beautiful honor that was presented to me at the convention that was held in Baltimore that year. It gave me a great opportunity to accept the honor on behalf of Cornell University and the Cornell Lacrosse team.

How long had that award been in existence at that time? Do you know?

I think the award went back to the '40s. It was called Morris Touchstone Coach of the Year Award. Morris Touchstone was a very successful lacrosse coach at West Point for a number of years, and the award was named after him.

You won it again in '77 and '87, too. Was there a big difference between those second and third times of winning it?

Again, it's an honor that you share with many people. The 1977 and '87 teams were remarkable teams. The respect that the program got was based on a tradition of Cornell athletics, including lacrosse. That tradition goes back to 1892, so when your program starts being recognized on a national level, it gives everybody a lot of pride. I can share that pride with many people and many players.

The momentum that your teams had there during the winning streak of '76, '77 and '78 obviously put you in contention to be the coach of Team U.S.A. How was that decision made?

We won the title in '77, and the process was the coaches that won titles in their various divisions were selected to the coaching staff for the United States team. Jerry Schmidt, the Hobart coach who has since passed away, was the Division III coach. Tom Flatly was the coach of the Long Island Athletic Club, and they won the club championship. I was the Division 1 coach.

I was hoping they would select someone from Division II, because I've always been a firm believer that there's really not that much difference between the divisions, especially in those days. We did play Division III teams and Division II teams, and those teams were very good.

As an example, Hobart was a D-3 program, but they could hold their own with anybody, right?

That is correct.

I know they ultimately moved to D-I.

Yeah. And then you had Adelphi and you had teams like UMBC and Towson. So those games were very powerful. Here again, it was a remarkable situation for the coaches and the players. We had players that were nominated to compete at the tryouts, and we had over 150 applicants. We had a meeting to discuss which applicants fulfilled the criteria for selection, based on their performance for that year and the year before.

The try-outs were held in '77, at Penn State. Coach Joe Paterno was kind enough to come to some of our practices to talk to the players who were trying out. I actually had an opportunity to spend some time with him, and he was very gracious and nice. At that time, I think he was preparing to assume two titles: head football coach and athletic director - he was a remarkable person.

Our practice plan called for double practices on Friday night and again on Saturday and a single practice on Sunday. The coaching staff felt five practices really gave us an opportunity to look at our talent.

Ultimately, we went from 100-plus applicants down to a logical figure of about sixty. We had a committee that was available to help us with the selection, so it wasn't just the three coaches that were making the decisions. The committee consisted of ten other coaches, including some club team and collegiate coaches. At that time, some of the players were playing club lacrosse. That was really big in those days. That was before professional indoor and outdoor lacrosse, so the selection was tough. To pick two goalies out of a group of twelve was not easy.

We made the final selections. One of the unfortunate things was that our team was not subsidized by anybody, which meant that when you were picked, you had to either raise your own funds or pay for your own trip. The games were in Manchester, England, and we were going to tour various parts of Europe. From Manchester, we were going to go to Oxford. From Oxford, we were going to go to Germany. From Germany, we were going to go to France. So it was quite an extensive tour. It was a hardship for some players, and in fact, two of the players we selected had to drop out because of financial reasons; they were very good shooters, but unfortunately that's going to happen when you have to rely on funding your own program. We did try to raise funds, but that's something that takes a huge effort. We put forth the effort, and we did raise some money and we were fortunate to have Joe Banks give us team blazers, shirts and ties.

Joseph Banks, the clothing guy?

Right... So that was very nice.

We brought everybody together and practiced at Cornell for 2 days before we left for England. It was an adjustment when we got to England. We look at sandwiches in the United States the size of Subway. They look at sandwiches in England the size of hors d'oeuvres, so we were running into a little bit of a nutrition problem, but we got that solved pretty quickly.

The games started, and we opened against Canada. Canada was going through some difficulty, as their goalie had to leave due to a family matter. We dominated Canada, and we then played the favorite to win the tournament that year, which was Australia. In a real hard-fought contest—physically, mentally, emotionally—we beat Australia. We were fortunate; we got a day off and I guarantee you all the players sat in a tub for a long time to take care of the bruises and bumps.

When we arrived in England, I felt it would be nice to get out in the countryside to enable our players to see a lot of the country. We went to Leeds and we put an exhibition game on against the team that was picked from an English All-Star group. It was quite a tough contest. I happened to have a number of boxes of Big Red gum, and I didn't realize how popular you can be in a place like Leeds when all these young boys and girls came up and you gave them gum. I'm sure they didn't know what the Big Red stood for, but it was really pleasing to give out the gum to these young children.

We also left some souvenirs for the people in Leeds. We had extra shirts, and Leeds was a very poor section at that time. It might have been that area in England where they did a lot of mining, and it was just gratifying that our players were so welcomed by them, and our players really enjoyed sharing with the people there.

After our game with Australia, we had a day off. We then went back to our training base, which was Stockport. Manchester and Stockport are a short distance apart, and we practiced prior to our game against England. That gave us an opportunity to rest our legs and get ready for England.

We played England in a quagmire. The stadium field had games on it before we played, and it had rained all day. I really didn't know if the North Sea was coming up or it was just the rain, but it was a very difficult field to play on. England played with a tremendous amount of pride. The cheers in the stands were echoing all over the stadium. "England! England! England!" While they played a tremendous game, we were fortunate to win by two goals.

At that time, the World Games consisted of four countries: the United States, Australia, England and Canada. We didn't have a day off before the championship game, which was played against Canada. In the process, we knew that it was going to be a game that we'd really have to be at the top of our game for because once you beat a team, they were going to come back and come back with a vengeance. The game went back and forth. Both teams played very well. We shot well, they shot well, and our defense provided excellent support for our goaltenders.

With 35 seconds to go in the game, we were up by one goal. Canada came down and put a lot of pressure on our goalie, who made some good saves. He threw an outlet pass to one of our defensemen. There was no stalling in those days, and we brought the ball up-field. We should have held the ball out. One of our defensemen decided to go to the cage, and he took a shot. The ball ricocheted off the goaltender. They picked the ball up, threw it up-field, and they scored the tying goal with about five seconds to go. We went into overtime, but unfortunately lost.

That was a real tough set-back, because anytime you represent your country, the red-white-and-blue is pretty important. I didn't fight the Revolutionary War. I wasn't in the colonies when England was dominating, but we played Canada on English soil and we got beat. It was very tough. Getting on the bus to go back to our quarters, it was complete silence.

I can imagine how that defenseman felt.... It's a team thing, right?

Correct. To this day I've never mentioned his name. I've been asked a number of times and I refuse to do that because we had a great team effort. The World Games had been played a couple of times before 1978, so we were the first U.S.A. team to lose. And that was a tough year for me. We lost in the NCAA championships and then we lost in the World Games.

Those were the first two losses you'd seen in a long time.

The magnitude was the thing that got to me. You always want your players to win a national championship, and I definitely wanted those players to win a world championship. In recent years, American teams have lost in the World Games, including last year, and the nemesis has always been Canada. So since '78, the games have been played every 4 years and we've lost on two occasions besides '78, including last year in Denver.

How many Big Red players were on that '78 roster?

Bruce Arena was on the team, Eamon, Dave Devine, Bob Hendrickson, Craig Jaeger, Dan Mackesey, Chris Kane, and Bill Marino. Rick LaFrance was the trainer.

What about Mike French?

He played for Canada. In fact, he scored some big goals in that championship game.

That's a crazy twist in the plotline.

Yes. In fact, he was voted the Player of the World Games.

I'd like to ask you about the Tewaaraton Award. Is it fair to say that it's the lacrosse equivalent of the Heisman Trophy?

Yes, it is to a player.

I know that Max Siebald and Rob Pannell of Cornell have won that prestigious award, and I'd like to know how it came to be, and what role you played in its creation.

Twenty-some years ago, I was in Florida and I got a phone call wanting to know if I would be available to be chairman of an award that the University Club of Washington D.C. was planning to create. The University Club of Washington D.C. is very famous. A couple of presidents – I know Howard Taft was one of them - were members. It is a club where everybody gathers. It generates a lot of interest, politically and socially.

Several members had a strong connection to lacrosse, and they decided that it might be a great thing to start an award that they could call their own, representing the University Club of Washington D.C. They had done some research on it, and had spoken to people that were connected with the various Native American tribes. They spoke to representatives from the Mohawk and Onondaga Nations, and word spread.

We then started discussing the trophy. There was a gentleman named Fred Kahl that did some beautiful sculptures. We commissioned him to do a trophy that we could present to both male and female award recipients.

When I came back from Florida, I went down to D.C. and spent a couple of days at the University Club. We were planning to have a dinner in May, after the championships, to honor the finalists. My duty, as chairman, was to set up a committee of coaches. We had a woman's representative set up the female committee. The committee consisted of coaches from Division I, Division II and Division III that were still actively coaching, and a few coaches that had retired but were still active in the game.

We had a conference call every week for the last 3 weeks of the season to determine what players would fit the criteria for finalists. We picked five. Films were submitted to us; information was gathered, and a lot of us went to see players in competition. We made every attempt to see as many candidates as possible. These players were recommended by their coaches as potential recipients of the award. The media staff at the various colleges and universities provided us with all the statistical data, all the information on the players. That gave the committee a tremendous amount of assistance in determining who the best male athlete would be. On the women's side they did the exact same thing.

The dinner was held at the University Club. Players arrived 2 days before the event and we held a dinner for them, their parents, and coaches. The next day, we had a remarkable tour of the Capitol. We had to submit material on all of us that were going to go to the Capitol - IDs, Social Security numbers, if you had a passport, they wanted you to bring it along.

Everybody went through without any complications at the checkpoint...except for me. I was asked to step aside. I was a little concerned. I knew that there was a mobster in Chicago back in the '20s, by the name of Bugs Moran, but I definitely wasn't a relative, so I was trying to figure out why I was being held up.

A gentleman came over to me and said, "Have you been to Ireland lately?" I realized I had two passports. I had an Irish passport and a U.S. passport. So of course, that raised some questions. I explained to them about me going to Ireland—my parents were born there - so I qualified for an Irish passport. After security personnel talked among themselves, they gave me permission to continue. I felt very secure because they were diligent in determining whether a person had the right to proceed.

So after the tour of Washington, D.C., we got together with young lacrosse players in the D.C. area and held a clinic. For the awards dinner that night, I asked Dick Schaap - who was a very good friend of mine - if he would be our M.C. It really was a great night. We had the Monsignor from Washington, D.C., do the invocation. It was wonderful that an award that people in the lacrosse world had thought about and planned for years was now going to come to fruition.

It was really a tremendous night for everybody that was connected with lacrosse. In fact, when tickets went on sale, they sold out in about an hour and a half. Each year, the event has gotten bigger.

I was really delighted that I was part of the committee involved with the founding of the award. I stayed on the committee for 6 years. Unfortunately, one of my good friends, Dick Adell, became ill, so I wanted him to be chairman, to give him an opportunity to stay involved in the game he loved so much. He stayed on for 4 or 5 years.

Over the years, the Tewaaraton Award started branching out with additional awards, including the Spirit of Tewaaraton. They also honored players that would have been recipients of this award. Since they didn't have it while they were playing, they started honoring them. Eamon was honored posthumously, and I was honored that same night for the Spirit award.

Other Halls of Fame:

Sewanhaka High HOF – Manhasset High School HOF - Nassau County HOF – Long Island HOF - University of Maryland Athletic HOF – Cornell University Athletic HOF – United States National Lacrosse HOF

Fulfilling a Dream

Richie, you were talking about your Irish passport, and it seems like a good time to ask this question: When you were at the World Games, were you wishing there was an Irish team?

That didn't happen until 2001. They did have lacrosse in Ireland until about 1933. In fact, they have plaques and trophies going back to 1875, but from what I gather, the Gaelic Athletic Association disbanded a lot of sports that we competed in against England back in the '30s, and lacrosse was one of them. There is a great history of Ireland lacrosse, traveling to the United States in 1904. They had a famous team called the Shamrocks that played in Canada. They also had teams in Belfast, so the history can be quite interesting.

In 2001, on a Sunday afternoon, I got a phone call and the person asked me if I had an interest in Ireland lacrosse. I said, "Yes, but to my knowledge, there's not a program." The caller said, 'Well, they put together a team last year and they went to the European Games." So, evidently, someone got information about European games and they invited Irish-American players and players from Ireland that had some experience with lacrosse. The games were in Sweden, and they didn't fare very well. I think the scores were up in the high 20's. Ireland didn't score many goals.

They found out that some of the other countries were very advanced in the game of lacrosse. The conversation started with the caller asking if I would help do some fundraising, and once I started hearing the scores, I said, "We have to do more than fundraise. We've got to build a program that people can have some pride in. We've got to see if the National Sports Council in Ireland will start contributing and maybe recognize lacrosse."

Because you can raise all the money in the world, but if you don't have a good product on the field, they won't support the effort.

Exactly... So the person said, "Thank you for your advice," and we hung up. I sat down and I said, "God, that's a strange phone call." And then about 45 minutes later, I got another call and this time it was "Would you like to coach the Irish program?" I said, "I thought you were going to say 'team' but we don't have a team." And they said, "We'd really like you to think about coaching the program."

And with that, I said, "Give me some time to think about this and I'll call you back tomorrow." So I thought about it. I always wanted to do something for my parents. So this was kind of a gift back to my parents, to take a sport that provided a lot of great opportunities for me and present it to young athletes in Ireland.

My wife has always been a great backer of things that I wanted to do, and has always helped me accomplish the goals I was reaching for. I think she realized at that time, although I was retired, I definitely was not going to build a patio or a new deck. And when it came to any kind of construction or home projects, I definitely was going to give her the Yellow Pages.

I needed some hobbies, and I felt that this would be a great hobby. With that, I started putting a staff together, and started checking with people in Ireland about facilities that we could use. I had wonderful connections with lacrosse companies in the U.S. and they were very willing to assist us. We had try-outs in the United States for Irish-American players, because we knew that if we were going to be in any kind of international competition, we were going to need some pretty good players. The try-out was at Hofstra. We had 75 people come to qualify for the Irish team.

The try-out was fantastic. We placed eight evaluators up in the press box, and they evaluated the personnel. We had a morning session and an afternoon session. We set up games so we could see players under game conditions, and we started getting an idea of who we would select.

You may be amazed to hear that Cornell alum Tim Goldstein tried out. His mother's name is Kathy O'Sullivan, and she and I went to high school together.

I grant you that Goldstein doesn't quite sound Irish.

How much time elapsed between the try-outs and when you were actually going to be in competition?

A year and a half.

That felt like a comfortable cushion for you to develop this team to where it needed to be?

Yes, and we had some people in Ireland start getting players ready. We finally got down the final squad and we had some exhibition games on Long Island, New Jersey, and Connecticut that were extremely well attended. They were great fundraisers. We would have events afterward at the various Irish headquarters that were frequented by many people. The club in Connecticut is enormous. It had three levels and we had close to 500 people come to that event.

That enabled us to start getting money to acquire equipment and uniforms. We had a uniform company by the name of Macwear, who actually was owned by one of the players that was going to be on the team, James McAleavey. James played at University of Massachusetts, and I actually recruited him when he was in high school. He was one of 16 children and his family sent him to St. Paul's School in Garden City, so it didn't work out for James to come to Cornell, but we always stayed friends. His company was great in providing uniforms for us which were dazzling, beautiful uniforms. He did a lot with the colors: green, white, and orange—the colors of the Irish flag.

During our exhibition games, we really started to mesh. For the games in Connecticut, we brought the players over from Ireland, and it gave them a chance to see lacrosse firsthand in a great setting.

Did you have a ratio of how many players could be Irish-American and how many players were actually going to be Irish?

The ratio really started the following year. As we saw the players develop in Ireland, we realized that we could mesh them in, put them into various schemes and various units and they would feel comfortable. And it would be athletic. One of the things in Ireland, you have young men that are great runners. Unfortunately, some of the guys we had play for us were not great runners. Paddy O'Leary was a cross-country runner; he could run all day and all night. So he sort of set the tone. The next time we had try-outs in Ireland, we started putting club teams together at the various colleges in Ireland.

So we started a farm system to try to get players to get as much exposure as possible, because if you don't play against top competition, you pretty much level off, and we needed to escalate.

If the squad consisted of 24 players, we would try to have twelve Irish and twelve Americans who were Irish passport carriers. And that worked out well. And then we started gradually going toward ten Americans and fourteen Irish. Then, for the first time ever, we had an under-19 team. Eleven of those players came from the United States, but it gave us a chance to start developing them at an earlier age because when we first started developing, the development was done at the club level. With colleges, that would put it in like an intra-mural program. So there wasn't consistency. Lacrosse is like tennis; you have to practice it. You have to put some mileage into it. You just don't pick the stick up one day and then put it away for a month. You have to stay sharp. So those are things that we were emphasizing greatly in Ireland.

That first year, we went to Australia with the help of a great benefactor from Cornell by the name of Charles "Chuck" Feeney. Mr. Feeney owned a huge complex in Brisbane, Australia, called Couran Cove, and we trained there.

Was it an athletic complex?

Yes. In fact, that's where I met the International Blind Runners. They were there at the same time we were. Also, the New Zealand Blacks rugby team was there. It was designed to be an athletic training ground. It also brought in the beauty of Australia back in the early 1900's. Homes were built on stilts over the water. It was right near the Pacific. They had a five-star restaurant there. When we were there, the German Olympic team was training. The Irish Olympic team was training there as well, which consisted mainly of swimmers. Greece had their runners there, so it was like an Olympic village.

Mr. Feeney was so gracious to us, and really helped us prepare for the games in Australia. Our first practice after we got to Australia was interesting. In my mind, the plane trip was short, and in everybody else's it was a long trip. Flying is mental, if you just enjoy it. Make sure you stretch out. Make sure your legs don't clot, and you will get to your destination with a smile on your face.

Well, we had everybody stretch out. The next day, we had a great practice. We had everybody go for a walk, get acclimated to the temperatures and to being on level ground after a long flight.

We gave everybody a program to work on in advance to get in top condition. It was obvious to me that if you were playing in the World Games, it was important to realize how important conditioning would be. Some realized it was important, and some probably had not opened the envelope yet. We started off with leg work. We built it up, and we went to do some heavy agility and quickness drills. Before you knew it, we had a couple of players that were coming up with the most unbelievable ailments that I've ever heard in athletics. I got the three of them together, and it was obvious that they had built this up in their minds that they were going to come on this trip for a vacation. I said, "You hurt your hip? You have a calf problem? And you have a thigh problem? Three different problems?" I said, "Well, I spoke to the trainers from New Zealand's rugby team. What I'm going to have you do is to go over there and practice with the New Zealand rugby team." I couldn't believe how quickly they recovered.

The former altar boy inspired a miracle recovery?

I know the Lord, and I know God performed a lot of miracles, but this miracle had to go down in history. Those three guys got right back in the action and they made up what they had missed after practice.

So they saw these monster rugby guys with no teeth and they didn't think they wanted any of that?

Yeah. I think what scared them is when one guy hit a blocking sled and blew it up to pieces! I don't know if it was the design but the matting came off and one of the metal bars popped off. And you could hear that thing just come apart. When they saw that, they realized that they were on safer ground with us.

Their "injuries" didn't hurt quite so much?

Right. Then, of course, we had policies about training, about respecting the other countries and the other teams that were there. We had breakfast with the gentlemen that were there for the international event for blind athletes. That was a thrill. They were remarkable athletes, and we enjoyed meeting the people that would be called caregivers or trainers….

Guide runners.

Guide runners—you couldn't ask for nicer people.

So we were on our third day of practice, and we wanted to get a chance to see a little bit of Brisbane. We had a policy that everybody should be back by 11, which gave them ample time. One of our policies was not to over-indulge, because that stuff stays with you for about 48 hours. We were going to have double sessions the next morning and a single session in the afternoon. You better make sure your body holds up. Ninety percent of our players understood that. The other 10 percent got to understand it a lot better at the practices that next day.

That night, they all went out, and we had a guy that evidently was still on California time. He got to the gates, which were locked at 11 o'clock to protect the athletes. They had guards in the area, and he attempted to come over the fence. They apprehended him and brought him back to my room. It was interesting… he became the night runner. I had him pack all of his equipment, and we had great travel bags. They were really beautiful travel bags—black, endorsed by NIKE, the side of it said "Ireland Lacrosse," we were very proud of them. I had him put the straps on his back, and he ran the track. Everyone said it was probably an hour. I thought it was only a half hour.

And he thought it was three hours…

I think I got the message across and it worked out better. It helped us tremendously. When we got to the games in Perth, we finished 5-0 and won our division. Since we were the new country, we couldn't play the teams up above us, but what a thrill it was to go 5-0.

What year was that?

That would have been 2003.

Here we are now, in 2016. When will you next be with the Irish team?

I'm working as an advisor right now. We developed other coaches, and I just felt as I moved closer to the century mark, that it's probably good to make changes. I'm not giving in to young people but I think it's good to create a different coaching culture.

You fulfilled your dream of helping to plant that seed there, in honor of your family and your heritage.

Yes. That's right.

Good on ya, Mate! Sorry… that's Australian…

They Made It All Possible

> Richie, as I go through the Cornell lacrosse archives, and I think back to growing up in this area (graduating from high school in 1974) I remember seeing you and your teams front and center in the *Ithaca Journal.*

If I drop a few names, would you tell me something about some of these players? I'd love to do a chapter about each one of them but given we don't want this book to be the size of Webster's Dictionary, that's not really a practical thing to do. We did a long piece about Eamon, and those are some great stories. I know that one of his famous partners in crime was Mike French. What can you tell me about Mike?

Cornell is extremely attractive to students from Ontario, and Mike came here for a visit. The close proximity, the educational values, and the fact that Ken Dryden, along with a number of other Canadian student-athletes, had such success here – all of those factors made it attractive. Mike was a good student and he was looking at Cornell. He was a superb basketball player and played box lacrosse, but at that point he had never played field lacrosse.

I happened to meet him when the admissions office called and said, "We have a gentleman by the name of Mike French visiting campus. He has played box lacrosse and he seems interested in Cornell." So I went over and met him; of course, Mike was a very good looking young man from the standpoint of size, and he had a great smile. He had blonde-reddish hair, and he really stood out.

We had a chance to talk, and I said, "Would you like to make the transition from box lacrosse to field lacrosse?" I had played box lacrosse and knew that his skill set was going to be tremendous because of his experience in box lacrosse. I said, "It can be done very easily. In fact, freshmen are not eligible to play on varsity teams at Cornell, and you would play freshman lacrosse, which would really benefit you and help your transition."

He became very enthused about Cornell, and we spoke on the phone a couple of times. He came from Niagara-on-the-Lake, which is a magnificent area. One of his best friends was a quarterback at Ithaca College, and they had a very fine team. In fact, his friend was also a boxer when he left college.

So we went through the admissions process. Mike was accepted, and he started developing as a player. Jonathan Levine and Bill Marino were on that freshman team, and they helped him refine his skills and transition to field lacrosse. Mike was a good shooter. Handling a field lacrosse stick is a lot different; it's a lot wider. His precision started to develop; his accuracy developed, and with his teammates working with him, you could see that this group could potentially be an outstanding team because they worked so well together as freshmen.

Of course they felt a little stifled because they had come out of very prominent programs all over the country, and they had played before big crowds. Now they're playing freshmen games before much smaller crowds, and it was a big difference. But they worked hard, they played hard, and they were starting to build our teams for the future.

Mike was a tremendous contributor and, if I needed one word to describe him, it would be "Dedication." He was very dedicated to his teammates; and still is today. He was very diligent in becoming a better player. His parents did a great job. Mike was the first young man in his household to go to college.

He also was an excellent basketball player. We had a barnstorming basketball team that I never knew about. In fact, if they had played for money, they probably would have made more barnstorming than they did upon graduation!

I'd also like to point out that Mike was the Lt. Raymond Enners

Award winner as the outstanding player in Division 1 in 1976. That same year, he was also the recipient of the Jack Turnbull Award, which goes to the outstanding attackman.

Nice. I remember a lot of the reading I did suggested that the McEneaney and French combo was kind of like Mantle and Maris, or Jordan and Pippen or one of those partnerships. The legendary "French Connection." They were a well-known and highly-respected duo, weren't they?

Yes, they were—no question, but the catalyst for that group was a gentleman by the name of Jon Levine. Jon was really interesting. He came from Long Island. I first met him at camp. He was a junior in high school and he had a twin brother, Harmon. Harmon was a lot more vocal, and stronger, but Jon was very wiry and quick. He had excellent feet and excellent range. Plus, he was a lefty, which is of great value in lacrosse.

I had both of them on my camp team (at St. Paul's School on Long Island), and both were wonderful young men. Their parents did a great job. Jon really wasn't a big scorer on Long Island, but I felt that he had potential. Once he started to fill out, get stronger, I knew he could be a tremendous asset to us.

To this day, I've not seen a left-hander with the moves that Jon had. He had the basketball backdoor move. He had the ability to change direction, do inside rolls, catch the ball in traffic, and shoot with accuracy even while he was getting knocked down. In fact, in one of our games, he got hit hard well after the shot was taken. A penalty was assessed to the opponent, and his teammates really rallied around him. They would really get upset because this was a brotherhood, and you don't do that to one of our brothers. The opponents paid the price that day because we became very physical. We were more of a finesse team, an agile, sportsmanlike team. However…

There was a statement to be made?

Yes. The other team was headhunting and we were shoulder-blocking. We didn't go for the head. So Jon was very accurate, and we wouldn't have that had the French connection without Jon Levine.

And it's interesting: The "French Connection" consisted of an

Irishman, a Canadian, and a Jew! If you ever go to heaven, all three of those religions will be sitting right beside each other. That was some combo!

What do you mean "if??" Thanks a lot! Who else would you like to mention?

Dan Mackesey. Dan is a local product; he grew up in Ithaca. His dad was a Vice President at Cornell, and was famous in the architectural field. His mother was a remarkable person. Danny's family members went to various schools throughout the country, and Danny was destined to go to Brown University. His uncle was, at that time, a Vice President at Brown. Danny was an outstanding soccer player. At that time, the Cornell soccer program was starting to build up. We had a gentleman by the name of Bill Pentland. Bill was from Scotland, but he also was vice president of Therm, Inc., so he volunteered to help out coaching Dan's soccer team.

Then, Bill found that it was really difficult because of being on the road to recruit. During my first year at Cornell, I helped recruit for him, and we got some good players.

So then, we had Danny Mackesey thinking about Brown. I always go to the Cornell reunions and I was really delighted when I went to the reunion in 1973. Dan's mother was there; her class was gathering. They had a great band, and I asked her to dance. I said, "Mrs. Mackesey, at Brown, the same coach leads the soccer and lacrosse programs, and I don't think he is a very good dancer." I added, "I want you to give us a decision based on my dancing ability." So that night, I think Fred Astaire and Gene Kelly touched my shoulder, and I became an outstanding two-stepper.

Whatever it takes...

You got it! And we laughed and laughed. I had a great conversation with Dan's dad. We were delighted that Dan decided to come to Cornell. He was tremendous in goal in soccer and in lacrosse. His stopping ability was remarkable. He was an All-American, All Ivy, just a great player. The wonderful thing about Dan, he was such a leader. He was an NCAA scholar, and he analyzed a defense like you would analyze a problem in chemistry or physics. He knew every detail. He would watch the opposing players in warm-ups, and knew exactly where they were going to be shooting the ball. So he was a student of the game—just a remarkable person to have on our team.

Danny was having a little trouble during his senior year; he was a left-handed goalie and he was having a trouble with balls going to his right side. I decided, "Dan, I think we should go get an eye exam." So he went to get an eye exam and Danny was suffering from what is known as a "tired eye." That's how it was described to me in the '70's. He was doing an extensive amount of reading, without good lighting, and his right eye was being affected. So, sure enough, they made some adjustments and prescribed contact lenses. In 1976, he had the only shut-out in the history of the NCAA play-offs.

Wow… Against?

Washington-Lee, 14-0, at Cornell. He also won the Ens. C.M. Kelly, Jr. Award as the outstanding goalie in Division 1 in 1976 and 1977.

Who's up next?

There's Jon Gordon, who is now a very successful writer and motivational speaker. He speaks all over the country, and in fact, I'm positive he's done some international speaking. Jon came from Smithtown, Long Island, and was a football and lacrosse player.

One of the things that was essential for me when I was recruiting, I never recruited a player that did not play more than one sport. That's because you develop a lot of instincts, a lot of skills, muscular structure, coordination and agility from playing other sports.

Jon was a running-back in football and a mid-fielder and a face-off man for us. In fall practice, about the fourth day, I always told the players, "When you come to Cornell, I'm available to you 24 hours a day. My wife and I will both be available. If I'm out of town, I want you to get in touch with my wife. She'll get back in touch with me. If there's a solution needed for your problem, we will have that within record time."

Well, embracing that open-door policy, Jon came up a few hours before a fall practice in October. He said, "Coach, can I speak to you?" I was doing some paperwork and I looked up and said, "Sure. Won't you have a seat?" He had a seat, I put the material aside and went over and sat next to him. I said, "Jon, what can I do for you?"

I know freshmen get homesick. I know freshmen are concerned

about what they're doing, why are they here, wondering whether they made the right choice. And you have to give them a lot of guidance and a lot of positive vibrations.

We talked about school; that was going well. We talked about his dorm; things were fine there. Jon was getting heckled by some of his teammates because he brought his football highlight film from high school. I guess one night in the dormitory he decided to let his friends see the highlight film, so, of course, they went wacky over this film. I thought maybe he was having a little difficulty with his teammates, but his comment was "Coach, I'm not playing enough. I think I could really help this team." I said, "Jon, there's no question. You're progressing quite nicely." He said, "Well, I think I should be up with the first unit." We hadn't even put units together. In fact, in my entire coaching career, the starting line-up was not known until game day. Players worked every day to make that starting line-up.

So I didn't put names up. As for statistics, the only statistic we ever had in the locker room was how many ground balls an individual picked up or what kind of defensive play was made.

So with that, I stood up and I said, "Jon, lacrosse players make this team every day. You just continue to work as hard as you are working. Don't worry about where you should be or where you shouldn't be, or where you want to be. Just keep playing. Just do it."

I patted him on the back. Now, as I mentioned to you, Jon's a motivational speaker. He spoke to the Jacksonville Jaguars. I had a friend who was an assistant coach with the Jaguars. He called me up and said, "Coach, do you know Jon Gordon?" I said, "Sure." He said, "Did you ever kick him in the ass?" I said, "What?" He said, "He came into your office one day and he wanted more playing time, and on the way out, you kicked him in the ass." I said, "Well, I patted him on the back and if his anatomy shifted then I probably did, but it was a pat on the back."

That's for the record? A "pat on the back?"

Right...For Jon Gordon. He made a tremendous contribution to our team. In the Army game, we were going into overtime. It was a great game. Jon faced-off for us, and the ball was rolling to the sidelines. He dove, picked the ball up, and threw the ball back to our offensive zone and one of our players - on a dead run - hit Joe

Lando with a pass. Joe turned, put the ball in the cage. So, we won the game in the first 14 seconds of overtime, thanks to Jon Gordon and Joe Lando.

Okay. Now, you've told me quite a bit about Bruce Arena's shenanigans when Eamon was a recruit. And we said that Bruce has gone on to become a very high-level coach in soccer. What did he bring to the lacrosse field?

Bruce played against my teams on Long Island. He went to H.F. Carey High School. I was coaching at Elmont, and we had just resurrected the program. We played Carey twice a year. We had some very fine mid-fielders, very good athletes who were also basketball players and football players. We also had one young man who was a tennis player with great wrists.

We played against Bruce's team, and Bruce and a couple of his teammates were players that we really had to mark very carefully. They were very good, and in one of the games, he had three goals. We won the game, and that was a time when we had all the teams line up and shake hands. I really don't remember doing that in high school when I played. As I was going down the line, I said special things to some of the players from Carey High School, and Bruce was toward the end of the line. I said to him, "What a remarkable performance you put on. Do you play any other sports?" And he said, "I play soccer." Well, the next time we played them was at their school, and after the game we were getting ready to go on the bus. He came over and he said, "You know, I told everybody that you talked to me after the first game." He said, "I would have loved to play football but I was too small. My parents were really worried about me playing"—even though his brother was a starting quarterback as a senior. So I said, "Well, just keep doing what you're doing."

Soccer is a tremendous sport. Bruce was a goalie. He always wanted to be in the action. I followed Bruce, and I saw him play in the summer league. I was still actively playing lacrosse, playing for a club team down at Jones' Beach, and Bruce was playing soccer on an adjacent field. They were playing a team from New York City, which consisted of a number of immigrants from Germany and Italy. It was a great team, and they could really move the ball. Bruce was called on to make some unbelievable saves. In fact, our game ended and a lot of the players came over and really rooted him on. Bruce's team might have lost 3-2, but it could have been 14-2 had it not been for his amazing goal tending against a highly skilled European team.

After that, I sort of lost track of Bruce. Bruce's parents worked very hard for the family, and it was very evident that all of them couldn't go to a four-year college. So Bruce went to a junior college, Nassau Community College. Richie Speckman, the coach at Nassau Community College and I are great friends. Richie was a tremendous quarterback at Cortland. He called me after Bruce's soccer season and he said, "Bruce Arena got stronger and bigger, and he said "I can't wait for him to play for me".

Every year, our "B" team played Nassau Community College. We played against Bruce, when he had four goals and two assists. The final score was 17-15, and we won, but it was a tremendous game. I was coaching at Cornell at that time. I was down on Long Island, where we had our "B" team travel to play Farmingdale and Nassau. Bruce wrote to me and said how much he wanted to come to Cornell.

So after his final year – during which he made Junior College All-American in both soccer and lacrosse - the doors at Cornell were hopefully going to open for him, and they did. Dan Wood was the soccer coach, and he was a remarkable coach. Dan Wood was, in my mind, almost like a Nobel Prize winner in coaching. He was also an excellent golfer. He was a kicker in football, soccer player, basketball player, baseball player. He could do it all. He went to Tufts, and I'm sure he's in the Tufts Hall of Fame.

Dan was delighted that we got Bruce, as he was developing a championship team. Bruce came to Cornell, and he played for me. He was captain of the team, he made All Ivy, he was named All-American, and he was just a tremendous, tremendous player.

We talked about Mike French, and his dedication; Jon Levine, and his perseverance; Dan Mackesey, and his intellect; Jon Gordon, and his durability. Bruce Arena's word is "inspiring."

It seems obvious that those seeds of inspiration just kept growing. If a person goes on to be the coach of the U.S. National team and pro franchises, they'd better be inspiring.

No question.

Who would you like to talk about next?

Jay Gallagher. I'd be remiss without mentioning what Jay Gallagher did for this team, as a player, and later as my assistant coach. He was very helpful in making sure that Bruce Arena was going to come to Cornell.

Jay was a 3-year starting defenseman, captaining the team as a senior when the Big Red was ranked third in the country and advanced to the NCAA semifinals. He was also a first-team All-Ivy player, and played in the 1974 North/South All Star Game.

We lost Jay on January 9, 1992, when he was only 39 years old. I think about him every day.

I remember Jay well, as a friend and colleague. He held his head high when talking about Cornell lacrosse. His memorial plaque is up there in the lacrosse complex, right next to Eamon's. I recall that Jay played a prominent role in the story about hiding Eamon's fraternity party injury from you.

Jay was a pathfinder, much like the Pied Piper. He would start piping and they would follow. He covered up for a lot of unusual things.

One night when he was a player, he was at the Pines Tavern, where the Collegetown Bagels shop is now. Ithaca College and Cornell students didn't really like each other at that time, and one of Jay's companions decided that this guy was pushing him around too much and was gonna punch him, so he did. A fight broke out, and the person that threw the initial punch jumped on the bar, ran across the bar to the exit by the kitchen, ran out of the kitchen door, and kept on running, right up Buffalo Street. The owner, Mr. Verrichio, was a state trooper but he owned this tavern. He came to my office a day later. He said, "Can you tell me the track guys that are really fast?" I knew immediately what he was getting at, once this was described to me.

Well, Jay took the brunt of that counter-punch being thrown, and the original punch was thrown by none other than Eamon McEneaney. After he punched the guy, he was on the bar, across the bar, out the door, and full speed up Buffalo Street. And of course, Jay covered up for him.

Again…

Yeah...That's what teammates are all about. My word for Jay would be "Brother."

I'd also like to say a few things about Aaron Jones. We talk about that young man to this day. I personally believe he would have been playing on Sundays, and I say this because he had an unbelievable vertical jump, remarkable speed, great hands, and as a freshman was a phenomenal player on the football field.

However, there was a little bit of a controversy about black athletes on the football squad, which was blown totally out of proportion. There seemed to be a battle at the quarterback position and I'm not really privy to all the details. But Aaron was pledging a fraternity and they recommended that he not play football. To this day, I regret it and I'm sure he does too.

There's a great picture that Jay got from a newspaper, when Aaron was in the 10th grade. It's a picture of Aaron and his mother - God rest her soul. She's telling Aaron that if he wants to go to lacrosse camp at Rutgers, he's got to do well in Math and English. Well, he did well in both. He went to camp, and when I saw him he was much more developed. His physical attributes, his speed—he could have been a tremendous sprinter. He just had it all.

Jay recruited Aaron Jones. Jay visited the Jones family a little bit more than you should, but it was something that he really wanted because we knew that he would benefit from Cornell and Cornell would gain an awful lot from having Aaron Jones here as a student-athlete.

To put a word in for Aaron Jones, it would probably be "determination." He was so determined to do his very best. Aaron wore his heart on his sleeve. I remember we lost a real tough game down in Philadelphia, and I had never seen players cry. Aaron was so brokenhearted, and I went up to him and I said, "Aaron, we'll be okay." And we were certainly more than okay. We got to the NCAA playoffs, and made it to the finals.

Someone described him to me just recently as one of the quickest defensemen they ever saw. His assortment of checks, his ability to cover—he would cover up for mistakes made by other people, and just gracefully do the job. His determination was at a level I haven't seen recently on the athletic field. In football, he would have been a tremendous receiver, and he was, when he was a freshman. He also would have been dynamite as punt returner. A lot of people would have been out of their shoes trying to catch him. He could cut on a dime. He would start at a gradual speed, put it into second gear, and all you would see is his heels. That's how quick he was.

On to Robert Henrickson…

Doctor Robert "Hondo" Henrickson?

Dr. Robert Henrickson, a veterinarian in Manhasset, Long Island. Robert's dad and I became great friends. His dad was a tremendous athlete, and was actually brought up in a few orphanages. He served in the Vietnam War, and was a very successful businessman. Unfortunately, he died from dementia. I lost a great friend. His nick-name was Whitey Henrickson, and he was so determined to do well for his family.

Robert was the only boy in the family. and he had two sisters. His parents – Whitey and Pauline - were just remarkable with that family. They did so many great things.

Whitey worked with a company called Burlington Mills. After that, he worked with the Worth company as an executive. That's a baseball and softball bat company. He had a lot of top baseball players at that time using their bats.

Whitey decided he was going to get a college degree, and he pursued that degree for 14 years, at night. He ultimately got his degree from C.W. Post. Whitey's dream was to be a coach and a teacher at a prep school, or possibly be a coach at a college. And he would have been a great one. He took a teaching job in the New York City school district. His first teaching job—if I'm not mistaken—was at John Adams High School, where he was a substitute teacher.

He went into the class and wrote his name on the board. He put down "Mr. Whitey Hendrickson." And with that, there was a roar in the classroom. Ninety-five percent of the class was black. And for Whitey to put his name up there as Whitey Henrickson I'm sure made for a lot of unusual comments and wise-cracks. But he loved teaching.

Now, Robert was making a decision about college. If he had received training earlier in life, this young man would have been an Olympian. There's not a sport he did not master. He played football and lacrosse at Cornell, and he definitely could have played basketball. His baseball ability growing up was second to none. His father was an outstanding baseball player. When it came time to recruit him, I would say he probably had offers from 15 top schools—including all the Ivies. So, considering the interest from all the Ivies, Columbia for football and basketball, and then all the other Ivy League schools for lacrosse or football... it was going to be tough.

I knew that he had an interest in veterinary medicine and we had a gentleman on Long Island by the name of Dr. Lou Schimoler, whose son, Paul, would later play for me. Dr. Schimoler was a very successful veterinarian. He's the gentleman that gave Eamon a job during intercession painting the vet hospital: the cages, the walls. And that in itself was a great story.

So when Dr. Schimoler and I sat in the living room with Mr. and Mrs. Henrickson, I think I said four words and Dr. Schimoler said all the rest. Bob came up for a visit with his parents, and spent a lot of time in the vet college. The professors in the vet school were just unbelievable. The people in the Agricultural and Life Sciences program met with him. The Arts and Sciences people met with him. He was an outstanding student and definitely a tremendous communicator. I was so delighted that he made the decision to go to Cornell.

Robert lived in Manhasset, Long Island, and after his visit, he was probably home for about three hours. I got a phone call, and he said "Coach Moran, I want to thank you for the remarkable visit I had. Of the schools I had visited, no one reached out to me like Cornell did." And he said, "I'm coming to Cornell."

With that, I knew we had a big piece of the puzzle, because he was also going to attract other players, because everyone around the country knew about him. He did remarkable things here. To give a name to him or one-word—I'd have to give some thought to it because it's really not easy. I'll keep thinking about it...

Oh, one outstanding memory... We were playing a league game and it was getting dark, so we had to turn the lights on. Evidently, the lights scared a dog. There's a picture in his vet hospital of this dog coming out on the field, going directly to him. And he's petting the dog. A ref came to me and told me to get the dog off the field. I replied, "How am I going to get the dog off the field when a future veterinarian is speaking to the dog?"

So… that's the description: He's the Dog Whisperer.

That's not bad... Okay. Let's go to Bob Rule.

You talked about him some in an earlier chapter, remembering his prowess in goal.

Bob Rule was a remarkable find for both our hockey program and lacrosse program. He could be one of the few in athletic history that have played on two NCAA championships in the same year. He won a hockey championship and a lacrosse championship. He was a very good hockey goalie. I was very impressed with him as an athlete. I happened to be recruiting on Long Island, and I always liked to take in basketball games, football games - sports that some of these young men I was looking at were playing. Bob was a tremendous linebacker at Manhasset High School, the same school that Jimmy Brown went to. And he had the same coach, Dr. Ed Walsh.

I really liked him as a player. He had played a limited amount of lacrosse; his main sport was hockey. He really used his hockey techniques in the first year he played lacrosse at Manhasset. He really improvised some techniques in goal-tending that people are using today. Bob Rule, Hall of Famer, has written a book about goal-tending, and his technique was super. He played on the winning USA team in the World Games. He was an All-American here at Cornell. In fact, he was First Team All-American in '71. Bob Buhmann, who passed away about a year ago; Bob made third-team. I don't know if that's ever been done.

What has never been done?

Two goalies from one team being named All American in the same season…. Bob Rule was a great catalyst for our defense. A rugged individual, and a very fine squash and tennis player. In fact, when John McEnroe needed a left-hander to practice against, he would call Bob Rule to work out with. To this day, Bob loves the fact that he came to Cornell. He started junior college for a year. He lived in Massachusetts, moved to Long Island, and got adjusted to becoming a Long Islander. He was just a remarkable player, very tenacious.

That's the word for him? Tenacious.

Yes. In 1971, Bob was the recipient of the Ens. C.M. Kelly, Jr. Award as the outstanding goalie in Division 1.

Let's finish up this section discussing Glen Mueller. What do you remember about Glen?

Well, Glen was recruited by Ned Harkness, just before I came to Cornell. Glen had played in an All-Star game on Long Island and Dick Belsito - whose father Luke Belsito was my assistant coach at Manhasset - recommended Glen to Cornell because his son, Dick, was playing at Cornell. His son had gone to the Naval Academy and transferred to Cornell, and that's how Glen got on the radar screen.

Glen could have played three sports in college. He was a tremendous football player in high school and a very fine basketball player. He did play on the varsity basketball team here at Cornell. He was also a tremendous lacrosse player.

Glen was about 6'4". Some people called him a monster.

What position?

He played attack.

That's a huge attackman, isn't it?

Yes, it is. He didn't really attempt to run by people; he ran over people. He was like a steamroller. That would shake up a lot of defensemen. We "rode" a lot—which means we put a lot of pressure on defense once they got the ball, after a shot or in a loose ball situation. I remember seeing players looking behind them to see where Mueller was because they didn't want to be anywhere in his zone. He covered ground tremendously. He had great strides. He was like a greyhound. He would go after you with a vengeance.

That's a game-changing skill, right? If somebody thinking not so much 'What am I going to do with this ball,' but thinking about 'Am I going to end up in the hospital?' that changes a few things.

It does. I watched Glen play against top athletes from other schools, top football players that were playing defense, and in those days, that was a big thing. You would try to get the biggest football players out playing defense, so we had size against size. And I saw a lot of people back down when Glen had the ball. He complemented his teammates so unbelievably. His work ethic made every man on that 1971 championship team want to work harder. It was contagious. Our scrimmages were remarkable. When we'd scrimmage each other, Red/White scrimmage, and sometimes we'd have scrimmages matching Long Islanders against Upstate New Yorkers. I wish I would have filmed those, because they were storybook.

What is the word for Glen?

For Glen Mueller, the word is "Overpowering."

Continuing with the people you wanted to mention on your trip down Memory Lane, who's up next?

Four-Star General John M. Paxton, Jr., assistant commandant, United States Marine Corps. I was very fortunate the day "Jay" walked into my office. It was right before Christmas vacation, during his freshman year.

What year would that have been, Richie?

1970.

So this was very early in your Cornell career?

Yes, he came in and I knew about Jay because he had also played football. He asked me if he could try out for lacrosse, and I told him I was always very enthused when we had athletes that had skills in one sport and could develop skills in another. That worked out very nicely for us at Cornell. As I have mentioned, I allowed walk-ons to try out, and that was very helpful to our program.

I gave Jay a lacrosse stick to take home during Christmas vacation. At that time, Cornell had a very lengthy break during Christmas. Students would complete their exams prior to the holidays, so everybody went home and had a chance to really let loose and relax. A lot of our players had jobs during the inter-session, which went from about mid-December all the way through about the third week in January. That was quite an extensive time. All of them were really delighted to get jobs, either during Christmas or right after Christmas, to help with the financing of their education.

I knew Jay would be going back to Pennsylvania, and I felt he was the type of individual that would be a great asset to our team. I could sense, from the meeting that we had, that he had qualities that all coaches look for. The young man was in ROTC, as were six other players on our team. Knowing that he played football, he was involved in ROTC, and also involved with a very tough academic program in the College of Engineering, gave me an overview of his character and commitment.

I would guess that the military piece of that puzzle gave you guys one more level on which to connect.

Pretty much so, and the wonderful thing—in the school of engineering, he was really doing an outstanding job. When I talked to him, I told him about the availability of scholarships in the engineering school, and I said I would like to endorse him as a candidate for one of those scholarships. And sure enough, he received it. To this day, he's thanked me greatly because it did eliminate a lot of financial burden on his parents.

So Jay came out for his first practice. As I have stated, our first practices were conditioning in Barton Hall early in the morning, or practicing in Oxley Arena, which was the polo field and equestrian center on campus. Jay was in great physical condition. I noticed his stick handling would need some work, but when someone is breaking into a new sport, you have to be very patient. His teammates were extremely helpful to him and the other walk-ons. That, to me, was a good indicator of the type of individuals that we had playing lacrosse. It was all about team.

In fact, the ceremony celebrating Jay's retirement from the United States Marine Corps was attended by over 75 Cornellians - his fraternity brothers, their wives, his former football teammates, and lacrosse teammates.

And that was 45 years after they all left Cornell, correct?

Yes. That was on August 4th, 2016, at the Marine Corps Barracks in Washington, D.C., which is very historic. That was built in 1801, and when the British burned Washington, D.C., that was one of the few areas that they did not touch. That evening was emotional and inspiring for everybody in the audience of close to 2,000 people. The Marine Corps Marching Band, which is terrific, was there. The Silent Drill Team... the ability of that team to present itself as one was remarkable. There were testimonials honoring both Jay and his wife, Debbie. Debbie received an award for all the work she did in Washington, D.C. for various organizations, a lot of them dealing with veterans and disabled members of the military and their families.

Ashton Carter, the Secretary of Defense, spoke. He and Jay had made a number of trips to war zones in Iraq and Afghanistan, on the front lines, and he spoke highly of Jay and his leadership. That was definitely recognized when he was at Cornell as a player. He was the first one out on the field, and the last one off the field. His discipline, his outlook on life, were amazing. When he graduated from Cornell, he had his pick of many jobs in the engineering field but he first had to fulfill his commitment to the Marine Corps. After his third year, he called me and said, "Coach, I'm going to re-enlist for a few more years." And those "few more years" lasted a total of 42. So he gave to his country almost everything that you can possibly give. He made extreme sacrifices, and he and Debbie raised a wonderful family.

When you say, "The United States Marine Corps," you have to look at all the men that have been in the Marine Corps. Semper Fidelis means "always faithful." Never leave a wounded or dead Marine behind. To me, that's a motto that represents Jay Paxton and the United States Marine Corps. His honor on August 4th was well-deserved. There were a number of Generals in attendance. Colonels, Majors, male and female officers, enlisted men, Sergeant Majors—which is a remarkable rank to receive in the Marine Corps—they were all there to honor Jay.

One Marine – Sergeant Major Anthony Spadaro - flew back from Japan, believe it or not. He's with the United States Pacific Command Post in Japan, where he worked under Jay. He flew back for the ceremony, and was going to fly back to Japan the next day.

Jay was kind enough to introduce me during his comments. I was very overwhelmed, humbled, and in all honesty, very choked up. He had me stand up, said a lot of things about our relationship and about my coaching. When the evening concluded, five or six people came up who had sons that either played against me or sons that played for me.

One of them happened to be a young man by the name of Anthony Spadaro, who actually came to my camp when he was 15 years old. The beauty is, he had such great memories of the Quick Stick Lacrosse Camp at Cornell. We hugged and took some pictures together. And yes, it is the same Anthony Spadaro who is now a Sergeant Major.

I met a number of other Marines that had participated in athletics. Some had played lacrosse. So it was a night of celebration. It was also a night of farewell, but to me, though, there will never be a closure with Jay Paxton, Debbie, and his family. I was very fortunate to have him play for us. He was a key member of our 1971 national championship team. In the printed program at his retirement ceremony, there was a picture of Jay in his lacrosse uniform - which was number 41. That was very special to me, that he would include that in his program.

We were all very lucky to have a person like Jay Paxton be a leader in the effort to protect our country. I have several wishes for him someday… He would make a remarkable college president, and he is what we need in Congress. I'm hoping that, after September, when he's fully relieved of his command and goes into retirement, I sure hope he considers some of those options. I know they're going to live in Virginia for a year to find out exactly where they want to settle. I'm probably a little selfish, but I wish he would relocate to Ithaca. He would be a great model for all our young people and our community.

It sounds like you're making an endorsement for Cornell's next president…

Yes, I am. I know Cornell's very liberal. I know that a person in the military would be looked at differently, but to become a Four-Star general is like receiving four doctorate degrees. So, figuratively speaking, he has a doctorate degree in organization, a doctorate degree in leadership, a doctorate degree in handling over 1,800,000 Marines, and he has a doctorate degree in being able to communicate at the highest level. His connections with all the top government officials would be an asset to any university or college. So,yes. I am endorsing him. If Dwight D. Eisenhower can be President of Columbia University, Jay Paxton has my endorsement for President of Cornell University!

Or whatever he wants to do next...

Exactly… I'm delighted that he came to Cornell. It was wonderful that he decided to come into my office to ask if a young man who had never played lacrosse had an opportunity to do so. To this day, I'm a firm believer in walk-ons in any sport. Give them a chance. Give them some time. Our fall practice allotment back then was

20 days, and the Ivy League decided to make it 12 days. And during those 20 days - which were maybe two days a week, three days a week - we had an opportunity to have these walk-ons work out and develop their skills. And believe it or not, here at Cornell, the total was probably about fourteen that made either All-Ivy, or All-American, or both.

That suggests that you had a keen eye for what you saw in a walk-on—the raw materials that you had to work with. I'm sure that there were some players that brought skill sets that were transferable to lacrosse, and others maybe not so much, but the fact that 14 walk-ons earned All-Ivy or All-American recognition indicates that you had a miner's eye for the proverbial "diamond-in-the-rough."

It's very interesting. A young athlete who excels in one sport can sometimes very easily convert to another athletic activity. Football, basketball and lacrosse are very similar with the movement, agility and teamwork, as are hockey, field lacrosse and box lacrosse.

Okay. You wanted to say a bit more about Bob Rule... you've mentioned him a few times in the book, but I'd like to hear a little bit more about your relationship with Bob.

Bob Rule was here before I arrived. His first season was 1969. He was our starting goal-tender. Bob actually had gone to Farmingdale Junior College, and after that year he transferred to Cornell. Bob came from Massachusetts. His number one sport was hockey, his number two sport was football, and his number three sport was tennis. So when he and his family relocated to Manhasset, Long Island, he took up lacrosse, and he brought some skills and technique to the game of lacrosse that he actually copied from his hockey skills. He was excellent in goal. His senior year, he was awarded the Ensign C. Markland Kelly Jr. Award as the outstanding goalie in the United States. He was also an All-American.

I will share a very interesting anecdote about his background... I went to visit Manhasset High School where I had coached, and still had friends coaching there. I didn't know about him until I went there to watch a football game. He was a linebacker and did a remarkable job. Little did I know that our paths were going to cross again on a lacrosse field. Once he started playing high school lacrosse, and got recruited by Cornell, there's no doubt he became a catalyst for our defense. He was an extremely hard worker. We couldn't ask for a better competitor. He also played with the U.S.A. team and played club lacrosse. He went into teaching, and just recently retired in 2015. He's an extremely caring, sharing individual, and I give him a tremendous amount of credit.

He's had two of his teammates diagnosed with cancer. One was his competitor at Cornell for the goalie position, Bob Buhmann. Bobby was diagnosed with a brain tumor. For a period of about three years Bob Rule visited Bobby Buhmann, and with Glen Mueller – another Cornell teammate - took him on trips. In fact, they took a trip out to the west coast about 4 months before Bob Buhmann passed away.

To know that these two men would find so many hours to encourage, to soothe, to assist, and basically to love one of their teammates was exceptional. When Bob Buhmann passed away, I happened to be down in Florida. We – his friends and family - decided to have a memorial for Bob, and for another gentleman that we had lost from the 1971 team. We had a beautiful program, and a number of people came back from all over the United States. It was a tribute to Bob Buhmann and his fallen teammate, Bruce Teague. It was a great tribute to what Cornell University meant to all these people.

From the locker room, to the field, to graduation, to a new lifestyle out in the world, these men found time to have love for one another. That, to me, is a blessing. It is what every coach desires for his teams.

Given you mentioned that Bob and Glen teamed up to help their comrade when he needed it the most, this is a good time to ask you a little bit more about Glen.

Okay. We might have mentioned how physical Glen was. I would not want to be a defenseman in lacrosse and have to cover Glen Mueller. He was a bulldozer. Glen is now a vice president at Cornell University. He was at Cornell in a similar position 10 years ago, when Stanford University came calling. While at Stanford, he and his wife raised their family, and as his kids graduated from college and went on to the various occupations, and relocated to various parts of the country, he was asked by Cornell to come back. Cornell's very fortunate that he accepted.

Glen is a doer. He's a man that turns every page. He's a man that, when something is on his desk and needs attention immediately, it will be done, and it will be done with expert talent, accomplishment, and work ethic. His ability on the basketball court, the football field, and lacrosse field was exceptional.

Glen led by example. He was tenacious whenever the ball was on the ground. He made sure that our effort was a team effort. He also played basketball at Cornell. I was at Manley Field House the night that we lost to Syracuse in overtime. Both he and Bob Shaw were exceptional players.

Bob Shaw made a terrific pass under the basket to one of his teammates, and I thought he got the shot off before the buzzer in regulation, which would have won the game. The referee saw it otherwise, and Syracuse won in overtime. It would have been a great upset and a great win for us.

In high school football, Glen dominated the conference that he was in. He definitely could have been a three-sport star here at Cornell, but the way he played, his body might have given out in his sophomore or junior year. You couldn't have a greater friend or teammate. Glen came from great stock, and his parents were remarkable people.

His dad and I were wonderful friends. In fact, his dad, Fritz Mueller, was a tremendous athlete at Cortland. He coached at Manhasset High School, and he helped coach football with Ed Walsh. He was also a great basketball coach. One of his outstanding players was Ken Howard, the actor.

The White Shadow!

You got it, and Fritz was an advisor on the White Shadow television show. Unfortunately, I just heard that Ken Howard passed away.

Yes. Sadly, he passed away in March of this year.

I was with Ken at Fritz Mueller's 90th birthday. We had a tremendous time together. I had seen the stage show "1776," and of course I watched the White Shadow. That show was based on Manhasset High School basketball. Ken went on to Amherst, and was a very fine athlete, and of course, a wonderful actor. His smile was unreal. We have a professor at Cornell by the name of Dick Booth. He went to Amherst and used to scrimmage against Ken Howard. Dick was on the basketball team, and Ken Howard was a big center on their team at that time.

So it's remarkable, as we write this book, the unbelievable connections. It's sort of like tentacles going out. You reach one tentacle, and it connects you with another. I've been so blessed to be able to associate with wonderful people in all walks of life. From my days as a "Sanitation Engineer" on a garbage truck, meeting some great young men, athletes, dedicated townspeople—it has been a wonderful experience.

So I was fortunate—whatever job I had, I worked diligently at it, enjoyed every minute. I always put some laughs and pranks into it. So it's been a good run.

Obviously, you believed in these young men and I know many of them point to you as one of the most significant mentors and influences from that part of their lives. The fact that they still show up for so many events says a lot about your relationship. The fact that so many Cornell-affiliated people showed up at Jay Paxton's retirement dinner - 45 years after their Cornell days—speaks volumes about that "band of brothers" concept we discussed earlier.

That's true. You know, some of these fraternity brothers admired Jay from the first day they met him, as a pledge, a fraternity brother, an athlete and a leader. That, to me, really is very gratifying.

My job in no way is done. I have a lot of areas to cover between now and the time when I move on. Hopefully my move is upward, and if it's upward, I'll be able to rekindle and be together with my family, mother and father, brothers, sisters, friends, and I couldn't ask for more. Every day, every minute should be very special to all of us.

We already made an agreement that now that you're turning 80, you have hit your home run and you're going to stay in the game and get to first base when you turn 100. We'll talk about the upward mobility after that, okay?

Definitely.

There are a few other folks you wanted to mention, right?

Yes. When I first came to Cornell, it was a beautiful October day. I remember coming in by way of Candor, 20 minutes south of Ithaca - and there was a restaurant called the "Brush and Palette." It had a beautiful design on the outside, so I stopped and had a cup of tea. A lady at the counter said, "Are you new in the area?" And I said, "Yes. I am. I'm going to be working at Cornell." And she said, "That's going to be wonderful. You're going to love every minute." I thought that was pretty nice because I was very apprehensive. I just left a job where I was Director of Athletics, I was coaching, I had about four summer jobs... recreation, driver education, you name it.

Things were good.

Yes. I was a manager of a bar and restaurant. I did some ticket sales for the New York Mets and the Islanders. My brother Bob was head of the ticket sales. I can remember when he called me and said, "We just got Julius Erving. It's going to be announced at 8 o'clock this morning." He called me back at 11 and said "We have already had 3,000 people-plus come in to sign up for season tickets." Bob and I were connected to the Shamrock Basketball Camp in Lake George, New York, and we invited Julius to be one of our guest athletes at the camp. So, it's remarkable, some of the things that can happen in your life.

As I recall, there were some high-profile personalities at that camp...

Yes, Bob Knight, who was coaching at West Point at the time. Butch van Breda Kolff, who was at Hofstra. Pete Carril, the famous Princeton coach who was then at Lehigh. And Lou Carnesecca from St. John's. Some pro players who participated were Kevin Loughery from the Baltimore Bullets and Wayne Embry, from the Cincinnati Royals.

Sorry for the detour... back to your stop at the restaurant in Candor...

Yes, after I left Candor, I drove by Ithaca College. My brother Bob had finished his education at Ithaca College after the war. In fact, he is in the Ithaca College Athletic Hall of Fame. When the war broke out, like all my brothers, he volunteered to go in the service to defend our country and our loved ones.

I continued my drive up to Cornell, and I went over to Teagle

Hall. I don't know if they had announced I was coming, but I said, 'I'm here." And that afternoon, lacrosse was having a fall practice. When I went out to the field, the first person that came up to speak to me was Mark Webster. From that day on, we developed an unbelievable relationship.

He was a student at that time?

Mark was an athlete, a very fine tennis player who was ranked high in New York State. At that time, Ithaca High School had a club lacrosse program, and Mark and his brother had played some lacrosse, but not a lot. Tad, who's also a doctor, played lacrosse at Cornell. Mark came to Cornell, and his parents were involved with the faculty here at Cornell.

And from that meeting, I felt that I was at home. And when I say "home," here I was dealing with a lot of indecision. Did I make the right move? Did I do the right thing? We were doing some work at Elmont High School on our facilities. The Cornell position was not presented to me until the end of August, and I just felt I could not get up and leave Elmont without making sure everything was in order.

So Mark Webster and I had a chance to sit down and talk after practice. We spoke for about an hour. I then went to dinner with Mark, and we talked about the players and about successes they had shared. I said to him, "I noticed that the head coach has had a number of assistants," and one of them happened to be one of my best friends, Jerry Schmidt. By the way, that didn't work out too well with Jerry. Mark said something to the effect of "You're going to have to let some of the comments that you may hear bypass you so that you really don't get affected by them." And I knew what he was referring to, because there are some coaches that are pretty stern with assistants. I had never been an assistant coach, so it was going to be new for me, and Mark helped me through the transition.

For all five minutes of your assistant coaching career?

That's correct. A few days later, I invited the two team captains to dinner with me at the Statler. They told me what I should do, and what I shouldn't do. And at the conclusion, I said to them, "This is really wonderful, getting the chance to meet you both, and a chance to realize what your interest is here at Cornell academically and athletically," but I said, "Ninety percent of the things you told me, as soon as I walk out that door I'm going to forget them." I think that was the first step for me to make sure that I wasn't going to let the inmates be in charge of the asylum, that I was going to have an ability to grasp what was going to be good for the players, good for the program, and good for Cornell.

Mark really helped me tremendously with that. His tennis ability made him a great lacrosse player. Mark was not very big; I think he was about 5'8". He had arms like a lumberjack. He could snap the ball into the top corners of the lacrosse goal faster than any man I've seen. We used a crease offense, a lot of cutting and picks. Very similar to what you may see in basketball today.

Mark would come off the pick, get a feed, and in a split-second the ball was gone. That was related to his tennis technique. Mark turned out to be an All-American player. He's in the Cornell Hall of Fame. He became a doctor in Old Forge, New York. He is extremely supportive of Cornell Athletics, Cornell University. He married a young lady from Cornell who was a swimmer. Old Forge is where he's presently living and he gets down to Cornell often. He still has the same smile. He still has this very positive approach to everything he deals with. I would say he was a major brick in building the foundation for me to go on to coaching here at Cornell. I can't thank Mark Webster enough.

Let's move on to Brooks Bradley.

Brooks Bradley is a great example of why coaches should take some time in evaluation. It was about the third week in August, and I always visited a place in Collegetown called Pop's Place. It was a combination diner and delicatessen - excellent food, wonderful atmosphere. You'd see faculty members there, local celebrities and administrators. I always liked to go there because, as a new coach, I thought it was important for me to get involved in the community. So I'd go to Collegetown or downtown for lunch. Sometimes I'd have breakfast, when we had early morning practices, at various locations just to let people know that I was truly interested in this community.

While I was sitting there, I happened to be reading *The New York Times*, and I looked up. I saw a young man sitting by himself. It was very obvious he had probably come from football practice. The reason I thought it was obvious is because he had the tell-tale sign on his forehead. When you wear a football helmet and you perspire, you usually get a ring around your forehead which is normally a little red from the pressure of the helmet.

I went over, introduced myself, and said, "Do you mind if I sit down here?" I said, "You're a student at Cornell?" He said, "Yes." And I said, "You're playing football." And of course, he was a little amazed. He said, "How do you know that?" I said, "Well, I can tell by your head."

We started a conversation and I hadn't really introduced myself, other than the fact that I said that my name is Richie and I live here in the community. As we went on in the conversation, I said I'd gone to University of Maryland. He said, "I'm from Baltimore, Maryland!" I said, "Where'd you go to school?" He said, "Gilman." I said, "Really? It's obvious you played football there." He said. "I was captain." I said, "What other sports do you play?" And immediately, I'm thinking he's from Gilman in Baltimore, he must be a lacrosse player. He said, "I was a baseball player."

So we continued our conversation, and I told him I was the lacrosse coach. He was a little disenchanted with football. I think sometimes when you're new to a school, and you're right out into the thick of things, you've just come off the summer where you've worked out, enjoyed some relaxation, home cooking, the tenderness that you receive at home—it's all gone. And now, you've got to be independent. You're in a rigorous sport. You have to maintain a good sense of what you want to accomplish, and possibly he was unhappy with football, which can happen to a lot of people. It can happen in any sport.

So I said to him, "You know, I don't know if you're going to play baseball, but if you don't, you ought to give lacrosse a try. It's obvious you're in great condition. You're a good size. You're about 6'3", right? I think you'd be an excellent defenseman in lacrosse." And I said, "By the way, Rennie Finney, the headmaster at Gilman, is a great friend of mine."

Rennie Finney wanted to come to Cornell and be a veterinarian, and we always talked about Cornell when I went down there recruiting. His whole family went to Princeton, and in fact, there's a field at Princeton named after his father.

Rennie Finney was a remarkable athlete at Princeton. He was All-American in three sports: football, lacrosse, and wrestling. And what a leader! He's been honored by the Ivy League, and he's been honored a number of times nationally. But once I mentioned Rennie Finney, I had no idea the connection that Brooks Bradley had with Rennie Finney.

Brooks described the connection by saying something to the effect of "Rennie's my second father." And when he said that, I really felt that I had a diamond in the rough. I had a young man that was great at communicating. I had a young man that had a strong desire to do well. We finished our conversation and I wished him luck, gave him my phone number, and my Cornell business card.

I said, "If you ever need anything, or you want somebody to talk to, or things are not going well with football or in school, I want to treat you just like I treat all my other players. We have faculty members here that have been great in helping our teams. A gentleman by the name of Professor Walter Pauk – who gained fame for his book "How To Study in College" -has helped out with instructing our players how to develop good study habits, take notes, prepare for essays and tests. That's the type of resource that we have that you're welcome to be a part of."

We shook hands, and I went up to campus. Three weeks later, this young man came to my office, and he said, "I'd really like to try lacrosse." He commented that he wanted to be a walk-on. So I said, "Well, give this a lot of thought before you make your final decision. We don't start fall practice for a while," as I knew he would be involved in football. He said, "Well, I've given up football," so that meant he would be eligible for fall practice. From the first day that he stepped on the field, there was no doubt in my mind, or my assistant coach's mind, that this young man was going to develop into a top player for us.

He wound up being an All-American. He was an All-Ivy League selection. His dad and mother were remarkable people. His dad actually was a mortician, very involved in politics in the state of Maryland. His close friend was Spiro Agnew. I think it had a lot of effect on his dad when Spiro Agnew was accused and convicted of wrongdoings on the political scene. There was no parental interference, as his dad just loved the fact that Brooks was going to be involved in the sport.

Brook's dad somehow found out that every once in a while I would bring Dunkin Donuts on the bus when we traveled. On one of our trips down to the University of Maryland, he decided to pull a prank on yours truly. On that trip, we also played against Mt. Washington Lacrosse Club which was a premier lacrosse club in the country. We stopped in Camp Hill, Pennsylvania, for a team meal. When we left Camp Hill, we went up a roadway where we were stopped by three state trooper cars.

We had a bus driver from Crispell Bus Company, which was a bus company here in Ithaca. He was extremely nervous because, obviously, when you're driving across the country, you're going to pick up some speeding tickets. He couldn't figure out for the life of him why he was being stopped by state troopers. He was so nervous he had difficulty reaching for his registration. With that, he opened the door and two troopers came in. I was in the first row. He said, "Did this bus originate in Ithaca, New York?" I replied, "Yes. It's the Cornell University lacrosse team." He said, 'We understand that there's some contraband on this bus." Hearing that, the bus driver almost passed out.

I had heard of strange things happening a year before. A good friend of mine took a prep school program to Bermuda, and at customs they opened up the bag of lacrosse sticks and found out there was marijuana in them. That was a very difficult time for the program and for the coach. I'm thinking, Oh no, I can see myself in chains someplace down in Georgia.

Do you look good in stripes?

It depends. If they're wide, I don't. Thin stripes are fine. Pin stripes are great.

So one of the state troopers walked down to about the middle of the bus, came back and said, "I think everything's okay." Then the next trooper came on the bus with four huge boxes of Dunkin Donuts.

The prankster was pranked…

I looked up and on a slight incline was Mr. Bradley, driving a hearse, waving to us. So, the Dunkin Donuts didn't make Brooks a great player. Brooks made himself a great player. To this day, he's a fanatic for working out. He's a very close friend. When I finish my phone calls with players, I always say "I love you." And when I said this to him for the first time a number of years ago, he called me back about 10 minutes later. He said, "Coach, do you know what you just said to me?" I said, "Yes." He said, "Is that unusual?" I said, "Not really. I say it to my children. I say it to my players. And I say it to friends of mine." And I said, "I really mean it."

Well, that message has carried over for all these years. Brooks is a very successful businessman in Maryland, owns a financial planning business known as The Bradley Company. His clients adore him. He could be competitive as a lacrosse player today, he's in such great shape. He has done wonderful things for me over the years. In the 1980's, Brooks spearheaded the dedication of a patio adjacent to the United States Lacrosse Hall of Fame, which was on the Johns Hopkins campus. It was dedicated to Richie Moran.

In what might be called "enemy territory..." Imagine that.

Yes, at Johns Hopkins. I don't know how many things they threw at it or poured on it over the years, but it definitely is a great place to have tailgates, parties, receptions, and it gets a lot of use. He led the campaign for that project, which was really a wonderful gesture. And then most recently, he led a major campaign to have the new United States Lacrosse Hall of Fame Museum and Gallery named after Richard M. "Richie" Moran. This campaign went on for 3 years. The dedication ceremony was held on September 11, 2016.

You know, you look at how lucky I've been. I'm not saying that the "reward" would have been what Brooks has done for me. Just his friendship is a reward enough. Meeting him at Pop's Place, having him come out for lacrosse having never played the game, and then develop into the player that he was, is reward enough. He was also captain of the team, along with Bruce Arena and Steve Sanford. To see him compete on the club level in Baltimore after his Cornell playing days, and then have a successful career, reminds me that I didn't know what it was, but something convinced me to go over and talk to him that day, and I'm a firm believer in that.

If I see someone that I feel I can assist or help, I'm going to be there. I'm glad that I was there for him, and he has been there for me for many years. I thank Brooks Bradley for the friendship, the kindness, and the generosity that he's extended to me and my family.

That's a wonderful story about a great 45-year friendship. The last thing I want to say to close out this chapter is to address your statement that you have "been very lucky." I have heard "luck" described as "that place where preparation and opportunity converge." It sounds like you align yourself with such a definition of luck.

Beautiful. I was going to say that. Plus, I think there's a guardian angel that either whispers into my ear or moves my body, and for it to move my body it's got to be a pretty strong angel.

Branch Rickey said (allegedly quoting John Milton), "Luck is the residue of design." And Thomas Jefferson once said—and I know you'll agree with this one – "I am a great believer in luck, and I find the harder I work, the more I have of it." All these definitions apply to the way you live, the way you teach, mentor and lead.

You got it.

Giving Back

You have been retired for several years, and I have heard you say that you have contemplated going back to work because you're busier now than you ever were.

I know that when you first came to Ithaca, you had an interest in working to help people with disabilities, and you made a connection with the Franziska Racker Centers. That connection remains strong, and I know you do some work with the YMCA, and with Gadabout. Would you please tell me a little bit about your involvement with the Ithaca community?

It really has been a joy. My wife mentioned to me that when I retire, we're going to get some projects done, and I think she is contemplating redoing the patio and a number of other things that would require labor. I decided to give her the Yellow Pages, and I told her she can pick out any plumber, any carpenter and I would pursue other endeavors.

Well, in my pursuit, I was very fortunate to meet Jack Murphy and his wife. We became inseparable friends. Unfortunately, they have since passed away. Jack encouraged me to get involved with the Racker Centers and, since I had done some work with young people with disabilities while teaching in high school, I thought this would be a perfect match. I got on the Board of the Franziska Racker Centers, and it was one of the best moves I made during that period of time.

I was still coaching so it gave me an outlet. The Board was extremely active, very productive, and efficient. Our client base gradually grew from approximately 300 clients up to about 1,500 at the present time. We have a staff of over five-hundred professionals, and a budget close to $17 million. There is a lot of fundraising involved, requiring a lot of expert executive work done by our CEO's, Roger Sibley and now Dan Brown. It has been an honor to be associated with the Racker Centers.

I'm still on the advisory board, and I still get involved in activities that they organize. I help with their fundraising and was actually President of the Board. So, that connection got me off and running and more involved in charitable work in Ithaca.

I'd like to interject something here, if I may. I know that one of their fundraisers could also be called a FUN-raiser, because they bring in several professional hockey players and former Cornell players, including some who currently play in the NHL. I know that you have a winning streak as the coach of one of those teams. You're a resounding 2-0, as I recall, and your tuxedo jacket/short pants/leather loafers ensemble raises many eyebrows....

Yes, that is true... Perri LoPinto – the agency's Director of Community Relations - is a dynamo. She and her staff have always come up with excellent ideas for fundraising. At one time, we had Merrill-Lynch sponsor a golf tournament, which was a huge success. But like most golf tournaments, after eight or nine years, it sort of wears out a little bit.

It also competes with about 20 other golf tournaments.

Right, so basically, the point was to come up with something else. With the help of Topher Scott – who is a former Cornell player and was an assistant coach - they came up with this great idea about hosting a hockey game at Cornell's Lynah Rink. It really started gaining momentum. Like you said, a lot of former players from Cornell, as well as some professionals, like three-time Stanley Cup winner Joe Nieuwendyk, and Dustin Brown, a young man who grew up here in Ithaca and has captained the L.A. Kings to two Cups, and a number of excellent hockey players....

Five Stanley Cups between those two guys... Not a bad attraction for a small-town fundraiser.

That's for sure. To have that in a community where you have two players that have been involved in five Stanley Cups, that I think could be a first.

The game also draws several players who were involved in Cornell's national championship effort as well, correct?

Correct. And then they have local skaters that come out and perform. Contact is limited, which is only natural in exhibition games. Males and females are on the ice at the same time. Plus, this year, we had a gentleman that was on the ice who is one of the world's best sled hockey players.

Yes, his name is Josh Pauls and he is a two-time Paralympic sled hockey gold medalist for Team USA.

That was fantastic to see him perform.

It sure was. He was born with no shin bones and he had both legs amputated at 10 months of age. He has become one of the world's best sled hockey players. They actually propel themselves with two short sticks, and then they turn the stick and shoot with the other side. It's an amazing skill to watch. That was a great draw.

It was magnificent for the young people that were in attendance, because it inspired them to realize that, even though a person has a disability, they do not necessarily have an inability.

I know that your community involvement means a lot, and that while you were coaching, it meant a lot to you to get your players involved, too. I know that benefitted the community, and I'm going to guess it benefitted the players as well.

It really did. When I was in high school, the high school football coach and my lacrosse coach thought that we should go out into the community and help out. One winter day, school was closed and we went out and shoveled off the tennis courts so we could play box lacrosse. Our coach came over and he said, "You know, you fellas can do a good deed. I'm sure there are a lot of people who need their sidewalks shoveled. Why don't you go ahead and do that today. You can always come back and play box lacrosse in the afternoon." That was my first taste of reaching out. Twenty of us went in different directions, and we made sure the people didn't think that we were doing something that was in violation. We just told "We're from

Sewanhaka High School, we are members of the lacrosse team and we'd like to help out." So we shoveled and we really weren't looking for rewards, but they'd give us some money anyway. We all agreed it would be a good thing to put that money into the Sewanhaka lacrosse program. We gave the money to our coach and it helped us buy t-shirts that we would need during the season. So that was a start, and I continued to do various good deeds in the community.

Lifting heavy shovels-full of snow wasn't too bad for your lacrosse game, either, am I right?

Definitely. It was great for your wrists and forearms.

Gradually we got involved with the Salvation Army on Long Island, and all those acts of charity stayed with me. As a coach, I wasn't going to have lacrosse players shovel snow unless it was my driveway! We did encourage them to volunteer for the Salvation Army, and I'm sure to this day, some of those gentlemen are still very involved with that organization.

Then I got involved with Gadabout. They provide transportation for the elderly and also people who are disabled. It's a non-profit, and just recently we had a very successful fundraiser to gain funds to help continue Gadabout's ability to provide the services that it does. Many of the volunteer drivers are men and women who are retired.

What a joy it is to see these buses go around the community, and see the advantages it provides, to take people who probably would have been confined to their houses and would have had to rely on expensive taxi cabs. The service is provided for a very low fee, and it really has generated some excellent opportunities for the people that are pretty much by themselves, all too often isolated. Now they are able to get out and about.

I was also involved in the beginning stages of the Make – A - Wish Foundation in Ithaca, a tremendous organization that helps young people realize some of their dreams. Some of these young people have a very tough diagnosis of cancer or another life-changing or life-threatening condition. To help fulfill some of these wishes and see them smile is very special.

I think it's fair to say that being in the community for so long, and having been a high-profile coach, that brings a degree of ce-

lebrity. Being able to use that familiarity and celebrity status—if I may use that term—for the betterment of the entire community is clearly something that has brought you a lot of fulfillment over the years.

It really has, Steve, and I always look back to my parents. It's something my parents could be very proud of. They were very caring, very sharing people. They really appreciated our neighborhood, which featured a strong ethnic mix. In the '30s and '40s, people really reached out to help one another. I hope that in the future we'll get the same type of approach throughout our country – that willingness to reach out and help. I would say, don't concern yourself with race or religion. Just be ready to help your fellow man.

I know this is a little off-topic in regard to community involvement, but it's fresh on my mind and it affected me deeply... I had a tough situation happen on Sunday. My daughter and her family were up in Lake Placid for a lacrosse tournament, and they asked me if I'd take care of their black lab. Emmy is her name, she's a wonderful dog, and it's a joy to take care of her.

In the process of going there Sunday, I was traveling down Perry City Road, going south. A car was coming north on Dubois Road, which intersects Perry City Road— and an unfortunate gentleman was going at a high rate of speed and did not see the stop sign. He hit the other car, spun that car around and that car missed me by, I'd say it was two feet, but I think it was a lot closer.

The car that caused the accident rolled over three times and landed on its roof. The gentleman that was hit—to me it was a miracle that he was not injured badly. I stopped my car immediately; and put my flashers on. There was debris all over the road, and I was sort of in the middle. Do I go to the left to help the man in the car that's not overturned, or go to the other car? I saw the gentleman that was hit get out of his car, and I went over and I called out to him. He was in a state of shock. He was coherent and he wanted to call his wife, so I had him sit down.

I went over to try and look at the man that was in the overturned car. I could see him move, but I couldn't see in the window. I pried the door open, probably less than a foot because it was dug into the ditch. He put his hand out and I said, "Please don't move. Just talk." And he was very coherent.

I witnessed two miracles on Sunday. And the fact that I was not hit is definitely a miracle. Even as the car spun, it could have spun right into me and knocked me off the road. I called 9-1-1, and within minutes there was an ambulance, fire department, local police, State Police. Both gentlemen were able to walk to the back of the ambulance to be tested and treated. And I just looked up at the sky and Sunday was a beautiful day. I just thanked God that both of these men were alive. You can always replace a car. I also thanked Him for letting me not be involved in the extensive damage and possible bodily damage.

I was really fortunate. I watched these two gentlemen, and one needed to go to the hospital because of some injuries that were not serious, and the other was able to walk away.

To this moment, I have no idea how either person could walk away. It was such a bad accident. So we talk about community, and there are a lot of things in the community that we're all going to face from time to time. I'm going to do every little bit that I can do to help out, and I plan to do that as long as I live.

Richie, when I wrote the intro, the lead-off chapter to this project, I said I remembered being on the phone with one of your former players who has written several books, and has really been an advocate for you to undertake this project. He told me that many hedge fund managers, Fortune 500 guys, and other people who have attained great heights professionally out there in the world, point to you as a mentor and an influence. I told him that I did appreciate that fact, but I also know several people have faced so many obstacles in life, people that believe that nobody in the world knows who they are, and it's very common to see you in a coffee shop with them when they're having a tough time. It's just the two of you, with nobody watching. I'm going to guess that while it does feel good to you to get some accolades, and have people say, "Oh, it's great that you're involved in all this volunteer stuff," I think your motivation to reach out goes way deeper than any kind of public recognition. I know that you like to pay forward your own blessings by helping people, whether or not anyone's watching.

That's the truth, Steve. As I mentioned earlier, I know down deep in my heart that these accolades are shared by my wife, my family, my children—Kevin, Jennifer, and Kathy. Without them, I would not be as inspired as I am. They've given me a lot of inspiration and a lot of strength to do, hopefully, good things.

I might have mentioned way back, that my first dealing with charity was when I was in the fourth grade and they had a program about Boys' Town. I remember I had 71 cents in a bank that was made in the shape of a baseball. It was a ceramic baseball with a slot in it, like a piggy bank. I was always hoping that the slot would get some greenbacks, but usually just change went in there. I opened up the bottom, which had a little rubber plug, and there was 71 cents in it. I remember taping the 71 cents on a card and giving it to my mother to put in an envelope. I addressed it to Boys' Town, Nebraska, U.S.A.. From that day on, I've always felt that if I can help in any way, whether it's monetarily or from the standpoint of just consoling somebody, or recognizing somebody that probably doesn't receive much recognition, maybe that's why God put me on earth.

I've always said to myself, "I wish I had the strength given to me by God to heal young people and old people, to help the homeless, to help people that have faced tragedy, just for one day to be able to cure them and help them." That would be one of the greatest satisfactions I could have. I know this is really reaching, and it may sound a little silly, but to me, looking at what happened on Sunday, that accident, that was a miracle. All three of us could have been killed. There had to be somebody there to help us. Somebody reached out to spare the three of us.

You had already been to Mass that morning, right?

Yes, sir.

Well, there you go…

Let me continue about the community… I'm also a member of the Elks Club here in Ithaca. It's called BPOE and that stands for "The Best People on Earth." It's actually the Benevolent Protective Order of Elks, and the beauty of it is that they, as a membership, provide tremendous opportunities for people with cerebral palsy. They are also very involved in activities for young people, providing opportunities to increase their education and knowledge. We have a dictionary campaign, where dictionaries are given out to every grade school in Ithaca.

They're not looking for a pat on the back, they're not looking for prestige. We all can help in some way. That has always been my feeling. I can always help out in some way.

You're on the YMCA board as well, right?

Yes.

What kind of work have you helped them do?

The YMCA has a scholarship program for children, so of course you have to raise funds. I was campaign chairman for 2 years. This community of Ithaca, New York, is unbelievable. We probably have the most resource groups for a town our size. Our population is about 38,000, and we have more resources available in this community than many cities that have a much larger population base.

Some people are concerned that we're being overrun by people that want hand-outs. Well, I disagree with that theory. The YMCA provides these scholarships for young boys and girls to go to camp. They have a wilderness program, and have built a beautiful camping area, trails, and a nature center. This all takes money.

The CEO, Frank Towner, is a remarkable leader. Our board is tremendous. People go out of their way to make sure that the YMCA will be very successful in this community, so it's a pleasure and a privilege to be a board member, to be involved in the campaign, and be available to help in any possible way. My wife and I donated items to the playground. I walk by and see eight to ten young children running in that playground. We also donated a sandbox, and looking at it, I think about the future architects that are working in that sandbox, and possibly future doctors, future teachers, and future people that are going to make us have a great world.

That's a positive outlook. I agree with you that a lot of people want to focus on the negative side of things. Like you said, the "People have their hand out" perception, and I embrace your attitude that if we have time, or money, or connections, or any of these things that we can turn into resources, we are better individually and collectively if we do that.

There's no question. I'm going to say this because I want it in the book: I admire you for all the things you've done throughout your life. I've seen firsthand how you've reached out to people at Teagle

Hall. How you did that at Challenge, helping people with disabilities find work. How you worked with the blind athletes, the people in the community, when you're out in public. How you say "hello" to people that probably nobody said hello to throughout the whole day. And to me, that's important. That little "hello" is so important.

I'll tell you why. A good friend of mine, Pete Noyes, was a football coach here at Cornell. We were in New York for an event at the Cornell Club and I said, "Pete, let's take a walk down to St. Patrick's Cathedral. Let's just walk in and have a period of solitude and reflection." I also suggested we look at that historic building that means so much to so many people, not just certain religions.

So while we're there, we looked at people that came into the church who were very poor. We looked at people who were from all over the world. We looked at rich people walking up and down the aisles.

On our way back, I said, "Pete, I'm going to bet you 50 cents. I'm going to say hello to everybody that we see within range on our walk back to the Cornell Club," which was about four city blocks. I said, "For everybody that doesn't respond, I'll give you a dollar." Well, of course, he jumped on that. It was like a free lunch.

As we started walking, I said hello to seven people and I got two responses.

You were already running a deficit...

Right...So I'm down five dollars. Well, the next couple of blocks, the word must have traveled that there's somebody that's saying hello to everybody because from that time, I got Pete for probably six dollars, which he never paid me.

Which would have delayed his retirement...

That's correct. He never paid me, but it was the joy I got from it that mattered. I remember saying hello to one woman. She looked like she had a lot of things on her mind. I said hello to her and she said, "Why did you do that?" I said, "I have a feeling in my heart that I want to say hello to people, and I want to recognize people." She said, "I'm going to have to remember that."

I appreciate those kind words you said about me. I can honestly say that I learned some of that from you. When I was working

at Cornell, I started running with that young man who had been blind since he was in the first grade. We needed some money for the trip to the Paralympics in Seoul. I remember the fundraisers, and that you helped me spread the word, and I picked your brain on how to do some of those things. I agree with you… I haven't lived too many other places, so I'm not sure how Ithaca stacks up, but I do know that when people need something, and they approach the community with sincerity and with gratitude, things get done.

Very true... When I was growing up—this is probably repeated from earlier—we didn't have coaches. We didn't have Little League. We had a league that was sponsored by *Long Island Daily Press* and Macy's. They gave us hats. They gave us a couple of balls to use. We supplied our own bats. We had to get our own umpires. We had to get our own fields. We just didn't have dads who were available, so we did our own coaching. We sold raffle books to get our first uniforms, and we copied the Yankees. They were pin-striped. Our team was known as the New Hyde Park Blue Jays. Some of the teams were very well established.

Another team was known as the Richmond Hill Saxons and the catcher on that team was a gentleman named Conrad Metzger. Forty-five years later, I met his son, Jim. He is now one of my best friends. Little did I know, when I played that double-header on July 4th in 1953 that I was going to meet Mr. Metzger's son. Jim's dad is still alive. We talk about that July 4th, and my dream is that someday when we get together he and I can play a game of catch. That is a great dream.

So the word "people person" sometimes rings out. I look at myself as a person for all seasons. When I say "all seasons," I don't want to take my personality and my feelings for people, and my love for people, and only have it exhibited around holidays. So I'm a firm believer in all seasons. I'll stay that way.

In fact, one time when I was playing football in high school, I gave the team a pep talk before our scrimmage with Iona Prep. One of my teammates had used the "N" word against our opponents in the huddle. I gave a talk to the team, and I made it optional for the coaches to stay or not stay. One of the coaches was in the background and he heard some of my comments. He said to me a year or more later, "You really should be a missionary."

The Friday night before graduation, my high school lacrosse coach, Mr. Bill Ritch, hosted a dinner for all the seniors. It was a very sad and emotional time, because it was the next to the last time we would ever be together. He said he had one dream for all of us: that we'd be happy and healthy, and that we'd always remember our time together. He said, "Wherever you travel, try to help develop lacrosse. Be a missionary for the game of lacrosse." A lot of us have done that.

It must be working on some level since the game has expanded so dramatically since you played.

It really has. There's no question about it. I think about our winning streak of 91 straight games. That was publicized, and it made a big impact on the growth of lacrosse. For example, on Long Island, we had eight high schools competing, and now, every town on Long Island has lacrosse.

You know, it's interesting, after the great Cornell team I had, I was asked to speak to various groups. I was invited to Cal-Berkeley. I stayed in a magnificent hotel right off campus. I decided to go and get a beverage. I was down at the end of this beautiful bar. The place was built about 1904-1905, and the woodwork was just magnificent.

The bartender evidently knew who I was. He said, "It's so nice that you're here. I've heard some wonderful things about Cornell, heard some things about you as a coach." I said, "Gee, that's really wonderful." It was so obvious to me that the host that invited me there had told the bartender. I said to the bartender, "I hope they didn't tell you I drink a lot!" He said, "There's another nice guy down at the end of the bar, and I'd like to introduce you to him. He comes here to get away from all the pressures that he's under." I'm thinking. Who is this guy? Well, it turned out to be Joe Kapp, the famous football coach at California. He had been a pro quarterback. He was the coach at Cal when they had the famous play where they ran through the Stanford band and completed several laterals on the way to the end zone for the winning touchdown. I asked Joe if that was a set play, and we both laughed.

I did the clinic for players and coaches, and also had a special session with some assistant athletic directors from the Pacific Coast

Conference. We discussed lacrosse and about adding it to the programs. At that time, some of the schools had it on a club level. The representative from UCLA raised his hand and said, "Coach, we realize how great this sport can be out here from the standpoint of agility and quickness, and that size is not imperative. But" he said, "We had a club team. After the first year they would not allow them to wear UCLA jerseys." I asked, "Why?" He said, "All they did after the games was drink and create problems on the field. We didn't want young people to see that. We didn't want our university to look bad."

In my opinion, behavior like that stymied the growth of lacrosse because some of those club teams might have been athletic, but it was obvious they didn't think as athletes.

They probably didn't have the kind of structure they needed. If they were a club team, whoever they had for a coach was probably a minimum-wage employee, right?

Exactly, or a volunteer… There was no discipline, so that created some key issues. Once the game started to get on television, people started seeing how great it is. Some young man who is 5'6" can beat some guy who is 6'5", and I'm not picking on guys that are 6'5" because I don't want them to pick on me!

Having known you for so long, and having spent many hours with you over the past few months, I am aware that there's a very important place in your life for a power much greater than yourself. Sometimes the things we do in this world can come back to us in unexpected ways, and I'd like to hear the story about when you went down to Washington, D.C., and some friends and former players bestowed upon you a gift that might be described as very generous...

What an evening that was… For the past 5 years, they have honored someone that probably would have been the Tewaaraton winner had the award existed. For example, Jimmy Brown was recognized as an elite player from years past, and Eamon was posthumously honored that evening. I received the Spirit Award for dedication and for having been one of the founders of the Tewaaraton Award itself, which, as you know, is similar to the Heisman trophy in football.

Over eighty former Cornell players came to honor Eamon, and

it was just beautiful to look out at that gathering. Mike French and I did the presentation for Eamon. Eamon's family was there, which was just wonderful. Then, Sid Jamieson - a gentleman of Native American heritage who coached football and lacrosse at Bucknell, and is a very close friend of mine, made the presentation of the Spirit of Tewaaraton award.

At the conclusion, we always go back to the University Club, which is, as I conveyed earlier, one of the older clubs in Washington, D.C., if not the oldest. Howard Taft was one of the club's first presidents, and as you know, he held the title of President in another capacity as well!

In an earlier chapter, you said that the University Club was instrumental in the creation of the Tewaaraton award.

That's correct. They backed it tremendously. And since the size of the group has grown so large, it's now held at the Native American Smithsonian location, which is magnificent. It's a perfect venue for this award. It has a huge auditorium which seats close to 1,000 people. It also has a gigantic area for dining and socializing. They have buses back and forth from the Smithsonian to the University Club.

Going back on the bus, I was with a lot of former players and coaches from other schools. It was really a beautiful night, everybody was enjoying themselves and thinking and talking about everything that happened that night. The most important thing for me was seeing all those players, most of whom I had known since they were teenagers.

We got back to the University Club and we had some beverages and food. We told stories, and the stories got better each hour. Then, someone made a suggestion: why don't we go outside and take a picture of the whole group. Many of those players had their wives with them, and we went outside to take the picture. Players and their wives had cameras. They had a videographer - a gentleman I got to meet, by the name of Mark Paoletta - who had a son, Joe, playing lacrosse at Cornell.

When I looked up, it looked a little bit overdone to me, all of the camera work and videotaping....

Were you getting suspicious that something was up?

Yes, I was. I said, "Wow, this is great." We were holding up a little traffic, so we moved to a safer area near the gardens at the University Club. Someone said, "Coach, we'd like to say a few words about you." First up was Dr. Jon Levine. He's a dentist in New York, and he and his wife, Stacy, started to speak about me. I thought that was beautiful. And then Bobby Cummings spoke on behalf of the players, and Mike French spoke about the traditions of the Cornell lacrosse program. Then Stacey Levine spoke on behalf of the players' wives, and said a few words about Pat and my family.

I thought to myself, "God, this is really overwhelming." Some may not perceive me as modest and humble, but the words that were spoken were very touching. We're now starting to draw in people who are walking by. They might have thought it was some type of big national event in Washington, D.C.

People were stopping and looking, and we had a lot of laughs and funny stories. And then finally, someone said, "Coach, we'd like you to look to your left." I did so, and immediately I saw a brand new car, and on the front of the car was a gigantic decal of a bear, the Cornell logo. And on the side of the car there was another logo that said, "It's Great to be Here."

I looked at it and I thought "This is going to be interesting."

How ironic that somebody would have a car with your favorite saying on it…

Right... And I said to myself, "God, I wonder who owns that car."

It wasn't really a 'car,' it was a brand new Acura SUV.

That's correct, a beautiful vehicle. Of course, as you know I had a 1993 Camry, and I loved it!

So they said, "Coach, this Acura is yours," and they came over and handed me the keys. I don't know why I said this, but I said, "I can't really take this." And with that, everybody started to laugh, and my wife said, "Oh, yes you can!"

So with that, my friend Jay Spiegel pulled out a green Irish derby, and of course, I put it on. I had some pictures taken, and I was definitely overwhelmed. It was unbelievable. Scott Crabtree - the car dealer - is a good friend of Jay Spiegel. Jay headed up the campaign and approached many players. *(Co-Author's note: Scott Crabtree, the car dealer who helped to make the gift of the Acura possible, has deep connections to the sport of lacrosse, as his two daughters were college lacrosse players. His daughter Summer played lacrosse and field hockey at Princeton and his daughter Shana, now a medical doctor, played lacrosse at Vanderbilt. Shana still holds the NCAA record for most saves by a Division 1 goalie, stopping 39 shots against Boston University in 1997.)*

In fact, I left out one detail... before the presentation of the car, they presented me with a wooden lacrosse stick that was made by Alfie Jacques, a member of the Onondaga nation who specializes in making wood sticks, which are now becoming treasured keepsakes. Antique style, handcrafted—it's just magnificent the way he designs these sticks and produces them all by hand.

I bet they're in high demand.

Very much so, and on the stick were the names of every player and person that contributed to the car. I was flabbergasted.

There was something in the car that reminded us of a prank I played on Bobby Cummings one time. I like Old Spice aftershave and deodorant. I dressed in the same locker room with the players, so of course, Old Spice was always on the top of my locker. They claim I used to put Old Spice all over me. I probably did.

Well, when Bobby came up to recruit some people for his company, I packed up two packages of Old Spice because he played a prank on me one time. He put this Cramergesic, which is extremely hot, that you use for aches and pains in my Old Spice deodorant and I proceeded to apply it underneath my arms and on my chest.

I'm glad you stopped there...

Yeah, me too! It was a great prank. So when he came up to visit, I presented him with a gift, wrapped beautifully in silver wrapping with a red Cornell bow. We met at the Statler and I presented it to him. He opened it up and, of course, it got a lot of laughs. I think he probably thought it was some jewelry I was going to give him, maybe a Rolex, but it didn't work out that way. It was, of course, Old Spice deodorant. On the front seat of the car, they told me there was a special gift and there it was: another pack of Old Spice deodorant and lotion, in case I needed it when I was traveling in my new car. It was quite a thrill.

And that custom license plate?

They did give me a CUAA (Cornell University Athletic Association) license plate, but I love my RMM5. They made frames that go around the license plate, and on the front it was “Cornell Big Red,” and on the back was “It’s Great to be Here.”

I was completely overwhelmed. I hadn’t had a new car probably since the ‘70s.

What does the 5 stand for in RMM5?

Family of five.

That’s what I thought.

Scott (the Acura dealer) had the car transported to my home, and everything was registered. Another gift was credit cards, which amounted to close to $2,000.

That’ll keep some gas in your SUV.

It sure will. I will never forget that feeling. In fact, I still have it. Every time I get into that car, I think about how generous my friends are, and what a beautiful gesture that was. In their minds, it was kind of a repayment for all the things we—WE—did together. Please underline “we” because nothing was accomplished as a solo act. It was all togetherness, teamwork, and love for one another.

That extended family you talk about so often and with such gratitude.

Exactly. The commitment not to quit, to encourage each other. And that really still goes on today. I hear stories every day about what some of our players have done, and how they help one another. So it was quite thrilling. It was an evening that I’ll never forget.

Afterward, we continued to celebrate, continued to laugh. Players came from: Texas, Florida, California—for that special night honoring Eamon and myself, and, of course, to be there for the beautiful presentation of the car.

You know, Richie, I kind of feel like I was there. Jay Spiegel was kind enough to send me the YouTube video of that evening. I will say that in the 35 years I have known you, I’ve seen you spoof some people pretty well, but they sure got you. If you

knew about it in advance, you sure fooled everybody because you looked completely bewildered by the whole thing. If you knew about it, there is an Academy Award in your future, because you looked stunned.

I was. In fact, one person made a great comment, saying it was the first time they saw me speechless! I definitely was overwhelmed. I was thinking of my Camry. I loved that car!

Where is it? I want to buy it.

Well, actually, Dan Joseph, who worked at the Gulf station in town said he wanted to get a car for his son. The car was spotless. The engine was great. I took great care of it. And Dan knew that because I would go to that gas station that was owned by his dad, and he worked on it. So I sold the car to Dan. I really feel I want to go back and see it sometime! Maybe I'll request that opportunity as a parental visit!

Maybe in 25 or 30 years, you can be buried in it!

Oh baby! That has been done, I guess. Some guy was buried in his Cadillac.

Let's be realistic. I'll probably wait 20 years, because, by that time, I'll be 100. If I keep hanging around with you, I'll definitely reach it!

I'm glad to hear that. I am so pleased that this book will be released right around your 80th birthday. That will make for a wonderful joint celebration. You are putting all this effort into sharing these wonderful stories, you are turning 80, and you're still the same guy you always were. It's a real blessing. You haven't lost a step mentally, although I don't know if you can still dunk a basketball like you once did...

I'll let you know…

And your crew cut's not standing up quite like it once did, but you're still looking and acting pretty tough!

Well, I appreciate that!

You've heard me say this before… Given that I have made a significant portion of my living as a sports writer, I have a tendency to frame life in sports terminology. That said, since the

average American lives to be 80, when you're 20 you're on first base, When you turn 40, you're sliding into second base, and at 60, you have hit a triple. You, Richie, are crossing home plate standing up, and you're going to dig in and try to get back to first base again!

That's good. I love being in the game. It's great to be here!

You have a lot of game left. Do you remember Sterling McAdam, the great Cornell softball fan?

Yes, I do.

I interviewed him when he was 102, and I told him he was the only guy I ever met who slid into home, and then made it to first again! He was 2 for 2! He laughed and said, "I don't think I'm going to make it to second base..." He didn't think he was going to make it to 120, and he didn't, but what a character that guy was.

That's a beautiful story!

My Heart and Soul

Okay, Richie, backing up to—and you can correct me on the year, 1958, 1957—you were walking with your buddy Charlie Wright and you saw a young lady coming down the stairs.

At that point, she was a stranger. Then she became an acquaintance, a friend, a girlfriend, a fiancée and a wife. Then ultimately, the DNA of Richard Moran and Patricia Smith joined forces in this world, making you and Pat "related" through the three children you've had. I know you have built many teams you're really proud of, but when I see you at your grandchildren's games, I get the sense that the "team" that you're the most proud of is the one you and Pat have built.

We're both very lucky. I was actually coming down the stairs in the biology building at the University of Maryland in 1957. I was with my roommate Charlie Wright, who was from the southern shore of Maryland.

I recall we joked that Pat almost found "Mr. Wright..."

That's correct! I saw this young lady walking up the steps and I said to Charlie, "Charlie, I'm going to marry that girl." Now, he went nuts. He was always a little apprehensive about New Yorkers, guys from Long Island. I don't know if he ever met anybody from New York or Long Island until we became roommates, even though he was in the Korean War. I guess he might have met some, but very few. We had a tremendous relationship.

That was probably one of the best stairways I ever walked up. They said there is a "Stairway to Heaven," so hopefully, I'll be able to walk up that stairway someday. I definitely don't want to go downstairs!

From that day on, I thought about her and happened to see her on campus with my fraternity brother's girlfriend. So I asked my fraternity brother, "Who is that girl that your girlfriend knows?" He told me her name was Pat Smith, and she was from Washington, D.C. And I said to him, "Is there any chance you could fix me up with a blind date?"

As we discussed earlier in the book, there's no doubt that I was very fortunate. I don't know if I said this earlier, but I would go out and watch her play intramural softball; she was a catcher.

You did not tell this story.

The funny thing is, I could tell my fraternity brothers and teammates, "That girl with the catcher's mask, I really love her." My buddies said, "What does she look like?" They couldn't see through the catcher's mask! Little did I know that our children would be involved in catching! My daughter Jennifer was a catcher. My granddaughter Kylie was a catcher. I was a catcher. Years ago, they used to make a comment that catchers wear "the tools of ignorance." Well, I disagree with that. It was a wonderful position.

Our relationship started blossoming. Our first date was not the greatest. She had difficulty understanding my accent, so I worked on that diligently before a mirror. Before you know it, everybody thought I was from Boston, and not Long Island. The Sopranos actually used the same dialect that I had, so you know exactly what that was like in 1957-'58.

I stayed on campus one summer to work in Washington, D.C. I took some courses at Maryland, and it was extremely warm and humid. It was a great summer. On weekends, I had an opportunity to see Pat and also spend time with her friends, and go to some great concerts. We got to see some wonderful tennis matches and go to some nice clubs. We were able to spend time at her parents' country club, and after putting in five hard days of work and school, the weekends were a wonderful vacation.

We started to enjoy each other's company a lot more. I invited her to Long Island, and she loved going to Jones Beach and Point Lookout with my friends and me.

Did you have to bribe those guys to be on their best behavior?

Well, pretty much so. I told them not to say "deez" and "doze." And don't trow the guy trew the window! That was pretty important. Some of my friends had gone to college; some had stayed home and worked. They had girlfriends at the time, so we were a happy group.

They were telling you not to mess this one up, right?

That's correct. They told me not to fumble.

We'd go to Jones Beach and have beach parties. We went to various concerts. One that stands out in my mind is one we went to at the Shell House, in Oceanside, New York, right near the water. We were there to see Tony Bennett but he became ill and couldn't perform. They substituted a young singer, who at that time, I don't think had sung anywhere in New York state. His name was Johnny Mathis. We had great seats. Johnny Mathis, instead of singing four or five songs, sang about fourteen. After about the second song, he was getting standing ovations.

There was a newspaper/magazine called *Variety* which used to talk about all the celebrities, and this was before *People* magazine. *Variety* would rate all the entertainment in and around New York. One of the most beautiful things is that his rating went up unbelievably after that night because there were a lot of people from *Variety* in attendance to cover Tony Bennett. So it was a great opportunity for us, and for Johnny Mathis.

So, given this is a sports book, Johnny Mathis pinch-hit for Tony Bennett and hit one outta the park.

No question about it. In fact, it was a grand slam because Pat thought I'd planned it because he was so entertaining. Of course, I did take credit.

Of course...

My friends loved it. She loved it. She would take the train every once in awhile from Washington to Long Island after I'd finished summer school and completed my summer job. I was home for probably three or four weeks before I went back to school. She worked for the National Science Foundation and, in fact, Father Theodore Hesburgh was very involved at the time. He was also the President of Notre Dame, and he is credited with elevating the standards of Catholic education, as well as being a key member of the Board at the N.S.F. Pat loved working at that foundation. It was really a sensational job for her.

She would get on the 5 o'clock train to come all the way to New York City, then take the Long Island Railroad. I remember the time she slept through her stop. I'm sure she was suffering from a lack of sleep, and was probably fatigued from the heat and from working all day. She actually wound up in Port Jefferson, Long Island. She forgot to get off the train at my hometown. When she woke up, she had to backtrack to get back to my hometown, which was New Hyde Park, about an hour away!

My dad had passed away when I was a sophomore in college, so she never got a chance to meet him, but her relationship with my mother was really outstanding. I could do nothing right with those two. It was really tremendous. It kept me on my toes. Pat knew she was very well accepted by my brothers and sisters, and of course, my mother.

That fall, when we went back to college, she was a cheerleader and I was president of my fraternity. We were very active on campus, and were involved in some charities. That fall, we had a Father/Son event at my fraternity and I invited Pat's father, Dr. Ashby Smith, to come and stay at our fraternity house for a weekend and spend time with me. It was a football weekend. We had father-son type dinners and other activities. He got to know me better, and I got to know him extremely well.

On Sunday morning, our fraternity had a brunch for all our guests and I said to him, "Dr. Smith, I realize this is going to be a strange question...." I paused, as there was a little hostility coming in my direction from his wife, who would be my future mother-in-law.

Why was that?

It was based on the fact that I was a Democrat, a John F. Kennedy fan, a Catholic, northerner, Long Islander. I wasn't going to be about doctor or a lawyer. But that's natural.

Everybody thinks their daughter can do better, right?

Yeah. That was definitely to be expected. I said to Dr. Smith at breakfast, "I'd really like to marry your daughter." And he said, "That's wonderful." I said, "Well, what's your wife going to think?" He said, with a wink and a smile, "I do all the thinking in the house." Little did I know that wasn't true...

So that fall, we got "pinned," meaning I gave her my fraternity pin, which was a big thing in those days. And, of course, her mother wasn't extremely happy. I had saved up some money from my summer job, and my mother was kind enough to extend me a loan, and I decided at Christmas time we were going to get engaged. I called Dr. Smith and told him. He said, "I will prepare my wife, your future mother-in-law, for this wonderful occasion." I said, "Your daughter is coming up here for Christmas. Do you mind that?" He said, "No. She talked about it and she'd really like to be with you at Christmas."

So, Christmastime was going to be time for me to give her the engagement ring. We were at midnight Mass. I held her hand. I took the ring out, showed it to her. I'm not sure if we both sat down or she sat down, but I put the ring on her finger. It was truly a blessing that we did it at that occasion. Midnight Mass has always been very special to both of us. By the way, Pat was not Catholic. She was Methodist, so that was another little detour in my relationship with her mom.

After the engagement and during the couple of years after that, the road to my mother-in-law's heart started to look like the yellow brick road. I was accepted into the family, although I know she was apprehensive.

Catholics have a lot of children. Catholics have rules that dictate how married couples were to raise those children, and my mother-in-law was not sure how it would unfold. .

And, they have that special meal on Friday...

Yep. And boy, I suffered through some of those. You talk about special meals.

Tuna casserole, right?

Yep. I would go into the Smith's house and they would host several friends and put on an elegant meal. I'd be sitting at the table in my coat and tie, and they'd bring out these gigantic steaks. A college guy doesn't see too many steaks, and unfortunately for me, Catholics could not eat meat on Fridays! I had a beautiful tuna casserole instead.

At least they fed you.

I'm glad I stuck to my religious beliefs. To prove my authenticity as a Catholic, I often went to church at 7 o'clock in the morning after being out carousing in Georgetown with Pat and our friends the night before.

When we got married, the weather gods were not too nice to us. We decided to be married in February. I had gotten out of the Marine Corps in January. Believe it or not, the worst snowstorm to hit Washington in years occurred that weekend. We had a rehearsal dinner on Friday night, and it was beautiful. Cold, but beautiful. My best man and I stayed together. My ushers stayed at various homes provided by friends of Pat's parents, in a neighborhood called Crestwood. About seven doctors lived in Crestwood, and they were all friends so a lot of my ushers and some of my very close male friends stayed in some of their houses. I stayed in a doctor's house directly across from Pat's house.

Outside of being in the Marine Corps, this was probably the earliest I ever woke up. It was about 5 o'clock in the morning the day of my wedding. I looked out the window and thought I was seeing a mirage. There was probably a foot and a half of snow, and there were some trash cans that were totally covered at the top. I was looking across the street; and all the bushes were covered, and it was still snowing.

I was thinking, they really don't do a lot of plowing in Washington, D.C. In fact, they probably only had one plow, and that was used for the driveway at the White House. I was thinking "How are we going to get to church?" Was the Good Lord telling me that I really shouldn't get married? I'm very superstitious. I thought that it was some message that was telling me "This is not your time for marriage."

It seems to me that if the Good Lord was to send some cautionary message, He would send it to Pat!

Granted…At about 6:15, I decided to call Dr. Smith. He had also been up for a length of time. He was trying to figure it all out, as there was no way the limousines were going to be able to get down the block. No way we were going to get out to make it to the church. And I didn't even think about our guests. I thought about the wedding party, Dr. Smith and his wife and family. I said to him, "Dr. Smith, do they plow here often?" He said, "If they plow like they normally do, they'll probably plow us out 3 days from now." I said, "Well, what does that mean?" He said, "You figure it out."

So I asked him if I could come over. I got the phone book and I looked up the sanitation division in Washington, D.C.

On a Saturday?

Yes. I put a call into their emergency number. I acted like an imposter, and I said, "This is Dr. So-and-So. We have a number of doctors on this block on Randolph Street in Crestwood, and we all have to, at certain stages today, get to the hospital." I hung the phone up and probably about 15 minutes later, there were three gigantic plows plowing the street. In fact, they actually plowed some of the doctors' driveways. He asked me what address I was at, and of course, I gave him Pat's home address, so they plowed the entrance.

In those days, there weren't a lot of commercial plow operators in Washington, D.C., like you have in upstate New York. It seems like every farmer in upstate New York has a plow hitched to his truck or some kind of maintenance vehicle. Well, the neighbors came out and shoveled sidewalks. They were overjoyed that the road was plowed. I think it was a couple of months later they found out that Dr. So-and-So was in charge of getting the road plowed.

How many confessions did you have to do to get squared away after that story?

Well, I told it to the priest, Father Gatto. He said, "Richie, there's such a thing as a white lie. Since it was snowing, there was no problem." So I frequently use that; I only tell lies when there's snow on the ground.

So the wedding proceeded. It was a magnificent day, a beautiful service. My wedding party consisted of men that I had played football and lacrosse with, as well as fraternity brothers. My brother, Al, was my best man. Pat had a beautiful group: sorority sisters, cheerleaders. One girl eventually went on to work in the White House. It was a great array of people, and just a beautiful time.

Father Gatto, of course, received a couple of phone calls from my mother-in-law before we went through our Pre-Cana program. She wanted Pat to consult a Methodist minister, and Pat did that. The Methodist minister thought what we were doing was beautiful. This opportunity to revisit the events of that time is wonderful, because it brings back some very fond memories.

Even though there was a little bit of friction, it never really bothered me.

I assume that after you had daughters of your own, you developed a clearer understanding of the level of apprehension many parents have.

No question. We're definitely getting to that.

Pat and I didn't go on a honeymoon because I was starting a job two weeks after we were married. At that time, Pat had a great job with Sperry Gyroscope, which was a huge instrument company that dealt a lot with military and corporate contracts. It was very convenient to where we got an apartment.

A lot of memorable things surfaced during that period of time. When you're husband and wife, it's certainly a special time. We shared each other's opportunities. And as I mentioned earlier in the book, she stood by me when I was teaching and decided that I wanted to do some coaching—and it appeared that I was going to lose my job. She said "go right ahead and do what you feel is best." And that's really been the approach that we've had during our 55 years of marriage. It'll be 56 years February 11th, 2017.

The beauty is, she always encouraged me. I could always share the good and the bad. The only thing I never really shared a lot with her, what I tried hard never to bring home—if we had a loss or if I had a bad day, I would try to leave that on the field or in the office.

You mentioned that you tried to decompress on campus before you went home.

Correct. Some coaches would go home after a loss and rip the shingles off the garage and yell at everybody. I probably did some of that, but I didn't rip any shingles. My voice was probably a lot louder than it should have been, but my family knew that my frustration was never directed at them.

After being married for about a year and a half, I was playing a lot of softball and lacrosse. We played in a great softball league, and in the Jones Beach Lacrosse League, which really helped develop lacrosse on Long Island. It was a very competitive league. I would play softball in the morning, lacrosse in the afternoon, and then we'd spend the late afternoon/early evening at Jones Beach. One Sunday after a game, Pat and I were in the water and she said, "I really don't feel good. I have a lot of pains in my legs and in my stomach." So immediately I thought she might have food poisoning, and we came out of the water.

Jones Beach is remarkable, with great security, medical assistance, the life guards and the cleanliness. Robert Moses was the designer, and was a visionary.

I decided to take Pat up to the first aid station but she had a lot of difficulty walking. I immediately called my brother and asked him to call Long Island Jewish Hospital which was near where we lived, and tell them that I was bringing my wife in. The medical assistant at the first aid station said that it could be cramps. He was also concerned about internal bleeding, and that concerned me.

We had a convertible at the time and I put the top up. We had some cold compresses, and as we drove, every time we hit even the smallest bump, it caused Pat excruciating pain. We had a towel; and she actually had to put the towel between her teeth.

We got to the hospital and my brothers met me there. They had spoken to a physician by the name of Dr. Tepper. He met us; took her immediately to the emergency room and started treating her, and decided she should stay overnight. I stayed with her as long as I could, within the rules of the hospital. I went back home, and I had a lot of difficulty sleeping. I woke up the next day and went to school. I was teaching a health class and the vice-principal came in and said, "Richie, you have to make a phone call to Long Island Jewish Hospital."

I made the phone call and Dr. Tepper was on the line. He said, "We need your verbal permission to operate on your wife. She's has an ectopic pregnancy." He said, "We can't wait for you to come here and sign."

My friend Tom, an usher at my wedding, was coming into town, and he arrived a couple of hours early. We didn't have cell phones in those days. He came to my high school to see me, as we planned to have dinner together and he was going to spend time with us for a day or two. The people at the high school told him I was at Long Island Jewish Hospital, and he came up there. My brothers and sisters were there, and Pat went through the operation. Dr. Tepper was really tremendous. He came out and told me in medical terms and layman's terms exactly what had happened, and that probably in about three or four weeks, she'd be fully recovered.

My main concern was about her, and her recovery process. My family was just unbelievable. They were with her virtually around the clock. When she got home, they made themselves available and would come to our apartment. I would be at work, and they would be by her side. It was just tremendous how everybody stepped up.

And then about a month later, I got a phone call from Dr. Tepper. He said, "Richie, I realize that you're concerned about having children in the future. The percentages at present may not be in your favor, but in a couple of months you ought to give it some thought." When you're a young couple, you see everybody with babies. A lot of my friends were having babies, and I was holding them, Pat was holding them. About three months later she went back for an examination and Dr. Tepper said, "Well, you can give it a try."

Well, it's obvious that it worked out beautifully because in February, our son Kevin Michael Moran was born. In those days, fathers-to-be didn't have all the training that they have today, and maybe that's good because I probably would have fainted during the birth.

You had been married for 3 years at that point, right?

Yes. We had a very healthy, beautiful baby. My friends felt a lot of compassion for me.

Where did you get the middle name?

It's actually my middle name. And it was a name that my brother John wanted my mother to give me. So I could have been Mickey Moran and I probably would have been....

Sounds like a mobster!

It does... I probably would have been a boxer, or an assistant to Bugsy Moran.

When Kevin was born - on February 6th, 1966 - I was told not to stay around, not to wait, as it could be a while. So I went home and I watched the Boston Celtics play Philadelphia on television. It was a tremendous game. And then I got the phone call. I'm not a cigar smoker so when I got the phone call, there happened to be a pharmacy up the block from where we lived. They carried cigarettes and cigars. I didn't even know what kind of cigars to get. That was the big thing in those days, to pass out cigars.

I got two boxes of cigars. The florist was open; I got some flowers. I went up to the hospital. It was February, and I was so excited I forgot my topcoat. I started to perspire. I never asked Dr. Tepper if the baby had ten fingers and ten toes!

Did you at least ask if it was a boy or a girl?

Yes, I did find out it was a boy. I got to the hospital and my family was there also. They had a chance to see Pat and Kevin. You can't put into words the feeling you have looking at your wife and your firstborn.

Especially after the obstacle you and Pat faced, and the ensuing uncertainty whether it would be possible to have any children.

Exactly... And it was just a beautiful time.

My friends gave me some strange gifts. Bill O'Connell gave us a sterling silver rattle that looked like a barbell. Another friend gave us a sterling silver cup that had footballs all around it. Another one gave us a sterling silver plate engraved with Kevin's name on it, and his date of birth. Flowers came to the house. It was just a magnificent time. It was a relief to know that what could have been a barrier in our life had been lifted, and it also gave us a feeling of unbelievable togetherness.

The good Lord definitely was in our corner because the initial diagnosis was that we probably never would have any children. I believe in spiritual guidance. I thank God every day for the gift of my children. It has made my life so much fuller, and continues to be a bright star in my life.

Pat and I are now grandparents to eight grandchildren. It's like the reincarnation every time one of those babies was born, my reflection, her reflection would go back to when Kevin, Jennifer and Kathy were born.

What were the time gaps between the children, Richie?

I would definitely have to look that up. I do have their birthdays written down someplace. After age 65, there's a mental void on anniversaries and birthdays.

I must point out another piece of irony that is, while amusing, sure to land you in hot water... It's ironic that you can remember who scored the third goal in the second quarter of the Maryland game in 1971, but the birthdays of your loved ones escape you. If I point that out, will we still be friends?

Oh, baby... Time will tell on that one... Hang on...I just remembered... Jennifer was born on May 20th in 1968,,,

So, Jennifer was child number two... When did it become necessary for you and Pat to switch from man-to-man to zone coverage?

Kathy, child number three, came along on May 22nd, 1970... I will never forget the happiness that came into our lives when our children were born.

When Kevin was born, the lacrosse season was getting underway at Manhasset High School. Our team attracted a large crowd, made up of students, parents, and townspeople. One of the players on our team was a young man by the name of Steve LaVaute, and his mother, Ann, was a well-known and successful realtor in the Manhasset/Great Neck/Roslyn area. She was at a game, and Pat was there with Kevin. Pat said "If you ever hear of any houses that are up for sale, we definitely are looking for a house."

Was that the first of many houses Pat has located for your family?

Yes. So Ann said, "I'm going to take you to look at a house. You don't have to go home for dinner," and she invited us to have dinner at her house.

Pat and Ann looked at the house she had in mind for us, and the gentleman who was the seller was with Fairchild Aeronautics Division on Long Island. Fairchild was transferring a number of their people out to the west coast, and he was one of them. If he were to set an asking price and couldn't get that price, Fairchild would pick up the deficit.

Pat looked at the house, and it went on the market at a very low price. That night, when we were having dinner, Pat broke the wonderful news to me that we had just put a down payment on a house. I said, "You put a down payment on what?" She said, "I put a down payment on a house."

I was happy. We had a very good game that day. Steve had played well and his mother had done a great job for us.

Pat has always been the financial genius of the family. I'd be a very poor man right now if it wasn't for her. To be honest with you, I don't even know what I made financially. She has handled our finances since we have been married. I strongly recommend her expertise to all newlyweds... I still get the same allowance that I got in 1961, so it's worked out pretty well.

So she has made you a rich man spiritually, emotionally, and financially.

No question. I said, "Pat, explain to me - how'd you get the down payment?" She said, "Do I ask you how you decide which plays to run?" End of conversation...

We drove by the house and it was very nice looking from the outside. The next day we purchased the house.

That's a big moment, a family's first house.

Unforgettable... In fact, one of our friends had what would probably be called a "jumpsuit" made for Kevin. It was white with blue trim and had his name - "Kevin" - stitched into it. I remember holding him up as we're going through the door of our new house, and it was sensational.

So, Pat's been involved in the acquisition of every piece of real estate that has ever had my name on it, sight unseen, and her choices have always been outstanding.

I remember you shared the story that when you were contemplating whether to make the move from Long Island to Ithaca, she had a lot of those things lined up, housing included, even before you accepted the job.

Yes, she did. So, the love of my life has done a lot of wonderful things for me and continues to do so. It's a beautiful relationship.

You and Pat are two peas in a pod. I've been around you for 35 years and hardly anybody ever mentions your name without mentioning Pat, and the other way around. You two are legendary as a duo.

Well, I can attribute a lot of my success to her. There were opportunities for me to move on from Cornell, to go up a level in administration at another school. There have been opportunities to coach at other schools, and to get back into coaching football. And all of them were a big step up financially. But my heart was loyal to Ithaca, and to Cornell. Each half of my heart told me that this is a beautiful place to be. Cornell University is a tremendous place. They've been extremely loyal to me and to this day, I am proud to be a part of the Cornell community.

I remember being on a plane going to a university where I was planning to take the head coaching job. I might have said this early in the book, but Bernie Olin, the great alumnus, took me to lunch at the Statler prior to my departure. As we were leaving the Statler, the chimes were ringing. He said to me, "I'll bet you they don't have chimes at noontime at the place where you're going to take the job." I still believe he had arranged for the chimes to be played. We talked all through lunch. He was such a dedicated and great man.

It makes sense that Mr. Olin's ashes would be placed in his beloved Schoellkopf Stadium. .

Very much so.

That's a great story. That was well played by Bernie, wasn't it?

Yes. It was. It just never felt right to leave Cornell.

All these things happen for a reason, and I couldn't have had a greater run. Pat actually is the head coach. I'm the assistant. It's really wonderful when you can combine feelings for one another, carrying on your career and your life together, hopefully being an example for your children, hopefully being available for friends, being there for your grandchildren. I try to make every effort to attend any activity they are involved in.

I try to get to memorial services, the funerals of the parents of all my players and friends, of course. Memorials are very important. It gives me a chance to reflect on the individual, how kind the individual was and what he or she meant in my life.

The memorials always remind me how blessed I am to have my family, my friends and my health. I've got a lot of things I haven't done yet.

It's a good thing you're only 80.

That's correct. I need another 15 years. If they want to stretch it to 20, I won't be upset. But I definitely need 15 more years because there are a lot of items on my list. They call it a "bucket list." I call it the Moran Menu, and the Moran Menu is going to be worked on very carefully over the next 15 years.

I do believe in miracles. Pat had that tubal pregnancy, ectopic pregnancy. It appeared that it was going to be very difficult for us to have children. Dr. Tepper at Long Island Jewish Hospital gave us both excellent advice. Before we knew it, we had a wonderful son, Kevin Michael Moran. Kevin was born on February 6th, 1966, and it was a tremendous joy for both of us.

So Kevin is 50... Wow, it seems like yesterday he was a freshman at Cornell.

I remember seeing him in the hospital. In those days, we didn't have a lot of the training that they have today for husbands, and it was a good thing. If I had been there at the birth, I probably would have passed out. But when I went to the hospital to visit him on that Sunday night, it was outstanding. His hands were moving; his legs were moving, and above all, I could see his beautiful blue eyes. That enabled me to really feel the joys of parenthood and the joys of having a son.

I want to ask you another father-to-father question... How

many times did you hear from your friends how lucky you were that Kevin looked like Pat and not like you?

Quite frequently.

That's a common thread, isn't it?

It was good to hear. Pat's a beautiful woman.

Yes, she is. Very smooth answer. I remember when I met you. Kevin was a young teenager and then he went to Cornell, and now he's a 50-year old man. It sure seems the fast-forward button is being pressed, doesn't it?

There's no question. I'm hoping to slow it down as I approach 80. I think it's important for me to put the brakes on.

Or at least downshift a little bit...

As I said, I have a full agenda I want to complete in the next 15 to 20 years.

Thinking back to the time we bought that house in Manhasset... We had a wonderful doctor in town, Dr. Nicosia. I coached his son Tom, who's also a doctor now, living in Manhasset. Tom actually went to Harvard and played against our teams.

When Kevin was about four years old, I would come home from practice and if he was taking a nap, I'd watch him sleep. If he was lying on our rug in the living room, we would have a chance to play footsie or do some things that would make him laugh. What a joy that was. If I was having a bad day, I had a great cure: open the door, see my wife, and spend time with my son.

Kevin did a lot for me. He made me realize how important it is to care about everybody. I say that because when you sit with a baby and you watch all his reactions, you realize that someday he's going to be a grown man. You watch almost every second, every minute, and of course, every year of his life. I remember when he was about two and a half, I came home from a meeting one night and went up to see him. He had a huge lump on the side of his neck. It really startled me. I was really concerned that he might have injured his neck somehow. Immediately, Pat came upstairs. We called Dr. Nicosia. The doctor came over and diagnosed it as a cyst. It had grown quite large.

We took him to the hospital and had that taken care of, removed. After going through the procedure, he had wonderful smiles, as if nothing had happened. He has actually kept that kind of composure throughout his life. He's a very caring, sharing, loving son. Those traits have contributed to all he has accomplished in his life.

Kevin was a fine athlete growing up. He played all sports. During his freshman year, he played football at Ithaca High School, and was a quarterback. I remember when he was playing against Johnson City, who had a very good team. On the first two series, he threw two touchdown passes. That was quite thrilling, especially since I had friends of mine from Maryland and Long Island visiting. I didn't bring them there to showcase my son, but he certainly had a great day. The Little Red upset Johnson City.

During his sophomore year, he decided to stick with hockey. I believe it had a lot to do with the starting date. Hockey started quite early, and that put a great deal of pressure on those young men as they prepared for the tryouts. In some cases, it was difficult to play a fall sport and try out for hockey. I disagree with that theory. I know this has changed in our school district. There is not as much overlap, and I believe in both programs —football and hockey. Kevin was very fortunate to make the team. They had a great team—or I should say, they had a very competitive team which turned into a great team. They were fortunate enough to win the 1984 state championship, which was a remarkable feat.

I would go to the games and my philosophy was similar to what my dad's was when I was playing, and that was to sit in a remote part of the stands. The games were in Lynah Rink in those days, so I would sit there and I'd bring some magazines. Of course, I never took my eyes off the ice. The reason I brought the magazines was that I didn't want people coming up and asking me "Why didn't they do this?" "Why isn't the coach playing So-and-So?" I pretty much wanted to stay away from some of the pressures that coaches are subjected to. I would not agree with some of the comments made by the fellow fans and parents, so I did my best to avoid those conversations.

The start of the season was very challenging. They won their first game and then lost three in a row. Two of those losses were against Rome and Massena – two state powerhouse programs that were always ranked very high. A gentleman I really admired was George Staller, a professor at Cornell. He was a remarkable man, and I am sad to say he passed away in 2009. He used to interview some of my recruits when they came to campus. His son was on the hockey team. Professor Staller had a foreign accent, and he came up and said, "Reechie, wat are we gonna do wit dis team?" And I said, "Don't worry about it. We're going to win the state championship." He looked at me in amazement.

Well, sure enough, after those two games, the team went on a twelve game winning streak and they got into the state play-offs. Guess who their first game was against? Rome. They played Rome up in Utica, and they beat Rome 4-3. Kevin had two assists and played very good defense. It was a sensational win.

The next night, they were playing undefeated Massena, and if I'm not mistaken, Massena had probably a 30-odd game winning streak. Ithaca beat them. I can't recall the score but it was great. Kevin had a goal and an assist. The jubilation after that game was unbelievable.

After the Rome game, they used the theory I had utilized in my coaching. It's a slogan: "Stay down on the farm," which means don't go overboard. You've got your win. Don't celebrate, so the opponent that you're going to be playing the next night will think that was as far as the team's going to go. So they were very calm after the Rome game, and I feel that sent a message to Massena. Massena really knew that they were going to be in for a very tough game, and they were.

From hockey, Kevin went on to lacrosse, and was a starter on the varsity team for three years. He was their top scorer. During that period of time, a game that stands out in my mind is one they played against Vestal. Vestal had some big local names on their team. Cal Harris was on that team, along with a number of other players that eventually went on to Hobart or other colleges.

The game with Vestal went into triple overtime, and then "sudden victory." A lot of people use the words "sudden death" but the lacrosse world is changing. They call it "sudden victory." I've always called it "sudden victory" because it has a better connotation.

They had a great game at Vestal, and went on to beat them. They won the STAC (Southern Tier Athletic Conference) championship and went on to the state championship tournament. After the Vestal game, I was so happy about the team's success, and how hard they played, that I went to a local grocery store and got four or five cases of soft drinks, and put them on the bus. I'm sure they had a little bit of a celebration on the way home. It was a great accomplishment.

How did they do in the state tournament?

They got to the semi-finals and lost to West Genesee, who eventually won the state title. That game was played in Ithaca in front of a huge crowd. It was a great game. West Genesee's depth and skill level was a little better than Ithaca's, but it was still an extremely competitive game.

During his time at Ithaca High School, Kevin was giving a lot of thought to college. He was a very good student. He took a lot of advanced placement courses, and he worked hard in the classroom, at home, and on the athletic fields and rink, and it was his choice to pick out where he wanted to go. At that stage, he was starting to be recruited very ambitiously by Virginia, Maryland and Princeton, and of course, we had an interest in him at Cornell. My assistant coach, Jay Gallagher - God rest his soul - did a great job recruiting Kevin. I was away for a weekend and he had Kevin come on campus, meet the players, and spend two nights on campus like all recruits can. You're allowed 48 hours on campus. That was very helpful, but it was still Kevin's decision to make.

He looked at Maryland. He visited Maryland. I had gone to Maryland; of course, I was leaning in that direction. The coach at Maryland at the time - a gentleman by the name of Dick Edell - was a great friend of mine, and in fact he still is. Dick was what you really wanted in a coach and that was one of the things that I was looking at. It wasn't particularly the school. I knew academically he would make the right selection, and athletically, I wanted him to have a great experience.

He visited all these schools, and I remember we were down on the New Jersey shore at Stone Harbor. Kevin and I drove up to Princeton and he spent a day there. During his visit, I went and visited one of my former players, Greg Raschdorf. I spent the day with Greg and Kevin spent the whole day with the coach at Princeton.

When it came down to decision making, I had just returned from a recruiting trip. Pat left me a note saying, "No matter what time you come home, go up and wake up Kevin." I sat on Kevin's bed, and he said, "Dad, I've looked at all these schools. I've looked at all the positives. None of them had any negatives. They were all a great match academically and athletically. And I've decided I'm going to come to Cornell." I got up and hugged him. I was delighted. It was a wonderful gesture on Jay Gallagher's part. I knew that Kevin would be an attribute to our school and our team. He became very active in organizations on campus. He was vice president of his fraternity and was very involved with the Big Brother program.

This is not necessarily the best comparison, but I think it's relevant: My mom was a very popular teacher, and when I was in that school with her there was some added pressure that both of us had to navigate in terms of expectations of how the teacher's son was supposed to behave, and produce. I'm going to guess that if Kevin had decided to go to a different school, it would have just eliminated that entire dynamic. I'm not putting words in your mouth, but if he had gone to another college, that would have provided another reason for you to be on board with the decision. It would have meant one less layer of complexity.

That would be accurate. He made it work, though. He played lacrosse for me, and he made a lot of great contributions on the lacrosse field. He scored three goals against Brown, which helped with the Selection Committee's decision to choose us for the NCAA play-offs in 1986. If we had lost to Brown, our season would have been over, but it gave us a chance to move on.

We played Massachusetts and beat the Minutemen before a very lively home crowd in their stadium. It was a great game, a great day. We played a fantastic Massachusetts team with a number of top players. Kevin had a goal in that game. He rode very well. Riding in lacrosse is very important because if you can steal a ball or force the offensive team to throw the ball out of bounds, you can get the ball back, and that gives you another offensive opportunity.

After that game, we were extremely happy in the locker room. We were selected on Sunday and we played on Wednesday. We were on the bus on Tuesday to Massachusetts. We had some time to prepare for them on Sunday night and Monday. In the locker room, Kevin came up to me and said, "Dad, I would like our bus driver, Dick

Sweet, and his wife to come on the plane with us to North Carolina." Now, I've always believed in lucky charms, and Dick Sweet was definitely a lucky charm. We had a better record on the road than we had at home.

We decided we were going to take Dick and his wife on the plane with us. I got permission, and he was delighted. His wife had never flown, so this was going to be an experience for everybody, and also sitting next to her to calm her down. That duty went to my trainer, Rick Lafrance.

I know that Rick Lafrance had a real talent for helping people calm down, and one of his techniques was known as "Pabst Blue Ribbon." He helped me calm down a couple of times with that technique. Did he have another technique for the lady on the plane that was having a problem?

We couldn't drink, so yes, Rick masterfully utilized one of his many other talents!

So Rick had more tools in his bag... Unbelievable... A Renaissance Man.

He had some tricks. After we took off and the plane got in the air, we hit some turbulence; and Mrs. Sweet made the hop along with the plane. I thought she was going to come out of her seat. When we got to North Carolina it was extremely warm. We were still dressed in tweed jackets, shirts and ties.

The bus driver was not very kind to us. Normally, they help put the bags under the bus. The bus happened to be a little smaller than the ones we normally used. Placing the team bags, luggage and suit bags underneath was going to be a chore. He said, "Y'all, I don't do those things." So invoking my best southern drawl, I said, "Well, guess what? We can get another bus." He said, "Y'all can't do that. We're hired by the athletic department." I said, "Well, I'll tell you what: You help us out, give me some idea of how you want these loaded. Otherwise, we're not going."

Of course, he was a little angry. He got on the bus and shut off the air conditioning. I would always sit in the front of the bus. I said to him, "You know, you and I are having a little difficulty. I'm going to tell you, in about five seconds, if you don't turn on the air conditioning, we're going to break out every window on this bus."

Sure enough, the air conditioning went on.

We arrived at Fetzer Field on the campus of UNC. We were greeted by a trainer and he had a bucket of water that I wouldn't take to the beach. There wouldn't be enough fluid in it to refresh a basketball team, never mind a 34-man lacrosse squad. I immediately asked him, "Can we get some additional water containers?" And he said, "There it is right there." In response, I immediately took that bucket by the handle and threw it over the top of the scoreboard. It's not that I was getting violent that day, it was just that the Southern hospitality that everybody talks about felt more like Southern hostility. No one had been hospitable to me – or to the team - since we got off the plane.

The trainer was startled and went in immediately and came out with four huge Gatorade jugs with cups, which was an adequate supply of fluid for our players. We had a light workout in preparation for Sunday's game.

We took the field on Sunday. Carolina had never lost a home game in the play-offs.. We talked about that Saturday night. It was a blue sky and a blue moon, because everything down in Chapel Hill is what I call Baby Blue. They call it Carolina Blue.

Once the game started, you could sense how physical it was going to be. The goalies were sensational. I can't tell you the goalie's name from Carolina, but he had over 20 saves and Paul Schimoler had 27 saves for us.

At half time, our opponent was up 4-3. We came back in the second half and scored two quick goals. Kevin got an assist on one of them. Our team was in great condition. We ran hard and played hard.

We scored a couple more goals. We ultimately won 6-4, and that, to me, exemplified what Cornell tradition and Cornell lacrosse was all about. Everybody thought Carolina would rout us at home, and the beauty was, we were flying back home as the winning team.

While in Chapel Hill, I had an opportunity to meet Dean Smith in the locker room. He was very cordial. I had written some motivational and strategic comments on the board, which I always did, so the players could see them just as they were going out on the field. He really liked a couple of the statements that I had written up there. A few years later, Coach Smith called me. The Tar Heels were coming up to play Cornell in basketball.

They played Cornell during the 1990-91 season, when King Rice - who was from Binghamton - was their point guard.

My side-kick here, Dr. Lawrence, remembers it as '91. I'm just enjoying every year so I am going to mix up some years here.

That's okay. As I recall, that's how they ended up playing at Cornell. Dean Smith tried to schedule a game as close to a player's hometown as possible during the player's senior year, and at that time, Binghamton University was not a Division 1 program.

Yes, that's right. So Coach Smith asked me about a place to stay, and I told him about the Statler. It was a good recommendation, as the Statler Hotel on campus is within walking distance of the athletic complex.

Back to that game in North Carolina…We had about three hours before our plane took off, so we went to a nice restaurant that had several televisions. The waiter said, "You had better come out here. They have some highlights of the Cornell-North Carolina game coming up." And sure enough, they replayed about 12 minutes of the game.

You know, when you're on the sidelines, you see things in "real time," but when you see them again, you can really reflect a lot more on what happened during that game. On one particular play, Carolina stole the ball and we were in a clearing pattern. The ball was probably about eight feet away from the goal, and there was really no chance for Paul to get back in the goal. The Carolina player that intercepted the ball was going directly towards the cage and one of our defensemen - Mike DeStefano – came out of nowhere and dove in the cage and stopped the ball. That would have made it 6-5. The fans went berserk, and on TV you could clearly see the reaction.

Our players very seldom saw the films of that magnitude, or on television. Television wasn't really kicking in that much as far as lacrosse was concerned, but it really worked out beautifully as we were celebrating our team's great accomplishment.

We got on the plane and found out that we were going to play

Virginia in the first round, and the victor would take on the winner of Syracuse/Penn matchup. We were in the Final Four, which was, as always, quite a thrill.

Whenever I think back to those great teams of the 1980's, I remember Paul Schimoler fondly. Sadly, Paul passed away in 2013, at the age of 45. He is, without a doubt, one of the finest goalies that ever played the game. He later became my assistant coach, and went on to become the head coach at St. Michael's College, in Vermont. An award in Paul's memory was established by his teammate, Joe Lizzio, and each year, in conjunction with the Cornell Lacrosse Association, the award is presented to an individual that carries on the Cornell Lacrosse tradition of caring and sharing.

Kevin was a great contributor to our team's success. He led in his own way, and it can be extremely difficult when coaches are coaching their sons. The pressures that Kevin faced were very challenging, and we sometimes talk about it. His career at Cornell has really helped him in his professional life. He's married to Dr. Melissa Van Buren Moran. She goes by "Van Buren."

Is she a medical doctor?

She actually has a doctorate in early intervention, and she works with children with autism. She and Kevin have three children: Eamon, Quinlan, and Finn. Those three young men are the apple of their parents' eye. Of course, when Eamon was born, Kevin kind of had the same reaction I had when he was born, and it continues to this day.

I don't suppose I have to ask who Eamon's named after.

Kevin definitely loved Eamon McEneaney. There's no question about it. He admired him as a friend, player, and as a fellow Cornellian.

So those three boys are really wonderful. Grandma and Grandpa are having a great time.

They're about a four-hour drive away?

That's correct. They live in Stratford, Connecticut.

I know that you and Pat put forth an effort to see them often. I hear you say quite regularly that you're on the road to see the

Moran Clan in Stratford.

Yes. It's great to get a chance to visit your family. No doubt about it.

Kevin was number 8 in the program, but he's number 1 in my heart and will always be. It was a wonderful experience for me to have him be a part of two teams that went to the finals of the national championship tournament. The only disappointment I have is that I couldn't get him over the hump in the final game, but in my mind, he will always be a champion. Those players will always be champions. I always say to my players, after I finish speaking to them, that I love them.

There's no question that on those two days that it didn't work out for the '86-'87 teams, as a coach, you definitely feel for them. Most of them will never get a chance again, and that really breaks your heart because they'll be remembered as a runner-up. But in my mind, they'll be remembered as great competitors, great teammates on great teams. I'll always love all of them.

I remember seeing Kevin often while he was at Cornell, because I was in the athletic department at that time. It was clear that he was going to work extra hard to make sure that any of the talk that he was playing because he was the coach's son was irrelevant. I know he recognized that there would potentially be some of those kinds of rumblings unless he worked as hard as everyone else. He saw himself as just one of the guys, and he paid his dues like everyone else.

That's correct. Everything he's done, he's always put great effort into it. Pat and I are very fortunate from almost not having any children to having our firstborn be a person like Kevin.

And then we were blessed again with the birth of my daughter, Jennifer. It's remarkable how you remember certain things. Jennifer was born at Long Island Jewish Hospital. I remember holding her briefly the first night and watching her with the other babies in the nursery.

My feeling is the birth of a child is such a miracle. It hurts me when I hear about children being abused, or neglected. When I looked at all those babies in the nursery, I was praying to God that everything continued to go okay for my wife and my daughter, Jennifer. I was thrilled that we now had another addition to the family, and my chest was out like a peacock. I was just so proud and so happy that she was going to be another link in the Moran clan.

Holding her was—I don't know what it's like to be in heaven, but if there's anything greater than holding your child, then it must be heaven. When Jennifer came home, Pat's mother had come up from Washington, D.C., and she was staying with Kevin. I remember that Kevin came to the front door. That fall, my brother and I had put a new sod lawn in at my house. One of Kevin's tricks was to slide down the lawn, and if I'm not mistaken, I think he had a white suit on. So he had his first grass stains. I wasn't concerned about that at all, but he came out and after he made his slide, he stood up and he was amazed at his baby sister.

So here was the start of a new life. Brother and sister together. I just enjoyed every minute, as did their mother.

One of the things that's wonderful about Jennifer is that she now has three children of her own. She loves being a mother. Mothers today have so many things to do out of the normal, everyday chores. Driving children here, driving them there, picking them up, taking them to activities, traveling long distances for various sports. Her three children are very involved in sports.

During her childhood, you could sense that Jennifer really cared about people. She was so well-mannered. She wanted to make sure every hair on her head was combed perfectly. She dressed so neatly. She loved stuffed animals, and whenever I'd go recruiting or traveling with the team, I'd try to pick up some stuffed animals. That was always the best, when she woke up and found a new stuffed animal in her bed.

Most children have a favorite blanket. Jennifer had this blanket for so long that I thought the Board of Health was going to call because Pat couldn't even get it away from her to wash it. She was very unique. She loved school. Everything in her room was neat; everything was lined up perfectly.

That's an interesting juxtaposition, Richie... You say how meticulous Jennifer was with her room, and her clothing and her hair, but in softball she was a catcher, and she was covered with dirt from head-to-toe after every game, right?

That's right. And she loved being a catcher. In fact, we did mention before, my wife was a catcher. I was a catcher. Jennifer loved competition. Her daughter, Kylie, also played for years and they were both catchers. She really loved high school, and still has tremendous friends from Ithaca High School. They're very close. She played volleyball and softball. She and my daughter Kathy helped put an intramural program together that was called the "Relaxers and the Laxers." It was a lacrosse program. I remember contacting a former player, Joe Taylor, who was a regional representative at Brine to get some equipment for the girls.

I did some consulting for the Brine Lacrosse Company, and they were kind enough to send some equipment and sticks. They started an intramural program which eventually built up to a girls' program from which Jennifer's daughter got a lot of value. Kylie played on that team for 4 years, and it was so wonderful to know that Jennifer and Kathy left a mark on the high school program.

People get awards for the most homeruns, most stolen bases, most goals, most assists and the like, but Jennifer got an award 4 years in a row for the best attendance in school. To me, that was remarkable. She enjoyed every minute of school.

From high school, she went to visit colleges. Like most children that grow up in Ithaca, they see Cornell, and they decide, "Wow, I want to go away to school." Well, she was planning to go away, and then at the last minute decided that she wanted to go to Ithaca College. It was a tremendous decision. She loved Ithaca College. She met her husband there. She made great friends. She is very supportive of her alma mater and she influenced Pat and me to be extremely supportive. We're part of the Blue and Gold Club. We're part of the Friends of Ithaca College, and these organizations do a tremendous amount of good for the students at Ithaca College.

I remember that during those years, the two most eligible Italian-American men in the world were Lou Ferrigno and Lou Sposito.

That is good. They'll love to hear that one.

So Jennifer chose Lou Sposito?

She did. We were very happy. He became a member of the family. I'm not old-fashioned, but I felt that Lou and I should have some conferences before he decided to get engaged to my daughter. The first one is probably part of Lou's history now, but he came to my house in a suit and tie, and he was wearing shined shoes. I was there with a sport jacket and, remember, shined shoes are very important.

I do remember that.

Lou and I sat in the living room, and the fireplace was going. I asked him if he'd like a Coke. He said no. I could sense he was extremely nervous. It was a fairly cool day, and I remember the heat from the fireplace was warming it up noticeably, and it was very obvious that he was starting to perspire.

We started talking about everything under the sun. I told him how much I appreciated him coming to talk to me and how much I admired his family. They're very hard-working people who owned Napoli's Restaurant in town. I just got to meet them. They were born in Italy. Lou was born in Italy. My parents were born in Ireland.

You mentioned early on that you had many Italian families in your neighborhood, and you were all very close.

Exactly. I've probably overused the word "ethnic," but I always believed in how wonderful these people were, and I admired the manner in which they conducted themselves, how hard they worked, their love for their family. So I knew that Lou had a wonderful foundation and he was going to continue to build on that.

As we concluded, I said to him, "Lou, if things work out and you get married, you better be really good to my daughter, Jennifer. If you step out of bounds, I have some friends that are in the business of dissolving a body and they probably won't even find your teeth." With that, I looked at him—and he's always got a nice tan, but he was as white as a ghost, so I didn't know if I was discouraging or encouraging him. It worked out beautifully because three years later, Lou went to Pensacola, Florida, with the intention of becoming a Navy pilot, but his eyesight was a problem. He changed direction and started working with Emerson Borg-Warner, in Ithaca. Given he spoke fluent Italian, and a lot of their business was in Italy; he took a position in the personnel department and really created a nice profession for himself and his family.

Jennifer, of course, would raise the three children as a stay-at-home mother and wife, which is wonderful nowadays. About 6 years ago, Emerson was sending a number of their main personnel and executives to Kentucky, and Jennifer and Lou went out there with their family. It looked like they were going to settle there, but Lou decided to open his own business. It's called Stonewell Bodies, and they do custom fabrication. He stayed in Ithaca, which was their desire. They bought our house on West Hill, on Oakwood Lane, which is magnificent that they're close to us. We're very fortunate as grandparents and parents to have them nearby.

I do want to ask the names of Jennifer and Lou's children but first I want to ask another question... You mentioned how meticulous Jennifer is with her hair. Does Lou share that meticulousness with his hair?

I feel it's pretty important to acknowledge the fact that men go bald for a couple of reasons. One, I firmly believe when you wear your baseball hat backwards, the metal that's on the back of the hat kills the roots in the front of your hair and it contributes to baldness. So, any of you young men that read this, I advise you to keep your hat on straight. Also, grass does not grow on a busy street. Luigi Sposito is a very busy man. He's a good-looking guy. He might hit Hollywood someday.

I know you are more concerned with what is happening on the inside of a person's head, and all's good in there with Lou...

It sure is.

And their children's names are?

Their children are Kylie, who is now a freshman in college, at Fairfield University in Connecticut. And then there is Ryan, who's going into his junior year at Ithaca High, and has expressed an interest in attending West Point. Chase, their youngest, is going into 7th grade. So Grandma and Grandpa have a great time

After Jennifer's birth, I was coaching and I was director of athletics at Elmont High School, which is right near Belmont Race Track—a wonderful high school, nationally ranked academically. We also created a very fine athletic program.

In August of 1968, I was asked to come up to Cornell to interview for the assistant freshmen football job and the assistant lacrosse job. I had a wonderful flight, and I was met by Frank Kavanaugh, a trainer at Cornell—a wonderful man. He was a very innovative person, born in Ireland, and he was my host my first evening. We went to the Station Restaurant; we had an excellent meal, and I met some townspeople because Frank knew everybody.

I came back home and told Pat about the interviews. I had a full day of interviewing with the vice president, of course Mr. Kane (the athletic director), a number of professors, and some people on the search committee that did interviews for potential coaches. That was a nice experience, and I met some wonderful people.

I discussed the job with Pat, and at that time, I didn't think it was the type of job that I really wanted. I had 2 weeks of Marine Corps Reserve duty in Virginia, and I went off to complete that. They called Pat on the phone while I was down there and said; "We'd like to offer the job to your husband. Would you like to come up and look at houses?" Well, Pat went up and looked at houses, she picked out a house—she's an expert at doing that—and called me. I was finishing up my first week of training. She said, "I was looking at houses in Ithaca." I said, "What for?" She said, "Well, they offered you the job and I personally believe you should take it." She said, "I put a down payment on a house."

So, of course, that whole week, I was looking at pros and cons of the job. I realized that I was working three jobs outside of coaching and being the Director of Athletics, and this might be an opportunity for me to get into college coaching, and maybe beyond. I think everybody in the profession has a dream of being a professional football coach, or perhaps a professional basketball coach.

When I got back home, we had a long discussion. I asked Pat if she was sure she wanted to make the move, and she said, "Yes. When do we go?" So I called up and told Mr. Kane I was delighted about the job offer, but unfortunately I could not leave Elmont that soon. Obviously, we worked it out.

When we relocated, the two children were young and I couldn't work with football because I couldn't get up there until early October. Pat joined me 2 weeks later. She was overjoyed, given the temperature was about 40-degrees, and she was wearing shorts and flip-flops.

And then, in 1970, I was getting ready for a game against

Syracuse. Pat was expecting our third child, and on Friday, while I was at practice, a friend of my wife had to take her to the hospital because it was obvious that the baby was on its way.

I came home and, in those days we didn't have cell phones, so nobody got in touch with me until I got home. I went up to the hospital, and that night Kathy was born. So I had a new baby girl, and once again, I experienced the feeling of heaven in my arms. Pat and I were very, very fortunate to have three wonderful children. God assisted in their health, their development, and their lives. What we did as parents was just to make sure that we were setting the proper examples.

I was overjoyed about Kathy's birth, and I was excited about the Syracuse game. I knew it would be a very tough game, my players knew that I had a brand new daughter and they were pretty happy about that. I might have been a little grouchy for a couple of weeks, and I guess on game day I was myself again. Like Bob Knight, I don't believe in a game face. I have no idea what a game face looks like. I looked in the mirror a couple of times; my face has always been the same.

We went out and beat Syracuse 11-7, and right after the game, I went up to the hospital. It was a joyous day.

Kathy and Jennifer were, and are, wonderful sisters. Jennifer was like a little mother to Kathy. Sometimes poor Kathy couldn't do anything right, and we had to tell Jennifer that she was only a baby. She, too, liked teddy bears and I remember bringing home to her a long stuffed toy —like a centipede, maybe a foot and a half long. It had tentacles that wrapped around it.

I'd always play games with them, and it was just a fun time in our lives. Kathy went on to Immaculate Conception School in her early grades, and I got them a plastic lacrosse set to use in the gym. Kathy loved to dance, she loved motion, loved activities. She was a cheerleader in high school and played intramural lacrosse and other sports.

One of the joys of my life took place when Kathy was 11, and she was playing in a local softball league. I have to think of the name of it... It was a very good league.

In Ithaca, it is the Dessie Jacobs League.

Yes, the Dessie Jacobs League. They were playing on a field down by Titus Towers, and I was sitting in the stands and Jennifer was catching. We were playing a team that was undefeated and picked to win the championship, and our team went up by one run. The opposing team loaded the bases, and there were two outs. For some reason, Kathy was in center field. This girl got up, hit the ball a ton to straight center field, and to this day, I can still see the ball. I can see the label on the ball, I can see the stitching on the ball, and I knew it was going directly to Kathy.

Now, Kathy was pretty good at catching the ball when we were close to one another, but here we had a well-hit ball that was in between a line drive and a fly ball. If she missed it, the opposing team wins. If she catches it, her team wins. Well, I didn't want to close my eyes but I started praying! I think that's where "the wave" was probably invented because everybody got up in the stands. As I said, it was a play-off game so a lot of people were there. Everybody got up, and I think it was total silence. Maybe the other team might have been yelling, I don't know.

With that, my baby - 11-year old Kathleen Moran - reached up with her left hand and made an unbelievable catch. As I said, I watched the ball all the way from the bat, I watched it climb up in the air, and I heard everybody screaming—and the ball was in her hand. I swear I can still see the laces, still see the label. And my girl made the great catch. Willie Mays, Duke Snider, Mickey Mantle—as the Brooklyn Eagle newspaper once said, "Mantle, Shmantle, (as long as) we got Abrams." Well, we had Kathy Moran make that great catch.

A lot of her friends were on that team, and to this day, they still talk about it. Kathy says, "I had no idea what I did." After that game, the victory celebration was held at Pudgie's Pizza, which is actually still there. So, that was her move to recognition, stardom - not that she needed it because she was a pretty active young lady.

It's in the highlight film of your mind, right?

There's no question. She went on to high school and took some dance lessons, but before high school, at age 12, she was on the playground and came home and her heel was really bothering her. I iced it, looked at it, and thought it was a heel bruise. I told Pat to take her to the doctor the next day, and she did. He thought the same thing, and he put a cushion in her shoe and wrapped it. The pain started on Monday. The doctor visit was on Tuesday, and on Wednesday, she had unbelievable pain. We were getting ready to play Washington-Lee in the first round of play-offs, and Pat took her to the hospital and they thought it was a lot more serious than a bruise. They wanted to do some tests to detect any further damage, and they put her in a cast and gave her crutches.

Well, as the game was being played, I looked up in the stands, and Pat and the children always sat in the first row, near our bench. It was a very good crowd, as we were on a winning streak and it was a big play-off game. Our opponents had enjoyed a great season too, and we knew we were going to be in for a real test. So I looked up and saw the cast on the edge of the railing, so I sent my manager up to find out what was going on. He came back and told me, and sure enough, that's when I first thought, "Wow, my little baby's got an injury and I hope it's not too serious."

I couldn't wait for the game to conclude so I could go see her. She was a very brave young lady, and she showed me how great she could walk on crutches. Pat and I discussed this, and we decided we had better see a specialist, so we went to the Dupont Institute in Delaware. We discovered that she had a broken bone in her leg but the pain was in the heel. It was difficult to understand how she had a broken leg with no pain.

So they did a lot of things to help her. The DuPont Institute recommended a device, invented in Germany. It's a coil that you wrap around similar to the cuff they use when they take your blood pressure. This was placed on the injured area at night, so she slept with that for about 4 months, and we were praying every day that this would be healed. The fear was that maybe, since she did not have pain in that area, but rather in her heel, that she may have cancer. Of course, as parents we were extremely concerned.

We took her to other providers to get exams. We found out that she actually had another broken bone! She had two broken bones in her leg, with no pain other than in her heel.

Kathy was in a cast for a long period of time, and then in braces and crutches, and she really fought it very hard because she couldn't do the things that her other friends were doing. But she always had a smile, and she would always say, "Well, other people have things that are much worse than mine." It taught me a lot because frequently I'll complain about what I would consider little things, and this was a major setback for her and she wasn't complaining.

I spent hours with her when she was in bed - rubbing her back, rubbing her head, hoping that this coil and the position that her leg was going to be in would be okay. Sure enough, about the end of her time in grammar school, she started to get stronger. She started dancing again, which I know was a great help to her. She had a slight gait at that time, but that is gone now. She recently went to Spain with a group of women and ran the marathon. So, she'll always be my baby. They're all my babies but she's my last. She's always given me a lot of courage.

Her life in school was great. She did very well in high school, and went on to Cornell. She was in the College of Human Ecology program, as she wanted to major in consumer economics or fashion design. In her junior year, she decided she wanted to go to law school, so she took the law boards, the LSAT's, and did well. She then started looking at law schools. She looked at Boston College and a couple of other schools, and decided that she was going to go to Pepperdine on the advice of a good friend of mine – Al Neimeth - that was at the law school at Cornell. Al was a neighbor, he played baseball at Cornell, and was director of the law school alumni group.

So Kathy went off to Pepperdine, she did extremely well, and she met a young man there that was eventually going to be her husband. He got the same treatment that Lou Sposito did, but only on different turf. It was out in California; as Pepperdine is in Malibu. The place was immaculate. She got a great education there. A professor asked students in the class if they would like to put some more time in the courtroom, and Kathy said yes. She went in for an interview, and the interviewer turned out to be Judge Lance Ito. Kathy was selected by Judge Ito to be a clerk. He picked four clerks that had no connection with California. He didn't pick judges' sons or daughters. He had a gentleman from Chicago, a girl from Michigan, a person from Illinois and Kathy Moran, from Ithaca, New York. So that was a jump-start. When we went out to the graduation, the O.J. Simpson trial was still going on. We had a chance to go to the trial, and what a joy it was to see our young lady – the one who fought off a leg ailment - succeeding in college and in law school, and to be part of a major trial.

Once again, we were very blessed. We had no idea she was a part of that trial. My son Kevin was living in Atlanta; he was watching CNN and they had scanned the courtroom. He called my wife and said, "Mom, I think I just saw Kathy in a courtroom. What is she doing in a courtroom?" Well, we called her that night in California. Kathy was very casual when she did things. She really didn't put a lot of hype to anything she's ever done. So she said, "Oh, yeah. I'm a clerk for Judge Ito in the O.J. Simpson trial."

Two days later, Robert Shapiro - one of the lawyers defending O.J. - asked Judge Ito who these people were that were coming up to him with notes. The judge said it was his clerks. He said, "Well, could you introduce them to us and tell us a little bit about them?" So evidently he did, and a day later, Bryant Gumble interviewed them on the Today show. Shapiro used to wear purple suits with various stripes, and one of the questions Gumble asked Kathy was, "What do you think of Mr. Shapiro's suits?" She said, "Only one guy can wear those and that's him." So, BINGO! My little baby was on TV, and she was a part of a major trial, and things continued to work out beautifully for her.

A year after her graduation from Pepperdine, Kathy married Bill Rogers. They met while they were both in law school. Bill's a lawyer, and he heads up the legal team for Chevron. Three years ago, Bill was assigned to a project in Aberdeen, Scotland. Pat and I were very fortunate to have the opportunity to travel there a number of times. It is a beautiful section of Scotland.

Now, Kathy, Bill and their family are in Nigeria for 2 years. They also just recently bought a house on Sullivan's Island, South Carolina. Our whole family spent time with them when they were there for 3 months this past summer. We were also there last Christmas, and we'll be there again this Christmas.

Kathy has organized a number of activities in Nigeria for the complex that they live in. There are over one-hundred "ex pats" families living there. Her two children - Lindsay and Adrienne - go to an international school, as they did in Aberdeen. The international schools are like a college campus, with top-shelf teachers and instruction. They're involved in dramatics, art - you name it, they're doing it. They speak different languages, they have visited twenty-four different countries, and it's really a joy to be with them. We try to speak to Kathy and Bill at least once every week. I'm delighted for both of them. Their next location will probably be either Australia or England, and then he'll come home to finish his career with Chevron. So God has blessed my children.

Moran

Motto:
They shine in darkness.

Moran is the name adopted by two distinct unrelated Irish septs. Ó Móráin and Ó Moghráin anglicised their name as Moran. The Ó Móráin sept had a chief in Ballina, Co. Mayo. The Ó Moghráin sept were part of Uí Máine tribal group and had a chief in Criffon, Co. Galway and another was head of a powerful family from near Ballintobber, Co. Roscommon.

General James Moran (1739-1794) who was part of Dillon's Irish regiment in the army of France was guillotined, although he was an excellent soldier and continued to serve France loyally after the Revolution.

Michael Moran (1794-1871), was a famous street singer and character. He was better known by his nickname "Zozimus". He was blinded as a child and made his living reciting poems and ballads on the streets of Dublin.

There were many eminent ecclesiastics of the name. The Most Rev. Patrick Moran (1823-1895), was a bishop in South Africa and New Zealand. Cardinal Patrick Moran (1830-1911), an Australian, was author of "The Life of Blessed Oliver Plunkett".

David Patrick Moran (1870-1936), was the founder of the weekly review, "The Leader". He had considerable influence on public opinion through his writings.

Moran is one of the sixty commonest names in Ireland and is now found in every county but is most common in Connacht. Other variants of the name is Morrin and O'Moran.

Game Strategy

16

Richie, your original outline included a chapter of X's and O's, but as the book evolved, its overall theme was more about your memories and your cherished relationships.

You have said that if anyone would like to discuss game strategies and those X's and O's, they can contact you, correct?

Yes, they can. I am happy to discuss game strategy and preparation, but I agree that this book is more about the other components of the game, like teamwork, dedication and love for one another.

I will say that I noticed that the NBA recently featured some of what they called "old school" offensive plays, and they used a lot of picks, off-ball cutting, and a great deal of rotation and back-door moves. These were components that our teams thrived on and executed to near perfection. Every player on offense was very skilled in carrying out his individual assignment.

On the other side of the ball, the moment the opposing goalie made a save, our defensive unit immediately went into an aggressive and tenacious riding technique, putting tremendous pressure on our opponent. Our defense did a remarkable job of causing turnovers.

As I said earlier in the book, I believe that a lacrosse goalie has one of the toughest jobs in all of sports – given the velocity of the shots and the many different angles they face - and we were very fortunate to have a legacy of great goalies.

In many sports today, there is a great deal of emphasis on offense, but I have always believed that ground balls, takeaways and assists were a major part of our game.

Many coaches are inclined to call a timeout immediately after an opponent scores, but I did it differently. I chose to let the opponent and their fans celebrate, and we would then get ready for the face-off, substituted a new midfield unit and then call a time out. This gave our coaching staff and players time to reflect on what just occurred, and enabled us to make adjustments. I would never call a timeout immediately after being scored upon. This entire process might take 2 or 3 minutes, but it could be the most important delay tactic available to a coach and his or her team.

I have also been asked about team travel and other components of getting the most out of a team. Regarding travel, we always made sure to make it possible for the players to study on the trip and we booked the best hotels with the best dining arrangements. We were very fortunate to have many alumni in the hospitality industry, and we gratefully utilized those connections. We saw it as a "business trip," knowing that our business was to do what it took to put ourselves in the best position to beat our opponent.

Superstitions frequently pop up in athletics. If we were not successful on a road trip, we would never stay at the same hotel. We also asked for the same bus drivers, and Dick Sweet and Jim Verrichio were great guys and very important "team members."

After games, our team would always leave the locker room together, whatever the outcome was.

Okay, one more story that we almost forgot... it was very heartwarming to read the beautiful testimonials offered by many of your friends and former players. It is clear that they love you dearly, and they know you love them just as much. If you were to ask a thousand players if Coach Moran would ever abandon them, nine-hundred ninety nine would say "No." Which player would disagree?

Tim Daly! He was the most "American" guy I ever knew! He once got arrested for kicking the hell out of four protesters that were burning the American flag, but it all worked out.

We were on a trip in 1982, and it happened to be Tim's birthday.

He played an outstanding game against Princeton, and I wanted him to go home with his parents to Baltimore to celebrate his birthday. He insisted on returning with the team, and we stopped at our favorite restaurant, in Easton, Pennsylvania, and on our departure the owner would always give us snacks and drinks for the bus. We realized we did not have any cups or ice, so I asked Tim to go over to a nearby convenience store. I was distracted, we made a head count and we utilized our "Is your roommate here?" drill, but we missed Tim. Dick Sweet asked if we were all set, I said "Yes," and we left Easton. Upon our return to Ithaca we had a policy of taking your own equipment bag off the bus, and I saw that Tim's stick and bag were still on the bus. I turned and said, "Tim, I know it's your birthday, and you had a great game, but you still need to get your things off the bus." There was a collective statement from the players, "Coach, we haven't seen Tim since Easton, PA!"

It was about 1:30 am, and I immediately got on the phone and called Bob Holt, who was an FBI agent based in Ithaca to get advice. While I was on the phone with Bob, Jay Gallagher was contacting the police in Easton. We were hoping that Tim would check into a hotel or contact us and we would return to pick him up. His real name was Thomas, and that's how he checked in. We were asking for a Tim Daly, so we did not locate him.

As the hours rolled by, I realized I should contact his parents to see if he had called them. Mr. Owen Daly answered the phone and I explained to him what had occurred, and he said he had not heard from Tim. Unbelievable thoughts went through my mind, I told Mr. Daly that I would go back to Easton to try to locate Tim, and with that he started to laugh and said "Coach, Tim took a flight from Easton to Baltimore, and I just picked him up." That was at 10 am, and at that moment, I took my first breath since 1:30 am!

Needless to say, we never had difficulty with head counts from that time on!

From the Shadows to the Light

Richie, you told me very early in our collaboration that you wanted to include a chapter about the time in your life when you faced the challenges brought on by a serious bout with depression.

The fact that you faced such challenges will come as a real surprise to many people, and I commend you for your courage and forthrightness in sharing such a difficult time.

In one of the earliest chapters we talked about the fact that you were the last of eight children. You enjoyed the security of having both your parents and all seven of your siblings in the family home. Then, World War II broke out and all of your brothers went off to serve our country. One made the ultimate sacrifice. Your dad was shipped to Tennessee for months at a time to work as a steam fitter in a ship building yard, because the U.S. couldn't risk having such work done near the coastal harbors. You went from having all that security to facing unimaginable uncertainty. You were the man of the house at 5 years old, and it's difficult to imagine how such a culmination of events might affect your psyche.

Since that chapter, you have talked about how blessed you have been to experience a lot of success and joy. You have a healthy family, you were successful professionally, you have financial security, enduring relationships, a lifelong sense of purpose, the

gift of a long life... I will be honest and say that it took me by surprise when I learned there was a time in your life when things took such a dark turn. Again, I feel it will be very helpful to many people to hear that part of your story.

Thank you, Steve. Sharing this is very important to me, having experienced a very acute case of depression, knowing what I went through, and knowing very little about mental illness at the time.

When was that?

It was in the fall of 1984. We had just completed an excellent fall practice, and during that time I was starting to have difficulty sleeping. I was very irritable, and very doubtful of many things I was normally very sure of.

You just didn't feel like yourself?

That's right. I felt I wasn't really nice to people. And the more I thought about it, the more it affected me. I knew I was not being kind, and it worried me. I found fault in everything, from where I lived to what I was doing to the people I was dealing with. The sun might have been out, but I didn't recognize it as a bright day. My days were really dismal and dark.

You were in your mid-40s at this point, so this had to feel so completely foreign to you.

Yes, very much so. I was taken aback. I wasn't sure what brought this on, or what it was. I couldn't sleep. I was finding a lot of reasons to come home late. I would stay in my office and pretty much gaze at the four walls. I would try to make some recruiting calls, and when I did I tried to make sure that my voice sounded happy on the phone. I know people sometimes describe conversations with others, and say "There might be something wrong with him." I really didn't want that to happen.

So over time, day-to-day tasks really became really difficult for me.

Over what period of time?

Well, it was about two and a half months. It was probably about the second week in November, and I happened to be in my office on a Friday night, and it was quite late. One of the reasons it was difficult for me was the fact that I had three young children at the time, a wife who had always been by my side, and I just felt I was creating a very difficult environment for them. When I say that, I mean it was difficult from the standpoint that I was totally confused about what was affecting me. My body was not really functioning well. I felt very weak and lethargic.

Then, on that Friday night, I once again chose to stay in my office and it was probably about 9:30. Dr. Russ Zelko, our team physician and the lead physician for the athletic teams at Cornell University, happened to pull into the back parking lot, which was below my office window. He had to pick something up in his office, which was adjacent to the training room. He saw the light in my office, and when I heard his car pull up, I went to the window and waved to him.

Dr. Zelko walked into my office, he looked at me and he said, "What can I do to help you?" I said, "Russ, it's obvious you're recognizing something, but I really don't know what it is or what I should do." We talked for a good half hour. That probably was one of the miracles that I frequently talk about, because he was coming up on a Friday night to get something that he had forgotten. And then he came into my office.

He recognized when he got into my office that I definitely was not myself. I had a problem that he recognized as an illness, and we immediately started talking about depression.

Had he been observing you informally since the onset of your illness? Had he seen that things were really different with you?

Actually, it happened that night because it was obvious to him from my actions, movements and facial expressions, but it wasn't that obvious to anybody else.

You put up a good front?

I think so. It's obvious I got help from somewhere, having Dr. Zelko just show up that night. When he walked in the office, and we started to talk, he immediately knew that I had a disorder. He made a couple of phone calls and made an appointment for me to see a psychiatrist the next morning.

I went to the psychiatrist's office, but before going there, I had a lot of difficulty getting out of bed. When I got out of bed, I felt so weak that I kind of crawled in to take a shower, and I struggled to shave, brush my teeth and get dressed. I made it to the psychiatrist's office here in Ithaca, and that was the starting point of working on recovery. I met with him twice a week.

Were you open to addressing this? Was there a period of denial or resistance?

Definitely not. I was so weak. When I was by myself, it was worse. Around my children and my wife, I would try to do my very best to not upset their lives, and the more I thought about this, the worse I felt.

You were very forthright with them about what was happening when you began your treatment?

Yes, I was. My wife was sensational. My children were great. They knew I was not the same father and husband that I was in September. So, from October through the time that I was advised and guided by Dr. Zelko to go get some help, I would not consider myself a good person. Little things, the normal things that children do would upset me. Loving comments and words from my wife I perceived as negative. Anything positive was not within my reach.

This is why I tried to isolate myself from as many people as possible. It was difficult for me to socialize. I was really worried about offending people. When you're irritable, strange things do happen in your life. I was finding fault with everything, from the clothes I wore, the way I combed my hair, to going to my office every day, not wanting to come home for dinner because I didn't want my children and wife to be burdened with the way I felt. It was the worst time in my life, because I felt like I had a lot of blank feelings for the people I loved.

Would you please define "blank feelings?"

I wasn't recognizing them as the people that I loved. They were just there. The chemical imbalance in my head was something that's extremely difficult to describe. At my fourth appointment with the psychiatrist, he prescribed Prozac. As I mentioned earlier in this book, when I was playing softball back on Long Island, I remember looking up on a hill and there was—unfortunately, they used the term "insane asylum." It was a place called Creedmoor Psychiatric Center.

We'd be down on the softball field on a beautiful sunny day, and I'd look up in the distance and see these people who were dressed in white clothing. They'd be walking around outside in an enclosed courtyard to get fresh air and exercise. There's no doubt in my mind that some of those people were probably there because Prozac was not invented at the time. And if they were going through what I was going through, the only cure or only help that could be given to a person with that disorder was probably to institutionalize them.

That sort of kept me on edge. I still think about those people. I still think about a few of my friends that, later on, I found out were suffering from depression and had committed suicide. You're just not yourself. Your mental capacity is all over the place. For some reason, I started to dislike colors that I normally loved—blue, green... The happiness that normally surrounds a family - I didn't recognize it. To this day I regret that because during that period of time, my wife and children were amazing. There's no way I would have made it without them. I've had discussions with them over the years to try to explain to them how difficult it was for me to go through that period of time.

I continued my visits, and the psychiatrist was a gigantic help. To help me piece this all together, he drew out sections. It was sort of like a grid. One part of the grid would be my personality. Another would be my negative outlook. Another was extreme irritability. And really, there was no cause for those. My personality changed completely. For a person that was normally so happy-go-lucky, I was very irritable. My physical strength was almost non-existent.

Little things set me off, which was really appalling because I remember my little daughter Kathy was helping me do things around the yard, and I loved her for that, but at that time, in the condition I was in, I really didn't appreciate it. Jennifer was so nice to me and trying to cuddle up and hug me and make me feel like I was extremely important to her. Kevin told me that he felt so sorry for me. He said I was like two different people, and the person that was created by my disorder really was not me. He was there for me. He helped me through tough struggles.

Have you any idea what triggered this, Richie? I know that many people have bouts with depression after some life-changing event. Obviously, in your case, it was not a divorce, but a

medical crisis, the loss of a loved one, or the loss of a job can be triggers. Can you put your finger on anything?

Not really. Over the years, I was wondering if it started because I felt sorry for myself. That wasn't the case because everything was fine. I was able to walk the walk and talk the talk and do the things that fathers and husbands do. And then, all of a sudden, it started to come into my life. I don't think it's proper to use the word "virus," but it was quite like that. It started to infect all parts of my body and my mind. My mind was in total disarray. I don't know how I functioned, day in/day out. The good Lord was definitely my guardian.

After about the eighth visit with the psychiatrist, the medicine kicked in. It usually takes about two to three months for it to take effect. Now, they tell me it kicks in much quicker. I was very fortunate. My medication started working within about five or six weeks. I started sleeping better. Up to that point, I'd get out of bed every morning and I'd be on my hands and knees and Pat would help me get going for the day. I'd get dressed in a sweat suit, put on a hat and gloves, and go out and walk. I had a walking stick. I'd go out about 6 a.m., because the exercise really helped the chemical imbalance. It gave me strength for the day. I'm so happy that it was not during the lacrosse season because there's no way I could have functioned properly and carried out my work assignments and coaching. My main focus was to get better so I could appreciate all the things I had appreciated four months earlier.

The walking helped, but then again I was thinking people were looking out their windows and saying, "He must have mental problems if he's out here walking at this hour." I was extremely concerned what people thought. I really don't know if anyone other than Dr. Zelko, the psychiatrist, my wife and children knew what I was going through.

I saw you 5 days a week during that period of time, and when you told me that one of the chapters of the book would reveal your personal challenge with depression that had its onset in 1984, it totally took me by surprise.

I understand. I got some very wonderful guidance and help. I started going to church a lot more. I'd go to mass every week. That gave me a chance to have some solitude, pray for my wife and family, and pray that I would be doing the right things and not offending anyone.

Our team had a wonderful faculty advisor, Dr. Phillip Marcus. I confided in him about my problem, so we'd go out and walk on the weekends. We would take strenuous walks to various locations, which I felt really helped me build up my strength. He heard all my confessions. He heard all my negativity. He reinforced me tremendously. It was essential for me to have someone on the outside of my family recognize that I needed help, and Dr. Marcus was a good friend that helped me take steps back to a normal life.

I am also very grateful to Dr. Jim Waite, a dentist and a friend who was there for me whenever I needed him. We did a lot of walking, had a lot of heartfelt conversations, and he, like Dr. Zelko and Phil Marcus, assisted me tremendously in my recovery.

I have another question about this period, Richie... A lot of people who have dealt with depression have said that they lost their hope for the future. You were literally at the halfway point in a very successful and high-profile career. Your children were doing really well in school and sports, and everything in your life was unfolding in what would seem an ideal way. Did you notice that you stopped looking forward? Did depression affect you in that way?

You know, it definitely did. I was having difficulty completing one day and focusing on the next. That was extremely difficult for me. I was sleep-deprived. I couldn't eat very well. I'd lost weight. I did not feel strong. I questioned every move I made, whether it was writing a thank you note, writing to recruits, sending out holiday cards… I totally doubted if I was doing anything right.

It was sort of like a repeat loop, every day. Just picture being extremely negative every day, and you look in a mirror and, and you're not the same person that you were yesterday. You're not the same person you were five months ago. It was like having a black crepe placed over your head, and you didn't have the strength to pull that crepe up. It was like wearing a mask that you could see through, but you didn't see anything that was bright. You didn't see anything that was joyous. You didn't see anything that was lovable.

You just saw visions of things you don't want to see. I started seeing visions of articles that were in the paper about people that committed suicide. And then, unfortunately, I had a person connected with a newspaper on Long Island call me about a coach and an athletic director that had just committed suicide.

Someone you had known?

Yes, and the reporter wanted me to comment on both of these people. Of course, he was on the other end of the phone and had no knowledge of what I was going through. I started to cry. I told him I was too choked up to really say anything. Eight years later, he found out what I was going through during that particular time. I was asked to give the keynote address at the National Lacrosse Convention in Baltimore, and Kevin had just graduated from Cornell. I told him I was going to be speaking and he said, "Dad, you could help a lot of people. I think you ought to talk about the depression you went through."

I thought about it. I had prepared a speech that was quite different. The theme was "Why We Are Coaches." I took Kevin's advice and I changed it. That's when the sports writer came up to me after I gave the speech. I was out in the lobby, and he came up to me and he said, "I really apologize. I had no idea what you were going through when I called you eight years ago." We hugged each other and my thoughts went right back to those two men that had died.

After that speech, seven different people came up to me and shared unbelievable stories, some very similar to mine. The most heartbreaking story came from a young man in his early 20s. He was very athletic looking, and he came up to me and asked me, "Coach, can I speak to you privately?" I said, "Sure." He said, "I wish my brother was here to hear you speak. It may have saved his life. Two weeks ago, he committed suicide." I was stunned, hurt, because in those years, we didn't talk a lot about depression. The connotation was negative, and it brought to mind some of what those people were going through at Creedmoor, when they walked around outside the building. If you were mentally ill, you were pretty much cast off. It broke my heart that this young man had committed suicide. Our teams played against him, and had actually played against him that spring. He was a wonderful young man, a great athlete. I can remember shaking hands with him after our game. Upon hearing of his death, I had tears rolling down my cheeks because I thought maybe we all should have spoken out sooner to let people know that they're not alone with a disorder of this type, and they should seek help immediately.

When you're dealing with depression, it's difficult to recognize what you really have. Now, it's being written about and talked about more, a number of people have stepped forward to talk about it. I personally believe more has to be done. I read and hear more about children with depression, and I've experienced it firsthand, since I had the disorder. Three players that were on my team had depression at an early age, and one of them had a relapse while he was here at Cornell. I was able to help these players, and the psychiatrists at Cornell were remarkable.

It's a tough hill to climb when you have a disorder of this type. Even when people reach out to help you, like my family did, mentally I could not accept their beautiful feelings they had for me. I came up with the strangest excuses on why not to stay involved, or connected. I had avoided social activities, events and speaking engagements during my illness, but after about two and a half months, I started to get stronger, I started to sleep better, and I continued to try to do as much walking as possible.

My spiritual values were definitely one of the things that got me through this challenging time.

Again, Richie, it's very generous on your part to be so forthcoming about your illness. When people think about who might be vulnerable to depression, you are not likely high on the list. You were – okay, are - a Marine, you played elite level college lacrosse, and you became a leader of men who went on to become leaders themselves. When people realize that you dealt with depression, it might make them feel much less alone if they're experiencing those symptoms. Given that you are a "tough guy" by any definition, it's very courageous to be honest about your own vulnerability. I believe this will help people realize they don't have to face such a challenge alone, they're not the first person to do so, and that there can once again be hope for the future.

I hope so. After that convention in Baltimore, I started being a mentor for six men that were recovering from depression. It's been a great network. If I think about one of those men, I call them, and I will sometimes call these individuals twice a month.

One of the concerns that I've had since that time in my life is that I worry about relapse. Once you're on medication, you can never make the decision to come off it on your own. I've spoken to people who have come off it, and, unfortunately, they regressed and that agony of being depressed comes right back. I think it's human nature that sometimes when you're feeling good, even though it's been prescribed by your psychiatrist or doctor, to be tempted to discontinue your medication every day. There's that feeling, "Oh, I feel great. I don't need that anymore." That is the biggest mistake anybody could ever make. You must stay on your medication.

If I was going to give advice, first it would be if you have signs similar to those I had, get immediate medical attention. See your family doctor. Get a referral to a psychiatrist. Start finding solutions to what your brain is doing to you and making you act a certain way. The person or persons that invented Prozac and other medications for depression and mental illness have saved an unbelievable amount of lives. There's no doubt in my mind that they saved mine.

There's not a day that goes by that, when I'm by myself, I thank my loved ones. I thank Phil Marcus. And I thank God that I had a chance to recover. I pray for those people who are going through depression. Please get help. Try to force yourself to look at the beauty that surrounds you. Try to embrace positive thinking. That's important for you.

It's like building up a structure that has crumbled. You have to recreate a foundation. You have to put the walls up with beautiful windows. Mine would be stained glass, I love stained glass, so somewhere in those windows there would be some stained glass—so the rays of sunshine can come through, brighten up your body and mind, brighten up your life, brighten up your future.

In the condition that I was in, it would have been very easy to give up. I had such wonderful support from five people – actually, counting Dr. Zelko and my psychiatrist—seven people. And I'm sure everybody that was around me—until they read this chapter had no idea that they played a major role in helping me recover.

Recovery is interesting... When I'm walking I often think, "Did I really recover?" When I look around me, I look at my friends, I look at my family, my grandchildren, former players, people, there is no doubt in my mind that I'm still going through a recovery period. I'm more happy-go-lucky than I've probably ever been because, in a way, I've made it. I fought through a blockade with help, with medication, with medical advice. I guess if you had to use a term,

I'm "stable." Thank God.

Richie, this conversation makes me think about our mutual friend, and the serious and debilitating mental health challenges he has lived with for 45 years. I now have a clearer understanding of your friendship with him. It is clear that you perceive the opportunity to reclaim your life as a real gift, and gifts mean more when we pay them forward. It seems this period in your life really helped you develop a deep sense of empathy for people who are facing similar challenges. I see that you purposely reach out when you think somebody's going through a tough time. It almost seems like you see that as a part of what you owe back to the greater good, or what you owe back to your Higher Power for having done that for you, for having provided what you needed when you needed it.

It's true.

I'm glad you're stable, and I'm glad you're more happy-go-lucky than ever.

Steve, you know, it's interesting. When I was going through this inability to function, I thought my condition was somehow related to coaching. Did I say the right things to the players? Did I do the right thing? Did I look at the person the right way? And I said, "This could be a coach's' illness," not knowing a thing about depression. And once I started to read about it, and started to check the boxes, I came to understand more about the chemical imbalance and what it was doing to me.

My biggest worry was, What is it doing to my family? That was the most difficult. Sometimes when you get injured, you may break an ankle, or fracture a shoulder or break your ribs. You know there's going to be a recovery. You know that if you follow the rehab schedule, that these injuries are going to be okay. You go through major surgery, you know that the surgeon is going to do everything possible to help you recover and rehab.

We often hear the term "Is there light at the end of the tunnel?" I didn't think I was going to recover. All I saw was darkness. It hurt me deeply to know that this was affecting my family. When you're around your family, you want to display happiness and joy in their achievements. I'm concerned that I put them through five or six months of misery. People say you can always make up the time to some degree. I've been doing that ever since I realized what my mental complication was.

There's not a day that goes by that I don't cherish the kisses I got from my children, their hugs, the touching, and the smiles that I experienced. Sadly, during the time when I was really down and out, I couldn't recognize any of those. Today, it has really made me a better person.

My recovery has brought me happiness, but I often think What if I had not gotten help? I frequently think Will this ever come back and repeat itself? And then when I look at friends, I look at people that have disabilities, I think of people that are - I don't like the word - "institutionalized." I feel for them because the way I look at it, I'm a very lucky person. It's remarkable how that Friday night visit by Dr. Zelko, the consulting and advice and feelings of friendship and support that Dr. Phil Marcus had for me, the love of my wife and my family. I worry about people that don't have that type of support.

So whoever's reading this, if you feel in any way I can help, I'll be available 24/7. I'll be happy to visit with you. But, please: Seek assistance immediately. This is an illness that could prevent you from enjoying your life and your future, and also may lead to thoughts about ending your life. Seek help. Accept it. Realize it's going to be a period of time in recovery. And don't ever, ever stop taking your medication.

I hope you can give yourself some credit for stepping up and making that bout with depression a six-month episode and not a six-year, or a six-decade ordeal. Some people are so rooted in their denial, so resistant to getting help that it just casts a pall over their life and their family's life for decades.

That is very sad. See, what happens, too, Steve—when a man is the provider for his family, he wonders when he has depression, How is it going to affect my employment? How is it going to affect my income? How is it going to affect my stability in the community? How is it going to affect my being accepted in the community?

Because, immediately, when you have a mental illness, many people think "I don't really want to be around that person." "I don't think he can really work for us." "I don't think he can function properly." So without medication, your chances are not very good.

Yes, I have heard several mental health professionals convey their belief that the most effective "three-pronged" approach to managing and recovering from depression includes the three components that you talked about: medication, exercise, and talk therapy. I'm sure that there are some people who may believe that taking medication throughout their lifetime will not be necessary. You made a valid point when you said that the most important thing is to find healthcare professionals that you trust, formulate a game plan with their expertise, and stick with it.

That's a powerful chapter. It's a very generous offer that you made, inviting people to reach out to you personally. That's a very Richie Moran kind of offer.

Email address: rmmlax@aol.com

Forever Connected

> ***Co-Author's note:*** When I mentioned to Richie that I'd like to include a chapter of testimonials, he squirmed a bit.

Understandably, he was a little uncomfortable with the idea of including an entire section of glowing praise in what is essentially his autobiography. I get that. I said to him, "Richie, a lot of people have thoughts and memories they want to share with you, and they are happy to do it publicly. I understand if that pushes you a bit out of your comfort zone, but we will make sure we specify that it was me, not you, that solicited these comments."

Marc Martone *(Richie's High School coach on Long Island)* - More than 65 years ago, as the assistant varsity football coach at Sewanhaka High School in Floral Park, N.Y, (which was one of the largest high schools on Long Island at that time), I welcomed a large group of enthusiastic men to try out for the team. Talk about my good fortune, for in this group was a young boy by the name Richie Moran. Richie, despite being small for a lineman, proved to be one of the toughest and hardest working players I ever had the pleasure to coach. He was the "watch charm" guard of high school football (I did not know how old that phrase was until I checked and found out that a Notre Dame guard by the name of Bert Metzger in 1929 was nicknamed the "watch-charm guard" by Coach Knute Rockne because of his relatively small size.)

Richie more than made up for his lack of size with an extremely fine work ethic — he didn't know the word "quit." I knew then that any coach of any team with Richie Moran as a member was always a winner regardless of the final score. Richie's attitude was infectious and inspired all his teammates, one of whom was Paul Rochester who played defensive tackle for the New York Jets, who beat the Baltimore Colts in Super Bowl Ill. However, after the football season, it was love at first sight as Richie discovered lacrosse and helped his team to four straight undefeated seasons.

After Sewanhaka, Richie headed for the University of Maryland where he played a dominant role on the 1959 National Championship team. History speaks for itself - Richie became an outstanding player at all levels in high school and college. He also had a college coaching career culminating in winning three NCAA Division 1 Championships as head coach at Cornell University. He has been inducted into the National Lacrosse Hall of Fame as well as numerous other halls of fame. Talk about covering the world - Richie has coached Team Ireland in world competition and currently serves as President of the Irish Lacrosse Foundation.

Everything can be summed up in the fact that one of Cornell University's most prestigious awards annually is the "Richie Moran Award" presented to a senior-athlete who has distinguished himself/herself through "academics, athletics, and ambassadorship." More importantly he is one of the finest individuals I know and I am happy to state that Richie is one of my closest friends as well as one of my most favorite 'sons!'

Richie Moran :

GREAT AS A TEACHER/COACH

GREATER AS A HUMAN BEING

Joe Capela - My name is Joe Capela and I played Lacrosse for Richie Moran at Manhasset High School in 1963, and we were New York State champions and Manhasset's first lacrosse championship team. Richie taught us many valuable lacrosse skills, but the most valuable skills he taught us were the skills that we could take with us into life, business, community, country and family. I made up a saying which is still valid today: "I take Richie Moran with me each day onto the toughest playing field there is, the playing field of life."

Bruce Cohen - I have known Richie Moran for 55 years, and though many people connect Richie and me and assume I played for him, he has never been my coach. That doesn't change how I feel, however. In fact, when I was inducted into the National Lacrosse Hall of Fame in 1989, I asked Richie to nominate me. Of course, he crushed it.

I first met Richie in 1961, after my freshman year at Cornell. He was then a successful coach at Elmont High School on Long Island. We played on the same team in the Jones Beach Summer Lacrosse league, and held practices, if I recall correctly, at Sewanhaka High School in Floral Park. Very fun time. I got to know Richie pretty well over those summers and, well, we just connected.

Fast forward... After finishing my playing career at Cornell in 1966 under legendary lacrosse coach Ned Harkness, I learned that Ned had decided 1968 was going to be his last year coaching lacrosse. I went to Robert Kane, the Cornell Athletic Director at the time, and recommended he talk with Richie. The rest, as they say, is history.

While Richie was a fabulously successful coach, winning 15 Ivy and 3 National Championships, 3 Coach of the Year awards, etc., his contribution has been far larger than great coaching. What Richie has meant to lacrosse, in general, not just to Cornell, has been recognized by the US Lacrosse's decision to name the Gallery of its new Hall of Fame facility in honor of Richie Moran.

In my view, however, Richie's most important contribution has been his incredibly positive influence on so many young men and, actually, on everyone he touches. He has a rare gift. I am so proud to have known him over all these years and to be able to exchange hugs whenever we get together.

Richie Moran is a very special person. His blend of warmth, humor, compassion and passion is rare. Happy 80th birthday!

Jay Paxton - Coach Richie Moran knows lacrosse. He also knows the human spirit. For over six decades Coach taught the former while he molded the latter. From his scholastic and club days on Long Island to collegiate success at Maryland, Coach mastered the skills and perfected the mindset of a great player. We all came to quickly learn that. He was a stellar member of many eminently successful and still revered teams at every level. He honed his habits and his approach to the game under renowned mentors. He consistently won alongside equally talented and committed teammates. Coach knew his stuff.

But Coach Richie Moran then gave back. He taught, epitomized, shaped and contributed - much more, much better and much longer than most peers. He did so in a unique way and at a storied place.

He came to build and to embody Cornell "Big Red" lacrosse. The spirit that is lacrosse had captured Coach. Add to that Native American spirit and his personal experiences such key intangibles as a large close-knit Irish Catholic family and upbringing, plus a stint in the United States Marine Corps, and you get an inkling of more key composite pieces of Coach. He brought all that to Ithaca and to Alumni and Schoellkopf Fields and to a generation of young men. When you then saw and you now say Coach Richie Moran you envision that whole package - technical skill, tactical acumen, sustained success, passion for the game, compassion for the players, and the spirit – his constant, irrepressible, inexhaustible spirit.

Who else but Coach Moran could be found walking the lines at Teagle Hall during freshman PE sign-up and using it as a recruiting landslide. Actually he stalked the lines. He moved with a mix of scout-sniper, sheriff and horse trader. Once he picked his target it was a rapid physical close, a lacrosse tale and an Irish sale. You then got a post-card, had an office call, were issued a crosse or stick, and quickly found a new sport and team and mates, and an open door to a real life-changing "ride".

Needed a testing ground? Wanted formative and bonding experiences? Let's practice on Upper Alumni in the mud and slush of a few lanes of snow melt above the cyclotron in February. Not enough? We'll swap for a midnight practice in the dust and fragrance of the Polo Barn. Weather finally broke. How about running to the Ag and Vet schools to check if the cattle are okay, and report back quickly down Tower Road. No hitching a bus ride. Hey, "... it's great to be here!" We had faint dreams of fields and conditions the "big money programs" and "those schools down south" were seeing for practice. No sweat, we were Cornell. We were Big Red "Spartan bastards."

School or school life hard? Plenty of help was there too. Coach found accommodating part time jobs, alternate course schedules, tutors, new living options, unheard of and family altering scholarships. It was "on you" to make it work, but Coach knew what the big dream was for us all and why it mattered. He helped you find a way to stay and pay and play.

Forty years after the incredible ride began, the movie re-run sometimes flickers. But, with a little focus, the right light and a periodic sound track refresh, it comes in crystal clear and technicolored. The ground balls and face-offs are script, the wins and the losses (the former clearly larger) are sub-plots, the names and the numbers are all best supporting players. It is the motion and the spirit that captures you. Constant motion and constant spirit. Positive motion and winning spirit. And at the center of the motion and the spirit is the man, Coach Richie Moran - always in the mirror, always in motion, always our spirit! Happy 80th Birthday, Big Guy! We love you Coach. Semper Fidelis ...

Dave Wohlhueter - Here goes about my favorite coach: I met Richie Moran on a Bucknell basketball trip to Cornell. We became friends at that point and forever more. When I began work at Cornell, Richie and I immediately bonded because we were going to paint his office in Teagle Hall. We did a great job, caught hell for being non-union painters, and our friendship continued. There are hundreds of stories I could tell about our close relationship, but I think this one tops them all and demonstrates Richie's fondness for everyone in Ithaca.

Near the end of his coaching career, Richie had thoughts of taking on a new challenge at his alma mater, Maryland. Did he want to go into athletic administration or not? When it was becoming decision time, he came into my office and left me a note that shouldn't be opened until he made his final decision. When he made the "correct" decision to stay in Ithaca, I opened the note that just contained the simple phrase: "Cornell With Love".

That's how I will always think of the greatest lacrosse coach ever, and his feelings that are genuine as the clouds up above. Thanks, Richie, for your friendship with love.

Bob Rule - When asked to write something about Richie and keep it to 200 to 400 words I found myself thinking that 2000 to 4000 words would not be nearly enough to describe this extraordinary man. So, I will try to give a sort of summary of the man from my perspective of fifty years in no particular order. First thing that comes to my mind is his tremendous energy and zest for life. My brother-in-law, Brian, who also played for Richie, commented to me that Richie was slowing down a little. We both agreed he now has the energy of two men instead of three men! The second is his extraordinary ability to connect with the people around him. I have never met anyone who has close to the memory for faces and people than Richie Moran. He makes you feel like you are the most important person in the room when he talks to you. The third was his ability to make you better as a player. His amazing record was the result of players believing in his leadership, believing in his system of work hard and be prepared. He treated all his players with respect and it did not matter whether you were a star player or sat on the bench, you knew he cared about you. His zest for life, his enthusiasm lights up any room he enters. I never had and still don't have the stamina to keep up with him during social events as he would just spin stories and thoroughly enjoy himself with the people he was with at the event.

He is one of the most genuine and kind people that I know. He doesn't have to work at these things because you know, instinctively, that they are part of his personality. His loyalty to his friends is legendary. He makes sure he visits his ninety year old former high school football coach when he visits Long Island. I will receive a call from him because he just wants to say hi and see how my life is going. I know I am just one of many that are lucky enough to receive a call from him. He always ends the call, "You know I love you". And you know he means it.

When all is said and done I want to give Richie my ultimate compliment. He is a good man who takes care of his family, takes care of his friends and takes care of his players. How lucky am I to have had the privilege of having this man be part of my life!

Robert Henrickson - When one thinks of Hall of Fame coaches, like Richie Moran, one would naturally think of records, wins and championships. However, when I think about Coach Moran, I reflect on all the things he has done for players, including me, after graduation. He was instrumental in getting me a job at Cornell's Veterinary School because he knew my dream was to become a veterinarian. He introduced me to the Admissions' Director of Cornell's Veterinary College which helped me to get into the school. I am now a vet in my hometown of Manhasset, and Richie still calls me for breakfast or stops by to visit when he is on Long Island. He has always taken an interest in my family and calls me every birthday! He keeps in touch with my Mom by "checking in" on the phone, and was one of my Dad's best friends.

I have always been amazed by Coach Moran's memory of players, hometowns, coaches, parents and siblings' names. He remembers players, games, scores and plays. And, as always, Richie is a consummate storyteller and the life of every party that he attends.

Brooks Bradley - I'm proud to have been asked to write this testimonial for my longtime friend and coach, Richie Moran, in celebration of his 80th birthday. Here is a bit of background before I really explain how important Richie has been in my life.

I had never played lacrosse prior to arriving at Cornell in the fall of 1969. Football and baseball were my sports in high school. By a stroke of great fortune, I played on the Freshman Team, which was a godsend because freshmen could not play on the Varsity Team and I had the opportunity to start all the games that year in the spring of 1970. I fell in love with the game!

In my sophomore year, I made the Varsity squad. In the spring of 1971, we went on to win the first ever NCAA National Championship. I was a bit frustrated that year because I hardly played....more on that later. I was a starter my junior and senior years. In my senior year I was team captain and an All-American Defenseman.

Richie's major impact on my life is something for which I will be eternally grateful. We first met in the fall of 1970 at the fall lacrosse awards banquet. I was fortunate enough to win the most improved freshman award, which gave me a real shot in the arm.

I came from a difficult home in that my dad was an abusive alcoholic. Richie filled a very significant void as a father figure to me. I felt very insecure when I arrived on campus in the fall of 1969. I had attended the same school from K -12 and I thrived there, as some of my teachers and coaches became significant father figures, especially my football coach. I felt very secure in that supportive environment.

In my sophomore year at Cornell, I quit the varsity football tryouts, and then in the spring I briefly quit the varsity lacrosse team as well. Candidly, I was "bouncing all over the place", completely unsure of myself. Richie came after me because he knew I was struggling and he also knew what the impact of being "a quitter" would have on my life in the future. He refused to let me quit and my life was forever changed. I don't know where I would be today if not for Richie's love, support and belief in me!!

I've stayed very close with Richie over all these 43 years since I graduated from Cornell. My three sons and my former wife came back to Cornell many times for games. It was an awesome experience for all of us. We would have dinner with the team on Friday night and Richie would introduce us to the team, Saturday morning breakfast with the team, in the locker room before and after the game, and then always a great dinner with Richie and Pat on Saturday night. On Sunday morning, there would be an "until the next time" breakfast before heading home to Baltimore.

As a member of the US Lacrosse Board, I knew that naming the new National Lacrosse Hall of Fame (located in the newly completed National Lacrosse Headquarters) would be a fitting tribute to my great friend and longtime coach and mentor, Richie. It has truly been a labor of love raising the funds to honor Richie in this way. The ribbon cutting took place on September 11, 2016 (ironically the day in 2001 when Eamon McEneaney tragically died in the World Trade Center terrorist attack).

I love you, Richie, for all the love and support you have offered me over these many, many years.

Chris Kane - I recently went out to dinner with Richie and his wife Pat in downtown Ithaca. What a pleasure getting to spend time with them like that. I asked him what he thought he did differently as a coach that made his teams so successful. He said he had policies versus rules. Rules are too easily broken by high-strung kids and there have to be consequences.

In my own words, his policy for our team was simply, "Do the right thing when no one is looking." That says it all. We bought into that big time. We never embarrassed him or the University. Ever.

You can't buy into this if there isn't love in the equation. In my own words again, another of his policies would be, "Be the first one to say hello." You say hello, you put a smile on someone's face, in turn, it makes you smile. Everyone wins!

We all loved each other and it started with him. He genuinely cared, you can't fake that with the cast of characters in our locker room. On top of the locker room board, he wrote a saying, "It's Great To Be Here!"

I've personally helped start over a dozen youth and high school lacrosse programs in South Florida over the years and nothing gives me more pleasure than to hear a bunch of little kids screaming at the end of practice, "It's Great To Be Here!"

As I've said many times, Love you Coach.

Mark Webster - I had the good fortune of playing on Richie's first two Cornell teams in 1969 and 1970. That first season was a challenge with a difficult transition from a very successful previous coach (Ned Harkness) and racially motivated unrest on the Cornell campus, both of which resulted in a team that was distracted and underperforming. We lost an unheard of 3 games in a row midseason – two in the Ivies – threatening to make that 1st year a disaster. Our team was lower than a snake's belly! That's where Richie's infectious enthusiasm and unbounded optimism took over. On the plane to Providence he took me aside and said, "You know Mark, if we beat Brown today and Yale upsets Princeton and Dartmouth upsets Harvard, we still have a chance to tie for the Ivy League title. All we have to do after we win today is beat Princeton (the preseason favorite) and Dartmouth." All of those predictions came to be and we shared the Ivy title with Brown and Yale – both of whom we had beaten. That enthusiasm carried over to the next year resulting in an undefeated season and paving the way for the establishment of first National Lacrosse play-off, won fittingly by Richie's 1971 team.

Bruce Arena - I had the privilege to be recruited by Richie Moran to attend and play lacrosse at Cornell University. Upon graduation (1973), Richie gave me the opportunity to work in the lacrosse program as the Freshmen Lacrosse Coach (1973-74) and the JV Lacrosse Coach (1977-78).

Richie was my mentor. He helped me grow as a person and athlete. He taught me how to work hard, how to become a winner, how to be dedicated, and how to be a fair and honest person. These invaluable lessons and qualities inspired me to become a coach. I've been a coach for forty years and I'm indebted to Richie's influence in my life.

I guess I could cite a number of stories and experiences I have shared with Richie. However, it is almost impossible to pick one over another. For all of us that had the experiences to be around Richie on a frequent basis, we would simply tell you that every day was a special day and a special experience. He was incredibly influential to all of us, and because of this most of us grew to be responsible and successful people. I think this is an incredible legacy for Richie, and all of us that have had the experience to be influenced by Richie are forever grateful. Richie Moran was a great coach and he is even a greater person.

Richie, I thank you, I love you and Happy 80th Birthday!

Wayne Meichner - Over the past 40 years, I am very proud to call Richie Moran my coach, a mentor and a friend. He is not only a Hall of Fame coach, but a Hall of Fame person as well.

As an un-recruited walk-on at Cornell, I was fortunate enough to make one of the greatest teams in lacrosse history. To this day, it is one of the things I am most proud of, and candidly, it never would have happened had it not been for Coach Moran. Trust me, Richie did not need me. He had a team loaded with All-Americans, and was coming off back-to-back national championships. Nonetheless, he gave me a shot to be part of the program and for that, I will be forever grateful.

Obviously, Richie is an incredible coach and teacher of the game of lacrosse, but he also was a great developer of character. He built his teams not only with tremendous athletes and lacrosse players, but with outstanding individuals who knew what it took to truly be a team. For this reason, Cornell lacrosse is like family and has become such an important part of each and every one of his former player's lives.

Over the years, I have stayed in touch with Richie. He has gotten to know my wife and my two sons. My oldest son just graduated from Cornell and Richie would take him to lunch from time to time and check in on him to see how he was doing. No specific agenda, just Richie being Richie, always caring, always being available to talk.

It's difficult to say everything I want to say about Richie since he has been such an important part of my Cornell experience and my life overall, however there were a few phrases he would always say at practice or in the locker room that have always resonated with me. The first was "stay down on the farm" which was his way of saying to stay humble, despite individual or team success. Another was "competition breeds success," which is so true and something I use as motivation in business all the time. And finally, "It's great to be here," which of course, it was, because of Richie Moran.

I love you coach. Happy Birthday.

Jon Levine - My lacrosse coach in college was Richie Moran. I walked on the field freshman year and I met amazing players; players with more skill and finesse than I'd ever played alongside. There was Mike French from Canada with his small box lacrosse stick, which he moved around in ways that were pretty magical. And there was Bill Marino, a Long Island midfielder I'd watched play in the Long Island championships at Hofstra, who was lighting it up on the field. I remember thinking, "Wow, this is a special group of lacrosse players." Little did I realize, the next 4 years would be the most special years of my life. It was a period of learning, laughing, crying, and building a bond with a band of brothers that would stay with me for a lifetime.

The architect, the producer, and the director of this lacrosse experience, on and off the field, was a fiery Irishman named Richie Moran. Richie was the Marine-type coach, who built a system, demanded a high work ethic, and expected 150% on and off the field. I had the honor of being surrounded by a group of young men, hand selected by Richie, who shared the same core values of hard work, family, integrity, and a desire to be the best in our chosen University. Richie instilled within us a determination of excellence and a brotherly bond on and off the field. He made sure we all knew what was truly important - love for your team, your family, and your country.

My greatest testament to Richie Moran is the impact he had on my two sons, Cody and Julian. Both boys played lacrosse for Cornell, and although Richie did not coach them, they played as if he did. They were inspired by Richie's values and commitment to excellence, on and off the field, and heard enough Richie stories growing up to know to keep the important aspects of life front and center.

As we remembered 9/11 this year, my son Julian posted a tribute to our hero and teammate, Eamon McEneaney. Eamon was part of the band of brothers, formed under the mentorship and direction of Coach Moran. His post reminded us of these words spoken by Eamon – "Devotion is love. For if you allocate the time to the things that are most important to you, then you will love them and you will succeed" – these words written by Eamon reflect the values that Richie instilled in all of us, which are now being passed down to future generations.

Richie, I thank you for enriching my life, my children's lives, and certainly, future generations to come.

Mat Levine - As one of the legions who have had the privilege to know and been influenced by Richie Moran's incomparable capacities as a teacher, coach, mentor, father, husband, and friend, so many things stand out in the 55 years I have known him. I have never officially played on any of his high school or college teams, but he will forever be "my coach." We are not related, but his devotion and friendship is so real and palpable, we are family. Through his love for my Dad and the game of lacrosse, the Levine family connected with this Irish wonder long ago. What is important to know is if you have connected with Richie yesterday or over a half century ago, THAT CONNECTION is "forever." You become one of the stars in his "constellation," you feel like you belong; your life enriched.

In my view, the principles behind his uncanny ability to "connect" and build relationships that endure "forever" were formed during Richie's upbringing on the South Shore of Long Island. In the 1950's, families were trying to get back to re-building their lives and their livelihoods. Richie described to me on many occasions how fortunate he was to grow up in post- World War II Long Island. In his neighborhood, families were close, people went to church, public schools and sports programs were good, and, more than ever, it seemed people shared common values coming out of the sacrifices made during the War. So, Richie took this sense of country, commitment, neighborhood, church and family with him as he left Floral Park and Sewanhaka HS to earn his college degree at the University of Maryland and then launch his legendary teaching/coaching career. We all know he has carved out an incomparable and storied career at the high school, college and international lacrosse levels. But I maintain, coaching lacrosse was just a metaphor. Through boundless energy, a magnetic personality, and unmatched selflessness, Richie has built an incredible constellation of relationships that have had a profound impact on all he has touched or included.

The Levine Family became part of this special "Constellation" in its formative stages. As a young 26 year old high school coach, Richie connected with my Dad, Al Levine, (brought him into the constellation) at a game Richie was coaching during the early part of his career at Manhasset High School. Captivated by Richie's coaching and leadership, my Dad knew there was something special about him and the rest is history. The Club teams they built together, getting a "coke" at the Waltz Inn after team practices, witnessing his success at Cornell, and even Richie taking the time to attend my brother's Bar Mitzvah (on the day he won his first National Championship, no less!). The occasions we shared and continue to share over such a long period of time, big or small, have brought a stream of unending meaning and joy into our lives.

So, on the occasion of Richie's 80th Birthday, we thank him for giving the Levines a small spot in his enormous constellation of friends, family, and colleagues. It's now a big, big group, but we all feel like we forever "belong." Happy Birthday, Richie, and, as we like to do at your gatherings, let's sing "God Bless America!"

Michael French - I was a naive high school kid coming out of a very rural community in Ontario, Canada when I met Richie Moran on my recruiting trip in 1972. At that time I had a very limited understanding about college and in no way understood what an Ivy League education might mean to me and ultimately my family. My mother came over to Canada from England post-World War II, and my father joined the Royal Canadian Air Force when he was 17. Neither had the opportunity to finish high school, let alone go to college. There were different priorities then.

I actually had my name in the que for a line shift work position at the General Motors plant, the largest employer in our town, when Richie called to inform me that I had been accepted at Cornell and that I qualified for a full financial aid stipend.

My life changed when I stepped on to the Cornell campus that late summer day for orientation in 1973, and that initiated the wonderful relationship and friendship that I established with Coach Moran that we've maintained for the past 43 years.

Coach Moran put together a very formidable freshman class of lacrosse player/student athletes, and playing together as a freshman group we had an undefeated season. In the classroom, I struggled at first with my busy schedule of washing pots at Sigma Phi fraternity(in exchange for meals), lacrosse and other sports(basketball pickup games) and homework. However, with a lot of support, by the second semester somehow I figured it out.

Coach Moran always had an open door. He made lacrosse fun and was always there (as were his assistant coaches, Mike Waldvogel and Scott Anderson) to keep all of us focused on the field and in the classroom.

After that first year, everything took off for me and my teammates which culminated in our 1976 undefeated season and national championship. The bond that I have with my teammates during my time at Cornell is deep and strong. Annually, many of us get together with Coach Moran to reminisce each fall at our reunion and memorial golf event in honor of our dear friend and teammate Eamon McEneaney.

Richie Moran is my mentor, but more importantly one of my dearest and closest friends. With his support and guidance, I became the first person in my family to receive not only one, but two college degrees. Cornell was the ultimate "game changer" for me. Richie opened the door for me at Cornell, which provided me the opportunity to learn and grow as a person and ultimately be a part of a team of athletes that achieved greatness. For that I will eternally be humbled and grateful.

Bonnie McEneaney - I first saw Richie Moran in 1977 running drills with his players at a lacrosse practice on Schoellkopf field. At one point he whistled—so sharp and loud and shrill- it was like an invisible arrow soaring from his lips; striking a bullseye on each player's back, simultaneously. It was the type of whistle that I imagine could shatter a glass. The team, almost in unison, focused on their leader, Coach Moran. Little did I know that 9 years later that same man yelling play specifics on the field, would be wildly dancing the tie dance at my wedding to Eamon McEneaney—who was, at the time I first saw Richie, just a friend.

It wasn't until I reconnected with Eamon in 1982 in NYC, that I really began to know the man who had become one of the most influential people in Eamon's life. Richie coached Eamon to two national championships-1976 and 1977- but he also coached him in life. He became a pivotal part of my life as well as the years passed—reunions, weddings, small dinners, lacrosse functions—and ultimately, eulogizing Eamon after he was killed on 9/11. Rarely do more than several months pass when I don't receive a call from him—devoted husband to Pat and incredibly proud father and grandfather. His first questions are always "How are the children?"—"How are the McEneaney's?" That's Richie through and through- family comes first before anything else.

Jon Gordon - Richie Moran changed my life. He recruited me to play lacrosse at Cornell University where I grew up as a man and became part of a team and community that would influence my life forever. I would venture to say that if it wasn't for Richie I wouldn't be writing the books I write today. The amazing thing about Richie is that I'm just one of the countless leaders he has influenced and impacted. I can't think of many people that have had the influence he has had. I'm thrilled that Richie now shares his wonderful and inspiring life story and journey with the world. We are all better for knowing Richie and now we'll be better for knowing his story. I hope you join me in reading this book!

Joe Lizzio - Either as a 10 year-old camper at Richie Moran's Quick Stick camp, or as a 50 year-old alumni of Cornell lacrosse, there are two things you always hear, or end up singing when you're around Richie. Those two things are "God Bless America," and "It's great to be here!"

Those thoughts resonate through your mind, and he makes you believe you're in the best place in the world possible. Even if it's 10 degrees outside, or you just lost a tough game, or you just had the worst day of your life as an alum, Coach Moran always makes you believe – because he believes. He's always going to make an impact.

Where that resonates the most is his memory of people's names, where they are from, what they're doing and making connections. We were playing in Australia after I graduated in 1988, and a guy on the Aussie national team had blown out his knee. Even though he was coaching the U.S. team, Coach Moran went over to him on the field, he knew his first and last name and remembered his town, he consoled him and the guy said his knee stopped hurting instantly when Coach Moran remembered him.

It seems that everything I do, or every speech I make, I work it in somehow that I played lacrosse at Cornell, and I have seen people come away from spending a few hours with Coach Moran and say that it changed their life. We as alums that had 4 years, and the rest of our lives with Coach Moran are very thankful to him for everything he has done for us, and I wish him a very happy birthday.

Michael LaRocco - It was my first day on campus as a freshman and I had no interest in going to the orientation programs the college had set for me. Instead I went to the one place that would become my second home during my 4 years in Ithaca, The Cornell Lacrosse office, and from the moment I stepped through that doorway I quickly realized what a "Home Away from Home" this truly was.

Coach Moran walked over to me and said "Mike LaRocco...do you want to be an All American? Then you better listen to me!" He then handed me a dust rag and a can of lemon Pledge and said "Now go dust off the chairs in the office."

I quickly came to realize "WHAT COACH SAYS, GOES." Even if it meant wearing 50 lb. re-issued lacrosse cleats to practice and games... Who was I to question this living legend? Back home in Smithtown, I didn't question my mom or dad, so why would I start with Coach? That was probably the smartest decision I made in my 4 years at Cornell University. Coach had the winning tradition...he had the titles...he had the list of All Americans...He was in the business of making Men...not just coaching great lacrosse players... He was the catalyst for an alumni network that is second to none...that still is going strong to this day.

My relationship with Coach has flourished over the years with much love, respect and admiration. We no longer speak of the wins and losses, but about FAMILY and the great memories we've shared. Now, during times of reflection, I no longer think about where I should make my outlet passes on the field, or what calls to yell from the crease, as he once instructed me to do. Instead, I think about all the life lessons I was learning from Coach... lessons I didn't realize he was teaching me at the time...In much the same way my mom and dad had taught me while growing up.

I am fortunate to say that I played at Cornell for Coach Moran, but the true blessing is that I consider him (and Mrs. Moran) FAMILY, and I always know when I'm with Coach that I'm at my home away from home.

Brian Conroy – When I was asked to write a little as to how I know Richie Moran, I realized my association goes back long before I attended and played lacrosse at Cornell University.

When I was a youngster my father, Don Ryan, Andrew Hegarty and two of my older brothers went to see my older brother Dave play basketball in the South Shore Semi's. Dave played at Uniondale High School. The opposing team, Elmont High School, which was not nearly as tall as my brothers team was coached by a young

Richie Moran. Before the game Rich stopped by to say hello, his older brother served in the Navy during WWII with my father, and he introduced himself to me. Little did I know at the time how our paths would cross in the future. Unfortunately, my brother's team lost, in a closely fought contest, which I could not believe because they were so much taller. Elmont went on to play for the Championship beating Roosevelt in the finals. In fact, Julius Erving mentions in his autobiography, a tough Elmont team that did not have a player over 6' 1" that beat his team three times his senior year in high school.

When I attended Nassau Community College, our paths crossed up in Ithaca, as we competed against the CU "B" lacrosse squad in a close contest and I met Rich again. My coach alluded to the possibility of attending Cornell. After the season my summer league teammate, Eamon McEneaney relayed Rich's desire to see me at Cornell. Eamon said it would be great to compete for a second national lacrosse title on the Division 1 level. It was a decision I'm glad I made.

While playing at Cornell, I developed a strong friendship with Rich, that has lasted to this day. We have done numerous lacrosse camps together after my playing days and always enjoyed our conversations in the locker room long after the campers had left for the day. I guess it's that neighborhood connection.

Rich is a frequent house guest here in Port Washington. He has his own keys and comes and goes as he pleases. He's Uncle Rich to my niece next door, as we have a two family home along with my youngest sister, Dorothy, who is also a Cornell Alumnus. Several years ago, I took Rich over to see my mom and brother Dave at my family's home in Uniondale. We brought over dinner and Rich had not seen my brother since his high school days. Dave served in the military as a combat medic in Vietnam after high school. He won the Silver Star and two Bronze Stars all with "V's" for valor. He suffered from the effects of Agent Orange and Hepatitis C. There was no cure for Dave and we all knew it. We enjoyed ourselves talking basketball, memories of my father in his basketball officiating days and life in general. On the way home Rich was quiet and spoke of the senseless nature of war and how proud he was to serve and the effects it has on people, his brothers and their terrible experiences. He was proud that he was able to do something positive in his life, helping young people. He spoke of a job opportunity at Grumman Aerospace many years earlier. He said he was thankful that his mother pushed him in the right direction in life.

His love of helping others was demonstrated earlier this year when Johnny Heil and I hosted a get together with the Johns Hopkins and Cornell Lacrosse alumni at Locale West near Penn Station. I told everyone that Richie was going to be eighty, to come out and celebrate. I did not lie, he is going to be eighty in January of '17. I was late to arrive and Rich came over to me stating that Pat called and people were calling the house to wish him a happy birthday, the only problem was that it was not his birthday. I told him that he's going to be eighty in January, so don't worry about it. It was nice to see him the butt end of a practical joke for a change! He did keep the Sewanhaka High School sweats, which I know have a special place in his heart. Later, I saw him staring at the room, watching the crowd of former players both for and against. He told me one of his greatest joys in life, besides his family, was the opportunity to have a positive effect and help give so many their start in life. I think Rich has always been a giver. Always giving a part of himself for the betterment of all. More importantly, he sets the mark for others to follow both on the field and throughout life. I'm blessed to have a friend like Richie Moran in my life. Happy eightieth Rich, the world is a better place because of people like you. All the best.

W. Buckley "Buck" Briggs - Many us of the pre-internet age grew up in homes cluttered with magazines, which were a primary source of news and entertainment and, of course, are becoming the dinosaurs of the information transmission game. One of the most popular magazines, *Readers Digest*, featured a story every month entitled "My Most Unforgettable Character." Sometimes the character was a famous or semi-famous person. Sometimes the character was just a regular person. But the character was always someone who influenced the writer in a profound and unforgettable way. Richie Moran is my Most Unforgettable Character, and I emphasize the word "character."

I matriculated at Cornell in the fall of 1972, and Richie was already legendary, having led the Cornell Big Red to the inaugural NCAA lacrosse championship, with a 12-6 trouncing of the University of Maryland in 1971. Long Island born and bred, this larger than life leprechaun, only in his mid-30's, sent shock waves through the collegiate lacrosse world with his north of the Mason Dixon champs. During my Cornell years, I got to know Richie in my role as Sports Director at WVBR, and his team provided one of the great thrills in my life with a double OT 16-13 win (over Maryland again) for his second NCAA Championship the day after my 1976 graduation. At that point, 40 years ago, I knew WHAT Richie was: a successful and charismatic coach, and a world class slinger of the blarney, but I did not really know WHO he was. That knowledge has taken 40 years to evolve, and continues to evolve to this very day.

The Richie Moran I now have come to know as a friend after years of interaction and observation, is possibly the most thoughtful person I have ever met in my life. He has accumulated hundreds, perhaps thousands for all I know, of friends, and he has the amazing capacity to make them all feel special, and I include myself in that group. The list of people who have told me what an important role Richie has played in their life is endless. Someone once told me that the true measure of a person is to see how that person treats people who are not in a position to be of any benefit to the person, and I know Richie counts as his dear friends countless folks on both ends of life's spectrum. I know from first-hand experience, as I am dealing with some serious health issues, that Richie is always one of the people there with a note of encouragement, or a phone call to check up on me. In his rich and friend-filled life, I cannot imagine how many people Richie extends such support to. The number must be staggering, and it is an honor to be in that group.

Frequently, when we actually meet a person who has accomplished substantial things in life, we are disappointed that the individual is less of a person in real life than we would hope. The Richie Moran I am honored to know is the polar opposite of that type of person. He has used his successful coaching career and his charismatic persona as a springboard to touch countless lives in a positive way. For that reason, I salute "My Most Unforgettable Character' and I thank him for being such a valuable part of my life.

Pete Noyes - King Richard I of England was known as Richard the Lionhearted because of his reputation as a great military leader and warrior. He was the "stuff of legend" and so is my best friend, Richie Moran ... and it continues to grow today.

When our family went to see the play, Lion King in NYC, I came away with an appreciation of what a lion represents: the leader, ferocious, a winner, never gives up, loves and protects family and friends first, totally loyal, full of passion - this is Richie Moran!

After knowing Richie for forty years, and watching him as a fellow coach, I say with full conviction, Richie Moran is the greatest coach in the history of Cornell University, bar none! He won three National Lacrosse Championships right out of the gate, and his team's 42 straight victories still stands as a record. To me, Richie is the Knute Rockne of lacrosse coaches!! He set the high standard for all others.

Richie played an initiating role in me finding out about a Cornell job in 1977 - my fellow assistant at Bucknell, Sid Jamieson (also a lacrosse coach) was visiting Richie, and Richie passed on info about Bob Blackman needing to hire a defensive coordinator. Sid gave me the tip, Blackman called me for an interview and the rest is history. I didn't know Richie at the time. Two weeks later, my family and I arrived in Ithaca and attended a welcome picnic and the first people we met were Richie and Pat Moran. We became, and still are, best friends!

Richie's legend continues to grow as he stays active in the lacrosse world. He gives back to his former players, encourages new players of the game, is loyal to Cornell University and is a generous volunteer for our Ithaca community. His contagious enthusiasm and generosity has touched us all!!

To know Richie, his awesome wife Pat and his children and grandchildren is to love them all. Yes, Richie Moran truly is Richard the Lionhearted and we love you and treasure our forever friendship!! Happy Birthday, dear friend and enjoy celebrating YOU and another year full of blessings!

Dick Pepper - I first met Richie Moran in the summer of 1972 as a wide-eyed sixteen year old at Walt Munze's All-American Lacrosse Camp. The campers were divided up into teams and each team was given a coach. I was stunned that the head coach for Cornell (who had won the 1971 NCAA championship) would be my mentor for the week. We learned a lot about lacrosse that week but also about being good sons and good citizens. He talked a lot about character and working hard.

Flash ahead to 1991. I had been coaching lacrosse since 1980 and had just transitioned into the world of men's lacrosse officiating. I had been hired to work at the All-American Lacrosse Camp and Richie and I were staff members together. It took a while for that to sink in! A number of years later my son, John, was a camper there. Richie and I were still on board as camp staff, and Richie treated John like he was his grandson.

Now the tough part of the story... My son, John, was killed in a car crash on August 30, 2001 about a week before his 16th birthday. John was playing lacrosse at West Genesee High School and was looking forward to his junior year. Some friends of mine from Camillus approached me about organizing a lacrosse tournament in John's memory to be held in August, 2002. Joe Taylor, a former player for Richie at Cornell, contacted me in June and said he wanted to arrange to have Richie as the speaker at the tournament. I was blown away!

Prior to the tournament, Richie and I were in Perth, Australia at the 2002 Men's World Championships. Richie was the head coach for Ireland and I was a USA referee. I was very excited to officiate the Ireland vs. Italy game on the last day of the tournament, and got to know Richie on a different level. If my memory serves me well, Richie made it quite clear he was not happy with one particular offsides call. A time out was used to make this abundantly clear.

A few weeks later, when Richie spoke at the John Pepper Tournament, he talked about people showing respect to each other and he addressed the subject of bullying. Again, he was focused on character and not primarily on X's and O's. At the end of the speech, he offered me the opportunity to represent Ireland as a referee and I enthusiastically accepted. I guess he was okay with the offsides call after all.

Shortly after that, the Irish Lacrosse Foundation was formed and Richie asked me to be a Director and Secretary. I have been actively involved with Ireland Lacrosse since then and it has given me the opportunity to referee on four different continents. It has also given me the chance to see lacrosse grow in Ireland and has been very personally rewarding.

If you ever had a chance to be in a public event with Richie you would really get a good feel for how well-liked and respected he is. No matter where you are, one person after another approaches him and he instantly remembers everything about them. His memory is remarkable. The opportunity Richie gave me to be involved in developing lacrosse in Ireland has developed a strong friendship between us. He has been a mentor, an inspiration and most importantly, a great friend.

Some descriptors for Richie: energetic, compassionate, upbeat, hilarious, focused, down-to-earth, motivational, respectful, disciplined, insightful, driven, and a great listener.

Jay Spiegel- I am delighted that Richie has finally decided to publish his autobiography as he approaches his 80th birthday. Having known Richie for over 40 years, I have long been concerned that were he to pass away (or become incompetent!) before his life story would be told, the world would be deprived of an amazing story full of anecdotes from a youth spent as the youngest of eight children, all of his experiences growing up on Long Island, his athletic career, a coaching career filled with highlights, his induction into numerous halls of fame, his work in the community for charitable causes, his mentoring of too many student athletes to list, his 50+ year marriage to Pat and stories about his children & grandchildren, his efforts and experiences as Cornell's greatest ambassador, and many other facets of his lengthy career and life.

My fear that this would not come to pass caused me to begin "encouraging" Richie to take on this task a number of years ago. At one point, I offered him the services of my secretary to transcribe written notes. That offer was refused. Next, I sent him a portable tape recorder and a box of at least a dozen tapes and asked him to record anecdotes and send the tapes to me for transcribing. Nothing happened. Next, while presenting the Richie Moran Award at Cornell's Athletic Hall of Fame Banquet a few years ago, I asked the 300+ attendees how many would purchase at least five books were Richie to publish the book? Everyone raised their hands. Richie was unmoved. During this time, I asked him when the book would be written during every conversation. I think Richie became annoyed with me.

Finally, for reasons never explained to me, Richie has come to the realization that his life story would be something many would be interested in reading, including coaches, players, politicians, and others, all of whom will be inspired to hear the story of a life of excellence well-lived. The book will be an important aspect of Richie's legacy. I anxiously await the results of Richie's efforts and thank Steve Lawrence for collaborating with Richie to bring this effort to fruition. The book will be a guaranteed best seller, transcending the lacrosse world and appealing to anyone coaching or playing any sport, anyone growing up in a large or small family, anyone looking for inspiration, anyone who values education, anyone aspiring to excellence.

Congratulations, Richie, for finally getting it done! Semper fidelis,

Mark Goldberg - There are a lot of people who make everyone laugh, who are the life of the party, who enable you to forget your troubles just by being around them.

There are those who demonstrate laser-like intensity, who outwork their competitors to overcome challenges on the way to success.

There are those who lead by example, who are a source of inspiration by how they treat others in providing an act of kindness on a daily basis.

There are only a handful of people who have all of these traits. Richie Moran is indeed a member of this very exclusive fraternity—an incredibly special person who was put on this Earth to improve the lives of everyone lucky enough to have contact with him.

I was a high school teenager living in Ithaca during the period when Richie was setting a new standard of excellence in college lacrosse in the mid-1970s. I only knew him by what I read in the newspapers, by what I could observe in stands during Big Red home games.

My relationship with Richie began when I was a Cornell student, having some interaction with him when I was the manager of the men's basketball team and a student-assistant in the sports information office. However, it wasn't until I became Assistant SID at Cornell in 1981 that I started to learn the greatness of Richie Moran.

I was assigned to handle the communication for the lacrosse program. Richie immediately made me a member of the team. He included me in almost all team functions. He gave me access to all areas of his operations. He made sure I was part of victory celebrations—whether it was going to dinner with a large group of family and friends or having a get-together at the Moran home. One thing was quickly apparent—success was never internalized by Richie. His greatness was primarily responsible for all of the victories and championships, but Richie was gracious when it came to sharing all of that success.

I had a front-row seat to all of Richie's famous traditions, superstitions, and, of course, the jokes he would play with unsuspecting players or program supporters. I watched him dance to "Thank God I'm a Country Boy" in a musty locker room in Geneva, N.Y., after a hard-fought victory over rival Hobart. I was forced to eat the same sandwich at lunch—going to the same restaurant at the same time—on game day to keep a long winning streak going (too bad I picked a sandwich that first lunch date that is really low on my all-time favorites list). And I was made a "post-graduate manager" of sorts during the team's run to the NCAA Championship Game in 1988 because the team was on a winning streak with me on the sideline; more important, Richie wanted me to share in the joy of that great post-season run.

Richie would make sure that Bernie Olin—the loyal Cornell graduate who was most remembered for his "Give My Regards to Davy" Winnebago—had a proper Jewish funeral. He was a caretaker of sorts to the late Bill Fuerst, involving him with the program year after year. I remember often meeting with Richie alone in his office when our discussions would be interrupted by a campus visitor who came in completely lost, looking for directions. Richie would treat these visitors with the greatest respect and care, providing detailed assistance. Little did these people know they were being taken care of by one of the most famous people in the history of lacrosse.

While I was working at Cornell, I thought I had witnessed all of the forms in which Richie could show his kindness and appreciation. Then there was a night in the fall of 1986.

I had left the University in June of that year to pursue a career in magazine publishing. In September, I took a position as an assistant editor with *Inside Sports* magazine, a national monthly sports magazine with offices in the Chicago suburb of Evanston.

I was planning to head back to Ithaca for Homecoming. The week before Homecoming Weekend, the managing editor of *Inside Sports* called me into his office. "We've decided to do a special article in the next issue on "College Football Homecoming"—what it's like for alums to come back to campus and enjoy a football weekend," he announced to me. "We're going to take a look at Homecoming for five college football programs around the country, and we want Cornell to be one of the five schools. We want you to cover Homecoming there. We'll fly you back to Ithaca on Friday to get there before Homecoming starts. We'll cover the cost of your flight."

I was delighted beyond words. I was clamoring to write for this national magazine rather than edit the words of other writers. This was my chance to show that I could be a national sports writer.

One of the first people I called with my news was Richie. "That's great news, kid," he told me. "In that case, I'd like you to come to our Awards Banquet Friday evening. I'll set everything up so you have an assigned seat. It will be great for you to be there."

I was planning to connect with my friends who were coming back to campus that night, but I couldn't say no to Richie. I had also worked with the 1986 team as part of my duties at Cornell, so it would be nice to be there to pay tribute to their season.

I spent most of Friday conducting interviews with prominent Cornellians for my Homecoming piece for the magazine. Then I headed to the banquet. I walked into the banquet room at the hotel and found my seat. My parents were already seated at the table. "What are you doing here?" I asked them; they had no involvement with Big Red lacrosse. "Well, Richie called us and invited us," they said. "He told us he had a few open seats."

I still hadn't put two-and-two together. The banquet ran very long (of course) and after about two and a half hours, it finally appeared to be coming to an end. My thoughts were drifting toward the anticipated reunion with many of my best friends who had just arrived in Ithaca. Richie returned to the podium. I assumed it was to say goodnight to everyone. Instead, Richie announced that he had a special award to give out. He called me up to the stage and expressed his gratitude for my contributions to Cornell lacrosse. He ended by presenting me with a framed collage of the lacrosse media guide covers that I had produced, centered around the phrase "Mark of Excellence."

I was in a daze—stunned by the way that Richie had honored me. But also, I have to admit, stunned that this was all part of a scheme designed by Richie to surprise me.

Before I joined up with my friends in Collegetown, I went to a pay phone to call the managing editor of *Inside Sports*. "Vince, I need to know—am I doing this story or not?" I asked. "We'll see," Vince said. "But this whole arrangement was set up by Richie. He called me (they had never talked before) and told me what he was planning, what he wanted me to say to you. He paid for your plane ticket to Ithaca."

I returned to Chicago and wrote my story. It never ran. And, not too soon after I wrote it, I came to the realization that it didn't matter. I knew what this experience was really about.

It was a snapshot of Richie—his extra effort, extraordinary kindness and devotion, and his penchant for mixing in a touch of humor. It is, indeed, the essence of Richie Moran.

Jim Metzger - Although I was recruited by Richie Moran to play lacrosse for the Big Red, I never made it to Cornell.

I chose to play lacrosse for the Harvard of Hempstead, also known as Hofstra University. Richie smiles when I tell him I too am an IVY League guy.

Through my superstar lacrosse player nephew Rob Pannell, I reconnected with Richie. Much to my surprise, after a 30 year break with no contact with Richie, he spotted me at a Cornell lacrosse event and made me feel like the only person in the room.

Richie is one of the most charismatic, passionate and electric people with whom I have crossed paths. My life has been significantly enhanced by virtue of our reconnection. We meet frequently for lunch,dinner and more.

Through my relationship with my nephew and Richie, my support of the game of lacrosse and my intense interest in the sport, I have been made to feel -by Richie- like a member of the Cornell family.

God bless Richie Moran.

With Gratitude

Richie, I'd like to thank you for the opportunity to be a part of this project. We covered a lot of ground talking about your first 80 years, and I really did love (almost) every minute of it.

I was reminded again and again why I have liked you so much and held you in such high regard for 36 years. While I surely considered you a "friend" for all these years, this book project has made me realize that you really were not joking when you said, "Pat has always handled our money. I have no idea how much I made." It is a real testament to your character that you have never measured prosperity in terms of money. The currency of your prosperity is your relationships, and by that measure, you are Bill Gates.

Given I enjoyed this project so much, I am really looking forward to collaborating on your next book when you turn 90. Its title, of course: "It's Great To (Still) Be Here".

Let's get out there and make this book a "million seller," and I do not mean a million copies in your cellar!

I have had many conversations over the years with friends, family, colleagues and former players, and I have told them how much I enjoy my trips down Memory Lane. Throughout my 60 years of teaching and coaching, my career in some ways is similar to four sports movies: "Field of Dreams," "Remember the Titans," "Rudy" and "Hoosiers" all wrapped into one.

The cycle of life has many twists and turns, and to be able, through this book, to reflect on the love that I had for my parents, brothers and sisters, my wife and children, my grandchildren, my daughter-in-law and sons-in-law, and the many dear friends that have crossed my path has been a real blessing. It's very interesting that in this cycle of life that we have joy, tragedy, love, loss, and the continuation of wonderful friendships. As you can see in this book, I have been inspired by many people, experiences and feelings for the people in my life. Working on this project for the past 6 months has reconnected me with my early years, with the past and the present, and I am extremely excited about the future. I hope people get as much joy from this book as I received from compiling and sharing it.

For many years I have been asked by so many people, "Why don't you write a book about coaching technique, philosophy, pranks, superstitions and highlights about games?" I wasn't very motivated to write the book until we had a family gathering. I looked at my grandchildren and realized how much I wanted to share my story with them and others.

The setting for writing this book has been the indoor and outdoor facilities at the Ithaca Yacht Club. This is a magnificent location on Cayuga Lake, here in Ithaca. The day I decided to seek assistance by engaging a co-author, one person came to mind. Steve Lawrence is a true Dr. of Knowology. Our long friendship has inspired me to read his sports column for 24 years, I have read his book, and his expertise in recording, documenting, and writing everything in this book was done with such elegant ease and deep feeling. Each day, he selected and directed our path, he inspired me to retrace the steps of my life, and I will forever be grateful to him and all the people that assisted me during this journey.

Thanks also to:

Jay O'Leary - Mark Goldberg - Maria Bise - Mike Townsend - Jenna Caruthers – Dr. Russ Zelko - Jeremy Schaap - Bruce Arena - Jon Gordon - Jay Spiegel - Vicki Brew - John Brehm - Eric Banford - Deb Moesch - Stub Snyder – John Murphy – Jim McDonald – Andy Phillips – John "Jake" O'Neil - Jim Case - Bernie DePalma – Tom LiVigne – Rick LaFrance - Tom Prior – Bob Deegan – Tim Weir - Pete Gogolak – Marc Martone - Jim Metzger – Jack Tierney –

Dick Pepper - Joe Taylor – Tom Howley - John Cavanaugh – James McAleavey – Bob Vogel - Vince Giarrusso - Pete Ginnegar - Bill Hall –Britt Britton – Chuck Feeney - Bob Vogel – Pete and Carol Noyes - Keith Reitenbach – Sam Carpenter –Butch Hilliard - Jerry DeMeo – Marty Rauch - Howie Borkan - Julie Greco - Jeremy Hartigan – Tom Gill – Warren Allderige - Larry Baum – Doug Pratt - Debbie Doolittle - Ithaca Yacht Club - Larry Carroll - Brian Conroy - Brooks Bradley.

(In Fond Remembrance)

Phil Marcus, Tom McGory, Dick Schaap, Alf Eckman, Dick LaFrance, Eddie Moylan, Bernie Olin, Jack and Gail Murphy, Jim Carroll, Harold "Whitey" Henrickson, Joe and Kay Rooney, Tom Nuttle, Bill O'Connell, Ken Molloy, George Boiardi, Henry Olivier, Dr. Jack Faber, Al Heagey, Bill Ritch, Craig Bollinger, Robert Buhmann, Larry Kenyon, Harry Nicolaides, Bruce Teague, Jim Nowak, Tom Mygatt, Jay Gallagher, Owen Daly, Ted Marchell, Eamon McEneaney, Paul Sadowski, Jim Sheehan, Paul Schimoler, David Von Rhedey, David Holder, Anne and Joe Taylor Sr., Ronnie Brion, Dr. Ed Walsh, and Bill Ritch.

...... // ......

Co-Author's Note: *Having spent hundreds of hours with Richie over the course of the past 6 months, I can attest to the fact that he put forth every effort to make these stories as truthful and compelling as possible.*

When it came time to thank everyone that played a significant role in his journey, and pay tribute to those who have passed on, Richie spent a lot of time worrying that he would inadvertently leave someone out. I assured him that if we were to get this book out in time for his 100th birthday, he could take all the time he wanted, but if we were to go to press in time for his 80th birthday, it was time to wrap it up.

Therefore, if we left anyone out, please forgive Richie and blame me!

– Steve Lawrence

The All-Cornell Team.

> "Richie, I know you have been asked many times if you could name an "All Cornell Team."

Do any players come to mind?

Yes, in fact I do have an All-Cornell Team. It is made up of these players:

1969

Paul Bloom
Stephen Bosson
Carroll Bryan
John Burnap
Charles Cook
Peter Coors
Richard D'Amico
Jeffery R. Dean
Robert Dean
Sam DiSalvo
James Doub
Peter Drench
Donald Dworsky
Richard Ellingsworth
Leo Fenzel
Alan Glickman
John Houston
David Irwin
Robert Kantack
Wayne Kingsbury
Paul Levine
William McCumiskey
Brian McCutcheon
Henry Olivier
Peter Peirce
David Pollak
Alan Rimmer
Robert Rule
Timothy Schiavoni
Brooks Scholl
George Sideris
Jerome Smith
Bruce Teague
Robert Wagner
Mark Webster

1970

Steven Alms
Craig Bollinger
Carroll Bryan
Randolph Bryan
Robert Buhmann
John Burnap
Robert Cali
Robert Christopher
Michael Conord
Frank A. Davis
Jeffery R. Dean
Robert Dodge
Donald Dworsky
William Ellis
Mickey Fenzel
Arthur Fried
Patrick Gallagher
Russell Greene
Brent Gunts
Frederick Hoefer
David J. Houston
David Irwin
Kenyon Lawrence
William McCumiskey
William Molloy
Ian J. Montgomery
Glen Mueller
Vincent Mulcahy

Harry Nicolaides
Frank Oda
Henry Olivier
Alan Rimmer
Robert Rule
Brooks Scholl
Robert Shaw
James Skeen
Bruce Teague
Robert Wagner
Mark Webster
Steven Woodford

1971
Steven Alms
Craig Bollinger
Jim Bradley
Robert Buhmann
John Burnap
Larry Croucher
Frank A. Davis
William Ellis
Mickey Fenzel
Arthur Fried
Patrick Gallagher
Russell Greene
Brent Gunts
Chuck Keibler
Tom McHenry
William Molloy
Glen Mueller
Harry Nicolaides
Jim Nowak
Matt Olenski
Henry Olivier
Bill Reed
Alan Rimmer
Robert Rule
Matt Sampson
Robert Shaw
James Skeen
Bruce Teague
Robert Wagner
Gregg Wellott
Larry Young

1972
Steven Alms
Bruce Arena
Craig Bollinger
Jim Bradley
Robert Cali
Robert Carell
Robert Clark
Richard Clifford
Lawrence Croucher
Frank A. Davis
William Ellis
Arthur Fried
John Gallagher
Patrick Gallagher
Gary Glath
Vernon Grabel
Russell Greene
Brent Gunts
Gregory Hunt
Douglas Johnstone
Chuck Keibler
David Kintzer
Garrick Kwok
William Latini
Stephen Lucas
William Molloy
Glen Mueller
Harry Nicolaides
Jim Nowak
Matt Olenski
Bryan Randolph
Matt Sampson
Robert Shaw
Gregg Wellott
Larry Young

1973
Steven Adams
Bruce Arena
James Bradley
Robert Brennan
Robert Carell
Richard Clifford
Michael Cunningham
F. Joseph D'Amelio
Michael Emmerich
W. Paul Fitch
John Gallagher
Steven Hall
Gregory Hunt
Douglas Johnstone
Peter Kaestner
Charles Keibler
Garrick Kwok
Stephen Lucas
Terry MacNabb
Steven Mann
Kenneth McCumiskey
Christopher Murison
Thomas Natti
Thomas Nolan
Walter O'Connell
Brian O'Sullivan
Matt Olenski
John Paxton
Richard Priester
Jonathan Ryan
Steven Sanford
Andrew Siminerio
Richard Weigand
Gregg Wellott
Kenneth Wingate
Larry Young

1974

Mark Black
Robert Brennan
Robert Carell
Richard Clifford
Michael Cunningham
F. Joseph D'Amelio
David Devine
Michael Emmerich
W. Paul Fitch
Michael French
John Gallagher
Thomas Haggerty
Albin Haglund
Cameron Hosmer
Douglas Johnstone
Jonathan Levine
Richard Liepke
Steven Mann
Ted Marchell
William Marino
Kenneth McCumiskey
Robert Mitchell
Thomas Nolan
Kevin O'Donnell
Brian O'Sullivan
Richard Priester
Steven Sanford
Andrew Siminerio
James Trenz
Kenneth Wingate

1975

Robert Annear
Robert Becker
David Bray
John Britton
Robert Capener
F. Joseph D'Amelio
Jon Davis
David Devine
James Duffy
Steven Dybus
W. Paul Fitch
Michael French
Albin Haglund
Timothy LaBeau
Brian Lasda
Jonathan Levine
Stephen Lux
Daniel Mackesey
Daniel Malone
Ted Marchell
William Marino
Eamon McEneaney
Robert Mitchell
Thomas Nolan
Kevin O'Donnell
John O'Neill
Brian O'Sullivan
Paul Patti
Richard Priester
Al Scazzero
Carl Scazzero
Scott Shane
David Sieger
Kenneth Wingate

1976

David Bray
John Britton
James DeNicola
Michael French
John Gerber
John Griffin
Albin Haglund
Robert Henrickson
Robert Jackson
Christopher Kane
Robert Katz
Peter Kohm
Brian Lasda
George Lau
Jonathan Levine
Daniel Mackesey
Ted Marchell
Thomas Marino
William Marino
Robert Mathisen
Reiley McDonald
Eamon McEneaney
Robert Mitchell
Frank Muehleman
John O'Neill
Paul Patti
Gregory Raschdorf
Keith Reitenbach
Paul Sadowski
Vincent Shanley
John Sierra
Joseph Szombathy
Charles Wiebe

1977

Bob Annear
Pat Avery
David Bray
Brian Conroy
Jeff Farrar
Ned Gerber
John Griffin
Scott Harrison
Robert Henrickson
Robert Jackson
Craig Jaeger
Christopher Kane
Robert Katz
Peter Kohm
Brian Lasda
George Lau

Daniel Mackesey
Gary Malm
Thomas Marino
Joe Marletta
Robert Mathisen
Reiley McDonald
Eamon McEneaney
Frank Muehleman
Steve Page
Gregory Raschdorf
Keith Reitenbach
Paul Sadowski
Vincent Shanley
John Sierra
Joseph Szombathy
Joe Taylor
Charles Wiebe
Charlie Wood
Warren Allderige

1978

Bob Barron
Tom Breen
Jim Buckley
Bob Capener
Cutty Cleveland
Brian Conroy
James DeNicola
Jeff Dingle
Tim Enright
Dave Furiness
Ned Gerber
Jim Gilbert
Jon Graham
John Griffin
Tim Guba
Scott Harrison
Robert Henrickson
Robert Jackson
Craig Jaeger
Christopher Kane
Robert Katz
Peter Kohm
George Lau
Thomas Marino
Joe Marletta
Robert Mathisen
Reiley McDonald
Wayne Meichner
Laurey Millspaugh
Frank Muehleman
Brian Myers
Steve Page
Jim Power
Gregory Raschdorf
Henry Reed
Keith Reitenbach
Paul Sadowski
Vincent Shanley
John Sierra
Craig Slaughter
Joseph Szombathy
Joe Taylor
Tony Verdi
Dave Walter
Charles Wiebe
Randy Wong
Charlie Wood
Warren Allderige

1979

Pat Avery
Bob Barron
Wade Bollinger
Jim Buckley
Bob Capener
Cutty Cleveland
Tim Daly
James DeNicola
Jeff Dingle
John Diviney
Dave Furiness
Ned Gerber
Jon Graham
John Griffin
Tim Guba
Doug Happel
Scott Harrison
Mike Haushalter
Robert Jackson
Woody Jay
Farrar Jeff
Skot Koenig
Peter Kohm
Reiley McDonald
Wayne Meichner
John Mutch
Jim Power
Gregory Raschdorf
Bruce Reitenbach
Paul Roland
Tony Sciabala
Bryan Stuke
Joseph Szombathy
Joe Taylor
Tom Wagner
Earl Weaver
Charles Wiebe
Charlie Wood

1980

Pat Avery
Bob Barron
Wade Bollinger
Rob Carey
Mike Cooney
Marty Cooper

Matt Crowley
Tim Daly
Carl Del Balzo
John Diviney
Sam Edwards
Norman Engelke
Tim Enright
Ned Ensor
Tarik Ergin
Steve Fitzpatrick
Dave Furiness
Jon Graham
Sam Happel
Mike Haushalter
Vinnie Ilardi
Woody Jay
Skot Koenig
Dave Lintner
Bob Lucas
Mike Lynch
Dave McDonald
Paul Mercer
John Mutch
Steve Newes
John Phillips
Bruce Reitenbach
Paul Roland
Dave Rose
Tony Sciabala
Jim Sheehan
Bryan Stuke
Joe Taylor
Tom Wagner
Earl Weaver
Charlie Wood

1981

Wade Bollinger
Rob Carey
Mike Cooney
Marty Cooper
Matt Crowley
Tim Daly
Carl Del Balzo
John Diviney
Norman Engelke
Ned Ensor
Tarik Ergin
Steve Fitzpatrick
Jon Graham
Sam Happel
Mike Haushalter
Vinnie Ilardi
Woody Jay
Dave Lintner
Mike Lynch
Dave McDonald
Paul Mercer
John Phillips
Bruce Reitenbach
Paul Roland
Dave Rose
Tony Sciabala
Jim Sheehan
Tom Wagner
Earl Weaver

1982

Jeff Baikie
Wade Bollinger
Dan Boltja
Bruce Bruno
Matt Crowley
Steve Dadourian
John Diviney
Ken Entenmann
Tarik Ergin
Steve Fitzpatrick
Tim Gordon
Josh Gully
Mike Higgins
Vinnie Ilardi
Kevin Loucks
Paul Mercer
Bob Miller
Bill Nordhausen
Greg Penske
Andy Phillips
J.D. Phillips
Peter Ruchkin
Jamie Smith
Tom Spaulding
Earle Weaver

1983

Peter Altman
Dan Boltja
Bruce Bruno
Rob Cappucci
Kevin Casey
Kevin Cook
Matt Crowley
Steve Dadourian
Frank DeCosta
Jeff Doughty
Ken Entenmann
Tarik Ergin
Steve Fitzpatrick
Kevin Frank
Bob Gilmartin
Tim Gordon
Tom Gundersen
Mike Higgins
Vinnie Ilardi
Monte Jiran
Frank Kelly
Nick Lantuh
Kevin Loucks
Paul Mercer
Bob Miller

Bill Nordhausen
Mike Pachino
Steve Paletta
Greg Penske
Brian Perry
Andy Phillips
J.D. Phillips
Greg Ripich
Peter Ruchkin
Jamie Smith
Tom Spaulding

1984
Kevin Casey
Kevin Cook
Bob Cummings
Steve Dadourian
Jeff Doughty
Pat Doyle
Ken Entenmann
Andy Eschner
Ray Floyd
Todd Francis
Kevin Frank
Bob Gilmartin
Tim Gordon
Tom Gundersen
Mike Higgins
Monte Jiran
Aaron Jones
Frank Kelly
Paul Kuehner
Nick Lantuh
Kevin Loucks
Rob Lynch
Mike Pachino
Steve Paletta
Greg Penske
Dave Petrosino
Andy Phillips
Tony Reece
Greg Ripich
Peter Ruchkin
Jamie Smith
Jack Tierney
Tim Vivian

1985
Jack Beany
Charlie Caliendo
Dave Cleary
John Colucci
Ed Cook
Mark Crawford
Bob Cummings
Mike DeStefano
Jeff Doughty
Ken Entenmann
Todd Francis
Kevin Frank
Bob Gilmartin
Tim Gordon
Tom Gundersen
John Hanko
Bill Hughes
Aaron Jones
Frank Kelly
Paul Kuehner
Nick Lantuh
Joe Lizzio
Steve Long
Chris Modesti
Kevin Moran
Matt Moro
Paul Mularz
Tim Mulligan
Steve Paletta
Dave Petrosino
Tony Reece
Greg Ripich
Jamie Smith
Chris Tierney
Dan Topoleski
Tim Vivian
Corky Webb
John Wurzburger

1986
Jack Beany
Dan Boltja
Charlie Caliendo
Kevin Casey
John Colucci
Evan Conway
Ed Cook
Bob Cummings
Mike DeStefano
Jeff Doughty
Dave Dunlap
Kevin Finneran
Todd Francis
Kevin Frank
Tom Gundersen
John Hanko
Bill Hughes
Aaron Jones
Frank Kelly
Paul Kuehner
Nick Lantuh
Karl Lehmann
Joe Lizzio
Steve Long
Tim McDevitt
Steve Meyer
Chris Modesti
Kevin Moran
Tim Mulligan

Steve Paletta
Tony Reece
Greg Ripich
Paul Schimoler
Chris Tierney
Tim Vivian
John Wurzburger

1987
Vince Angotti
Charlie Caliendo
Jim Ciquera
John Colucci
Evan Conway
Bob Cummings
Mike Cummings
Mark Davis
Mike DeStefano
Dave Dunlap
Todd Francis
Matt Gleason
Tim Goldstein
Geoff Hall
Larry Hallock
Mike Hayes
John Heil
Aaron Jones
Paul Kuehner
Karl Lehmann
Joe Lizzio
Steve Long
Chris Marzullo
Brian McCormack
Tim McDevitt
Steve Meyer
John Miller
Chris Modesti
Kevin Moran
Tony Morgan
Tim Mulligan
Bill O'Hanlon
Steve Paletta
John Rossettie
Paul Schimoler
Matt Schultz
Paul Shea
Chris Tierney
Tim Vivian
John Wurzburger

1988
Vince Angotti
Scott Burnam
Charlie Caliendo
Jim Ciquera
Mike Cross
Mike Cummings
Mike DeStefano
Dave Dunlap
Tom Dutchyshyn
Dave Edwards
Kenny Fidje
Matt Gleason
Tim Goldstein
Geoff Hall
Mike Hayes
John Heil
Pat Leahy
Karl Lehmann
Joe Lizzio
Pat Lorian
Chris Marzullo
Brian McCormack
Tim McDevitt
Steve Meyer
John Miller
Kevin Moran
Tony Morgan
Bill O'Hanlon
Eric Rao
Chris Reynolds
John Rossettie
Paul Schimoler
Paul Shea
John Snow
Ted Tarone
Chris Tierney
Paul Tully
John Wurzburger

1989
Todd Adler
Dan Alexander
Vince Angotti
Larry Barrett
Scott Boomer
Gregory Boyce
Justin Brown
Bob Budington
Scott Burnam
John Clarke
Michael Connelly
Dave Dunlap
Jeff Earle
Dave Edwards
Brendan Flaherty
Steve Gray
Chris Hartley
Mike Hayes
John Heil
Joe Lando
Pat Leahy
Frank Marino
Chris Marzullo
John McCarthy
Tim McDevitt
Glenn Meyer
Steve Meyer
John Miller
Brad Minnich

Tony Morgan
Bill O'Hanlon
Chris Reynolds
John Rossettie
Paul Schimoler
Paul Shea
Timothy Shea
John Snow
Joseph Solomon
Cregg Sweeney
John Tillman
Dave Varriale
David Von Rhedey

1990

Todd Adler
Dan Alexander
Vince Angotti
Tom Benson
Ted Berkery
Scott Boomer
Bob Budington
Scott Burnam
John Busse
Michael Connelly
Mike Cross
Mike Cummings
Jeff Earle
Jon Frey
John Gaensbauer
Jon Goldman
Steve Gray
Brian Hannafin
John Heil
Travis Lamb
Joe Lando
Pat Leahy
Timothy Lee
Michael Levine
Frank Marino
Chris Marzullo
John McCarthy
Glenn Meyer
Brad Minnich
Tony Morgan
Bill O'Hanlon
Chris Reynolds
John Rossettie
Paul Shea
Timothy Shea
Eric Smith
Chad Snopek
John Snow
John Tillman
Dave Varriale
David Von Rhedey

1991

Tom Benson
Ted Berkery
Patrick Blair
Chris Brown
Errol Brown
Scott Burnam
John Busse
Boyd Chastant
Michael Connelly
Mike Cross
Bill Duffy
Dave Edwards
John Gaensbauer
Jon Goldman
Josh Gonnella
Steve Gray
Brian Hannafin
Kevin Kiely
Travis Lamb
Joe Lando
Michael Leahy
Pat Leahy
Tim Lee
Mike Levine
Ted Lynch
Frank Marino
Kevin McCarthy
Glenn Meyer
Tony Morgan
Chris Reynolds
Hunter Ross
David Schneid
Timothy Shea
Ben Smith
Eric Smith
Chad Snopek
John Snow
John Tillman
David Von Rhedey
Brent Welch

1992

Todd Adler
Tom Benson
Ted Berkery
Gregory Boyce
Errol Brown
Ned Burke
John Busse
Boyd Chastant
Michael Connelly
Chris Danler
Bill Duffy
Michael Fronk
John Gaensbauer
Jon Goldman
Josh Gonnella
Steve Gray
Geoffrey Gross

Oliver Guinness
Brian Hannafin
Ty Hearon
David Holder
Ben Hutchen
Eric Johnson
Kevin Kiely
Travis Lamb
Joe Lando
Tim Lee
Mike Levine
Ted Lynch
Mark MacLachlan
Kevin McCarthy
Matt Norfolk
J.P. O'Brien
Anthony Pavone
Brian Rodgers
Hunter Ross
David Schneid
John Scott
Timothy Shea
Andy Slocum
Ben Smith
Eric Smith
Chad Snopek
David Von Rhedey
Brad Younge

1993
Todd Adler
Tom Benson
Ted Berkery
Ned Burke
John Busse
Boyd Chastant
Chris Danler
Bill Duffy
Michael Fronk
John Gaensbauer
Jon Goldman
Josh Gonnella
Jeff Green
Geoffrey Gross
Brian Hannafin
David Holder
Ben Hutchen
Eric Johnson
Michael LaRocco
Travis Lamb
Chris Langdale
Tim Lee
Mike Levine
Ted Lynch
Mark MacLachlan
Frank Marino
Matt Norfolk
Anthony Pavone
Graydon Ripley
Brian Rodgers
Hunter Ross
David Schneid
John Scott
Ben Smith
Eric Smith
Chad Snopek
Clayton Weber
Dan Wolff
Brad Younge

1994
Matt Amato
Alex Baydin
Chris Braceland
Ned Burke
Andy Cahalane
Boyd Chastant
Kevin Cronin
Chris Danler
Bill Duffy
Reed Fawell
Michael Fronk
Geoffrey Gross
David Holder
Buck Holmes
Kris Hopkins
John Horowitz
Jud Howson
Kevin Kiely
Dave Krauter
Michael LaRocco
Chris Langdale
Mark MacLachlan
Matt Norfolk
Anthony Pavone
Jay Pieroni
Graydon Ripley
Brian Rodgers
Hunter Ross
John Scott
Ben Smith
Matt Steinwald
John Sullivan
Ian Twers
Clayton Weber
Dan Wolff
Brad Younge
Greg Zorella

1995
Matt Amato
Jay Billings
Chris Braceland
Andy Cahalane
Dave Casillo
Kevin Cronin
Chris Danler
Ben DeLuca
Michael Fronk
Ryan Geller

Geoffrey Gross
Ian Hafner
David Holder
Buck Holmes
Darren Hopkins
Jud Howson
Ben Hutchen
Brian Keller
Dave Krauter
Michael LaRocco
Chris Langdale
Mark MacLachlan
Kevin Matthews
Dan McNulty
Glenn Minerley
Matt Norfolk
Anthony Pavone
Fred Peightal
Joe Perriello
Brian Rodgers
Joe Rossettie
Scott Seidelmann
Adam Shaivitz
Rob Snyder
Matt Steinwald
John Sullivan
Luke Turton
Clayton Weber
Matt Wise
Dan Wolff
Brad Younge
Bryan Younge
Greg Zorella

1996

Matt Amato
Zach Bard
Mike Bock
Chris Braceland
Matthew Burks
Andy Cahalane
Tanner Campbell
Dave Casillo
Ben DeLuca
Patrick Dutton
Dean Gurney
Ian Hafner
Brandon Hall
Kevin Healy
Buck Holmes
Brian Keller
Dave Kennedy
Dave Krauter
Chris Langdale
Mark MacLachlan
Kevin Matthews
Danny McCormick
Dan McNulty
Glenn Minerley
Eric Morgan
Josh Morgan
Fred Peightal
Joe Perriello
Joe Rossettie
John Schwartz
Scott Seiffert
Adam Shaivitz
Matt Steinwald
Sean Steinwald
John Sullivan
Chris Tousant
Michael Voris
Clayton Weber
Brett Wilderman
John Wilkinson
Matt Wise
Dan Wolff
Bryan Younge
Greg Zorella
Greg Zumas

1997

Eric Bertelson
Mike Bock
Evan Boulukos
Chris Braceland
Ronnie Brion
Dave Brostek
Matthew Burks
Andy Cahalane
Tanner Campbell
Dave Casillo
Devon Channer
Shaun Creegan
Ben DeLuca
Patrick Dutton
Troy Gorman
Ian Hafner
Kevin Healy
Craig Kaufman
Brian Keller
Dave Kennedy
Rory Linehan
Brad Little
Glenn Minerley
Brian Morgan
Josh Morgan
David Nachman
Chris Packard
Fred Peightal
Joe Perriello
Joe Rossettie
Tom Scott
Adam Shaivitz
Chris Tousant
Phil Tretola
Michael Voris

Brett Wilderman
John Wilkinson
John Wise
Matt Wise
Rich Yost
Bryan Younge
Greg Zorella
Greg Zumas

Richie Moran

Husband, Father, Coach, Friend

Most of what I need to know I learned from Richie Moran

1. Always call your mother on Mother's Day, then go to church and the library.
2. Big Red is the only gum there is.
3. When you're thinking of someone, call them; otherwise they'll never know.
4. It's great to be here.
5. Enthusiasm is contagious.
6. Never burn a bridge, some day you might want to go back.
7. Stay a little bit hungry. It's great to be be the underdog.
8. Respect all, be intimidated by none.
9. The value of game preparation.
10. Sometimes it's best to turn the other cheek and walk away.
11. There's no such thing as a bad day; it's just that some are better than others.
12. The value of family, friends and education.

Written by Steven "Farmer" Sanford, BS '75 DVM, '79

January 22, 2015

The brainchild of Cornell alum Jay Spiegel in early 1989, the Richie Moran Award was first given that fall to women's soccer player Jennifer Smith '90. Spiegel's idea was to honor a scholar-athlete who also exhibited the type of Ivy League spirit Cornellians seek to emulate — that of not only excellence in scholarship and athletics, but also in service to the community. At the same time, Spiegel thought it was appropriate to name the award after someone who was a great example for these attributes.

"Only one person came to mind — Richie Moran," Spiegel said. The excellence of his teams was unquestioned, but one little known fact outside of the Athletic Department was that his players consistently had the highest grade point average among all of Cornell's teams. Richie's service to the greater community at Cornell, in Tompkins County, and around the globe was legendary. Who better to bear the name of a prestigious award to be given to one senior scholar-athlete?"